# ABRAHAM LINCOLN

## *and* JOSEPH SMITH

HOW TWO CONTEMPORARIES CHANGED
THE FACE OF AMERICAN HISTORY

# ABRAHAM LINCOLN *and* JOSEPH SMITH

HOW TWO CONTEMPORARIES CHANGED
THE FACE OF AMERICAN HISTORY

## RON L. ANDERSEN

PLAIN SIGHT PUBLISHING
AN IMPRINT OF CEDAR FORT, INC.
SPRINGVILLE, UTAH

© 2014 Ron L. Andersen
All rights reserved.

No part of this book may be reproduced in any form whatsoever, whether by graphic, visual, electronic, film, microfilm, tape recording, or any other means, without prior written permission of the publisher, except in the case of brief passages embodied in critical reviews and articles.

This is not an official publication of The Church of Jesus Christ of Latter-day Saints. The opinions and views expressed herein belong solely to the author and do not necessarily represent the opinions or views of Cedar Fort, Inc., or The Church of Jesus Christ of Latter-day Saints. Permission for the use of sources, graphics, and photos is also solely the responsibility of the author.

ISBN 13: 978-1-4621-1416-0

Published by Plain Sight Publishing, an imprint of Cedar Fort, Inc.
2373 W. 700 S., Springville, UT 84663

Distributed by Cedar Fort, Inc., www.cedarfort.com

Library of Congress Cataloging-in-Publication Data

Andersen, Ron L., author.
Abraham Lincoln and Joseph Smith : how two contemporaries changed the face of American history / Ron L. Andersen.
    pages cm
Includes bibliographical references and index.
Summary: Addresses how Lincoln laid down his life for his work, as did Joseph Smith, and how he had premonitions about his impending assassination, much like those of Joseph Smith.
ISBN 978-1-4621-1416-0
1. Smith, Joseph, Jr., 1805-1844. 2. Lincoln, Abraham, 1809-1865. 3. Church of Jesus Christ of Latter-day Saints--History--19th century. 4. Mormon Church--History--19th century. I. Title.

BX8695.S6A53 2014
289.3092--dc23
                                        2014002530

Cover design by Angela D. Baxter
Cover design © 2014 by Lyle Mortimer
Typeset by Daniel Friend

Printed in Canada

10  9  8  7  6  5  4  3  2  1

Printed on acid-free paper

Special thanks to Dale Broadhurst for his kind permission to use the newspaper articles from his site, Uncle Dale's Old Newspapers (www.sidneyrigdon.com/dbroadhu/artindex.htm), throughout this book.

Please note that in most cases, spelling, punctuation, capitalization, and grammar have been retained from the original source material.

# CONTENTS

*Chapter One*

# "SOMETHING MORE THAN COMMON 'INFIDELS'"

M ore books have been written about Abraham Lincoln than about any other person except Jesus Christ.[1] What is it about this man that has captivated the interest of hundreds of millions of people for more than a century and a half? And what could Lincoln possibly have to do with Joseph Smith, an obscure farm-boy contemporary of Lincoln's best known for founding The Church of Jesus Christ of Latter-day Saints. Certainly, Lincoln's life and accomplishments hold a particular significance to members of The Church of Jesus Christ of Latter-day Saints, commonly known as Mormons. With the exception of Lincoln's first two years in office (when Brigham Young felt he and his people would fare better with a Democrat as president), Latter-day Saints have been universal in their high regard for Lincoln. Much like the rest of America, they revere him for his magnanimous character, his unparalleled leadership, and his world-changing accomplishments. Heber J. Grant, the Church president from 1918 to 1940, made the following declaration in February 1940:

> Every Latter-day Saint believes that Abraham Lincoln was raised up and inspired of God, and that he reached the Presidency of the United States under the favor of our Heavenly Father. . . . We honor Abraham Lincoln because we believe absolutely that God honored him and raised him to be the instrument in His hands of saving the Constitution and the Union.[2]

This statement is significant in light of the fact that Lincoln freely expressed his own personal belief that he was placed in the presidency not only by the vote of the people but also by the hand of God. He would frequently express that his role as president was nothing more or less than carrying out the will of God concerning the nation.

Abraham Lincoln was born just three years before Joseph Smith, who organized the Church on April 6, 1830, in Fayette, New York. Joseph was beloved by his converts for his role as their prophet but was maligned by most everyone else as a fraud. For five years, Abraham Lincoln and Joseph Smith both lived in Illinois, Lincoln in Springfield and Joseph in Nauvoo, which was then a city of twenty thousand residents, mostly Mormons, situated on the banks of the Mississippi some one hundred miles to the northwest. Joseph Smith spent time in Lincoln's hometown on several occasions. While it is entirely possible that they met, there is no record of such an acquaintance being made. However, Lincoln, like many other Americans of the era, would have read dozens of newspaper articles on the notorious Mormon prophet, and Joseph most certainly knew of Lincoln's support for the Nauvoo Charter in the Illinois state legislature.

The extraordinary lives of these timeless frontier icons shared remarkable parallels; this exhaustive treatment of their extraordinarily congruent lives has no precedent. Both men would declare themselves candidates for the presidency of the United States; one would succeed. Both would embrace unique and surprisingly similar interpretations of the Holy Scriptures; one established a global religion. Abraham Lincoln would not only win in his bid for the presidency but would also become revered across the world as one of the greatest leaders in history. Joseph Smith's peculiar religion, which his murderers predicted would disintegrate into nothing more than a blemish on America's religious history, has not only defied their calculations but has flourished with unparalleled resiliency across the globe—even while membership in most established Protestant religions has declined. The names of both the president and the prophet are known around the world, but in fact, each of these men was both presidential and prophetic.

## RELIGIOUS FOUNDATION

These two presidential prophets were derided as infidels throughout their lives for the religious convictions they each espoused and expounded, and both would give their lives as martyrs to their separate causes. Abraham Lincoln, both as a local politician and as President of the United States, would play an unanticipated supporting role in the turbulent development of The Church of Jesus Christ of Latter-day Saints. Lincoln's astute and unrelenting mission to preserve the disintegrating Union, his emancipation of the American slaves, and his preservation of the Constitution contributed to the development and preservation of all religions in America.

Each man unabashedly declared that he acted as a humble instrument in the hands of the Almighty God. Each believed that he was charged with a sacred calling, Lincoln to preserve the freedoms guaranteed by the Constitution and Joseph to establish what he called the restored gospel of Jesus Christ.

In light of the cumulative impact on religious thought wrought by early European Protestant reformers like John Wycliffe, William Tyndale, Martin Luther, John Wesley, and Roger Williams, it must be acknowledged that Abraham Lincoln and Joseph Smith might be numbered among these reformers. Lincoln should also be considered a pivotal contributor to the preservation of the free religious expression sought by these reformers, an American freedom that was being seriously disregarded in the years leading up to his presidency.[3] All of this was solidified by the role of our Founding Fathers, upon whom many Christians believe God moved to establish this government of freedoms. These liberties would foster the hoped for emergence of tolerance and respect for religious beliefs and practices of all types.

## GUIDED BY GOD

By the mid-1800s, there were an estimated four million slaves of African descent in America. Abraham Lincoln feared that God was angry at the sad mistreatment of these men, women, and children by slave owners in this land of freedoms. He also expressed his conviction that over the years government leaders in America had drifted far from the original Constitutional moorings. He believed that God did not approve of the politically powerful Southern merchants and slave owners who had taken it upon themselves to carve up and weaken this almost chosen nation, as Lincoln once called it, by seceding from the Union for their own personal gain.[4]

It is a historical anomaly to find at the helm of a nation in its most critical hour of civil war an awkward, self-educated backwoodsman with singularly remarkable humility, intellect, and trust in God. Some would call it divine design. As a president, Lincoln relied on God to a remarkable degree and repeatedly addressed his people with messages that one would expect to hear from the mouth of a prophet, not from a politician. As Christian writer John Wesley Hill wrote of Lincoln, "The thought that appeals specially to the hearts of men is that he was here as a prophet of the Most High on a divine mission."[5] Lincoln, through his words and out of his personal experiences, expressed his personal certainty that God acts directly upon human affairs. He said:

> I have had so many evidences of His [God's] direction, so many instances when I have been controlled by some other power than my own will, that I cannot doubt that this power comes from above. I frequently see my way clear to a decision when I am conscious that I have not sufficient facts upon which to found it. But I cannot recall one instance in which I have followed my own judgment founded upon such a decision, where the results were unsatisfactory; whereas, in almost every instance where I have yielded to the views of others, I have had occasion to regret it.[6]

Lincoln had a consuming conviction that God had created the United States for a higher purpose and that the political events culminating in the mid-1800s had been diverting the nation from that destiny. Another noted Christian author, William J. Wolf, explains in *The Almost Chosen People*:

> The country was founded upon the belief expressed in the Dec-
> laration of Independence that all men were created equal. Slavery
> was a living lie in contradicting that fundamental principle which for
> Lincoln had the force of divine revelation. The Civil War he came to
> understand as the punishment visited by God upon a nation denying
> its true destiny by its refusal to put slavery "in process of ultimate
> extinction."[7]

Lincoln believed that the political and moral drift from the original intentions of the Founding Fathers was an offense to God. In
presidential proclamations to the American people, Lincoln openly
expressed his view that the Civil War was the Almighty's judgment
upon the nation for its sins and His means to change the nation's
direction. Of the founding of America, Lincoln said:

> I recollect thinking then, boy even though I was, that there must
> have been something more than common that those men struggled
> for. I am exceedingly anxious that that thing which they struggled
> for; that something even more than National Independence; that
> something that held great promise to all the people of the world
> to all time to come; I am exceedingly anxious that this Union, the
> Constitution, and the liberties of the people shall be perpetuated in
> accordance with the original idea for which that struggle was made,
> and I shall be most happy indeed if I shall be an humble instrument
> in the hands of the Almighty, and of this, his almost chosen people,
> for perpetuating the object of that great struggle.[8]

As president, Lincoln frequently referred to his unmatched
resolve to do the will of God. Once, in a White House conversation
with a group of ministers on the subject of emancipating the slaves,
he said, "It is my earnest desire to know the will of Providence in this
matter. *And if I can learn what it is, I will do it!*"[9]

William J. Wolf explained:

> In this sense Lincoln is one of the greatest theologians of Amer-
> ica—not in the technical meaning of producing a system of doctrine,
> certainly not as the defender of some one denomination, but in the
> sense of seeing the hand of God intimately in the affairs of nations.

Just so the prophets of Israel criticized the events of their day from the perspective of the God Who is concerned for history and Who reveals His will within it. Lincoln stands among God's latter-day prophets.[10]

On another occasion during the Civil War, Lincoln said:

We are indeed going through a trial—a fiery trial. In the very responsible position in which I happen to be placed, being a humble instrument in the hands of our heavenly Father, as I am, and as we all are, to work out His great purposes, I have desire that all my works and acts may be according to His will; and that it might be so, I have sought His aid—but if after endeavoring to do my best in the light which He affords me, I find my efforts fail, I must believe that for some purpose unknown to me, He wills it otherwise.[11]

Joseph Smith's claim of being guided by God is similar to Lincoln's. The difference is that Joseph described the sources of his promptings as visions, revelations, and heavenly visitations. Lincoln was relatively silent on the source of his divine inspirations. But while the general public seemed to accept or at least tolerate Lincoln's frequent expressions of divine guidance, Joseph Smith found no such acceptance except that offered by his own followers.

Joseph Smith taught that the beliefs, practices, and organization of the church he founded were patterned after those of the church led by Jesus's apostles.[12] He further taught that the martyrdom of Jesus's original apostles resulted in a gradual corruption of doctrines and religious practices in Christianity.

Most prominent Protestant sects, such as the Methodists, Baptists, and Presbyterians, formulated their core beliefs and identities during an unprecedented period of religious zeal in the late 1700s and early 1800s known as the Second Great Awakening. Over time, some of these sects fragmented over doctrinal differences while others united. American-born religions such as the Campbellites, the Millerites (which later became the Seventh-Day Adventist Church), the Assemblies of God, and the Church of Christ, emerged during this same religious revival. While these Protestant groups gained wide acceptance in America, they were quite uniform in their derision of Catholics. But Joseph Smith's followers alone encountered the stunningly violent fury of opposition and persecution for their beliefs and practices.

The Revolutionary patriots won their freedom from England and established a government of unprecedented liberties. Freedom of religion fostered the development of the Protestant Churches so prominent in nineteenth-century America. It provided a safe haven for all of these religious groups with the exception of the Mormons and the Catholics. Opposition to the Catholics came gradually as their numbers increased in the mid-1800s with the mass arrivals of Irish and Italian immigrants. Mormons, however, were met with instant disdain.

As America established itself, an ominous threat to national unity already existed in the form of slavery. By trampling the human rights and dignity of millions of black men, women, and children, whose fundamental difference from white Americans was merely the color of their skin. This disregard for the inalienable rights of these Americans was fueled by unparalleled wealth on the part of the slave owners. This wealth would move men and women to accept and embrace every conceivable measure, including the creation of discriminatory and unjust laws and judicial rulings, to justify slavery—all for the purpose of protecting the lofty aristocrats' source of free-flowing wealth. When the institution of slavery became threatened by strong anti-slavery sentiments in the Northern states, the avarice of the Southern planters would deal a dangerous blow to the government of America in the form of secession and the Confederacy. The slave states' eventual break from the United States was founded on racism, prejudice, and the denial of freedom. The end result, had the Confederacy been successful, would almost certainly have been a continent dotted from coast to coast with individual nation-states, many of which would have continued the inhumanity of slavery. Instead of becoming the strongest nation on the earth, America would have been a collection of weak, self-interested nation-states.

## A HOUSE DIVIDED

At the Illinois Republican State Convention in June 1858, Abraham Lincoln expressed his controversial yet firm conviction of the impending national danger by using a Biblical phrase to describe the tenuous threat of secession in America: "A house divided against itself cannot stand" (Matthew 12:25). Three years earlier, in August 1855, he wrote a letter to a friend in Kentucky, George Robinson, reflecting his grave concern for the nation: "Our political problem now is: Can we, as a nation, continue together permanently, forever half slave and half free? The problem is too mighty for me. May God, in His mercy, superintend the solution."[13]

Sensing a transcendent purpose for which the founding fathers strove, Lincoln carried a deep conviction that this nation was formed for a wise purpose known to God. He believed that its preservation was of the utmost importance to not just America but to the entire world. And while much of the North passively watched and some encouraged the dramatic division of the Union in 1861 through the secession of the Southern states, President Abraham Lincoln would stand resolute in preserving the Union of all states, believing and frequently expressing his conviction that God willed that this nation remain whole, that the freedoms proffered in the Constitution be preserved, and that the slaves be set free.

The abolition of slavery and the preservation of both the Union and Constitution came at the ghastly price of the Civil War, a maelstrom of death and destruction that was never imagined by the proponents of secession and slavery. It was, however, anticipated by Lincoln at least two years before the war began. In aforementioned speech in 1858, he spoke of his fear of an impending crisis:

> We are now far into the fifth year, since a policy was initiated with the avowed object and confident promise, of putting an end to slavery agitation. Under the operation of that policy, that agitation has not only not ceased but has constantly augmented. In my opinion it will not cease until a crisis shall have been reached and passed. *"A house divided against itself cannot stand."* I believe this government cannot endure permanently half Slave and half Free.[14]

The following sums up, in Lincoln's own words, the value system that he took to the White House and by which he saved the nation:

> I believe in God, the Almighty Ruler of Nations, our great and good and merciful Maker, our Father in Heaven, who notes the fall of a sparrow, and numbers the hairs of our heads.
>
> I believe in His eternal truth and justice.

> I recognize the sublime truth announced in the Holy Scriptures and proven by all history that those nations only are blest whose God is the Lord.[15]

There is an ocean of recorded examples of Lincoln's character, his sense of purpose, and his leadership. Yet of the thousands of books that are written on Lincoln, only a few of them have focused on his faith in God. One of those books, written in 1920 by a Protestant minister named William E. Barton, is entitled *The Soul of Abraham Lincoln*. Barton interviewed hundreds of those who knew Lincoln and collected thousands of letters, manuscripts, and documents about his life. Barton's inquiry ultimately brought him to one conclusion: "Abraham Lincoln believed and professed faith in the Christian God. He read the Bible, believed the New Testament message, and believed God both listened to and answered his prayers."[16] "I talk to God," Lincoln once told General Daniel Sickles, "because my mind is relieved when I do." He added, "When I could not see any other resort, I would place my whole reliance in God, knowing that all would go well, and that He would decide for the right."[17]

## THE SECOND GREAT AWAKENING

Abraham Lincoln was born in Kentucky on February 12, 1809, a little more than three years after Joseph Smith's birth in Vermont on December 23, 1805. Both grew up in the midst of the evangelical, Bible-based Second Great Awakening. Joseph wrote of its intensity and impact on his young life while living in the frontier of upstate New York:

> There was in the place where we lived, an unusual excitement on the subject of religion. It commenced with the Methodists, but soon became general among all the sects in that region of the country. Indeed, the whole district of the country seemed affected by it, and great multitudes united themselves to the different religious parties, which created no small stir and division amongst the people, some crying "Lo here!" and others "Lo there!" Some were contending for the Methodist faith, some for the Presbyterian, and some for the Baptist. (Joseph Smith—History 1:5)

As intense as Joseph described this tumult to be, the religious contention experienced by young Lincoln may have been even more ardent. Western Kentucky was regarded to be the epicenter of this great religious revival.[18] During this era, one often paid a price for expressing doubts about the contents of a preacher's delivery. William J. Wolf observed, "The tactic of backwoods religion in meeting skeptical criticism was to shout it down as a work of the devil."[19]

The teenage Joseph Smith found this to be painfully true. He described a "scene of great confusion and bad feeling" as preachers and converts alike fell into "a strife of words and a contest about opinions." (Joseph Smith—History 1:6). Joseph writes that while reading the Bible and pondering this religious turbulence, he became deeply impressed with a scripture found in the book of James: "If any of you lack wisdom, let him ask of God, that giveth to all men liberally, and upbraideth not; and it shall be given him" (James 1:5). It was in the context of this religious confusion that young Joseph decided to ask his questions to God in prayer, with a hope of gaining clarification on the truth of the scriptures. This prayer would set his life on a most unexpected and tumultuous course. "In the midst of this war of words and tumult of opinions, I often said to myself: What is to be done? Who of all these parties are right; or, are they all wrong together? If any one of them be right, which is it, and how shall I know it?" (Joseph Smith—History 1:10).

In the spring of 1820, fourteen-year-old Joseph entered a secluded grove of trees and took these questions to God in prayer. He emerged with the conviction that he was to join none of the existing churches. At about this same time, young Abraham Lincoln was having his own personal struggle with the winds of doctrine that swirled about him. Abraham's father Thomas, a man of faith and an itinerate, unsuccessful farmer and carpenter (much like Joseph's father), was caught up in the spirited revival of conflicting doctrines that broiled in Western Kentucky and Southern Indiana, where the Lincolns moved in 1816. There, Thomas was chosen by the local church committee to direct the building of the Little Pigeon log meetinghouse. Thomas built the pulpit, window casings, and cabinets for the tiny chapel. It is very likely that his only son, Abraham, assisted with the project.

In 1823, three years after Joseph Smith's life-changing prayer for guidance, Thomas Lincoln and his wife and daughter joined the Pigeon Creek Baptist Church in Illinois, but like young Joseph, fourteen-year-old Abraham made no move to join. This was not due to a lack of religious interest on young Abe's part. His mother, Nancy Lincoln, was a woman of deep faith in God and had a profound influence on her son. She read from the Bible to Abraham and his sister from the time they could understand, and they were eager listeners. By age fourteen, Abraham himself was an avid reader of the Bible, and he continued to willingly attend the sermons with his family. Lincoln did not leave us the descriptive account of his youthful religious feelings and experiences as Joseph did, but there are a number of accounts by Lincoln's acquaintances that confirm a deep faith in God as well as some doubts regarding certain widely accepted doctrinal tenets espoused by the Protestant religions. We do, however, have record of him speaking and writing often, as an adult, of his love for God and the Bible and his determination to follow them.

Though a frequent attendee to various churches through periods of his life, Lincoln never joined any of them, a fact that rankled many and for which he received abundant criticism. He received so much harsh derision for his deep-seated and divergent religious convictions that sometime in his early thirties he began shunning religious conversations entirely. Later in his life, campaigning political rivals would use this point against him, referring to him as an infidel, a harsh and loosely employed label for one who expressed doubts about accepted Christian doctrines.

William J. Wolf states, "While [Lincoln] eventually attained to a deep faith, emotionally the bitterness of sectarian prejudice must have been repellent to him, and was probably a cause of his lasting reluctance to affiliate with any sect. . . . The divisiveness of frontier denominationalism left a wound that never fully healed."[20] Evangelists made strong appeals to get Lincoln to join their churches, but he was unmoved. He once said to a friend on the matter that "he couldn't quite see it."[21] The issue with Lincoln was never an absence of faith in God and His power, nor was it disagreement with the teachings found in the Bible. His contention was with Protestant Christianity's interpretation of certain doctrines that he "couldn't quite see." He viewed them as having deviated from the Bible's original intent. Wolf records a concise description of Lincoln's religious stance as "singlehearted integrity in humbly seeking to understand God's will in the affairs of men and his own responsibility therein."[22]

Lincoln's grasp of Biblical teachings was vast, and he often recited verses from the Old and New Testament from memory. Referring to the religious contention in Lincoln's own community of New Salem, Wolf explains:

> The crude emotionalism of these gatherings can hardly have commended itself to Lincoln. . . . What must have disturbed him still more was the violent feuding between the jealous denominations. One form of Baptist predestinarian opinion held that its church members were created by God for heaven whereas the greater part of mankind had been destined for eternal flames. Methodist and Baptist denounced each other on whether the road to heaven passed over dry land or water. Local roughs tossed logs into the Sangamon River when baptisms were scheduled.[23]

Yet through all of this, Lincoln would make a point throughout his life to not speak ill of any religion, and that probably included the Mormons of Illinois, even though many of his fellow citizens in Springfield had little good to say about them. Some months after becoming a resident of Springfield, Lincoln wrote to a friend: "I've never been to church yet, nor probably shall not soon. I stay away because I am conscious I should not know how to behave myself."[24] There was probably deep seriousness in Lincoln's statement. Expressing his true beliefs would sometimes cause a stir and tumult akin to that experienced by his fellow "infidel," Joseph Smith.

Considering on these experiences, one cannot help but believe that young Abraham would have had more than a passing interest in fourteen-year-old Joseph Smith's experience near Palmyra, New York, in 1820—had Abraham known about it. When young Joseph took his questions to God in prayer, he reported seeing heavenly messengers in the grove. Joseph reported the following:

> I was answered that I must join none of them [the churches of

his day], for they were all wrong; and the Personage who addressed me said that all their creeds were an abomination in his sight; that those professors were all corrupt; that: "they draw near to me with their lips, but their hearts are far from me, they teach for doctrines the commandments of men, having a form of godliness, but they deny the power thereof. (Joseph Smith—History 1:19)

One of Lincoln's childhood friends remembered Lincoln saying, "My mother was a ready reader and read the Bible to me habitually."[25] Lincoln's stepsister Matilda Johnson recalled that, as a teenager, Abe would frequently speak to the family on Bible topics:

When father and mother would go to church, Abe would take down the Bible, read a verse, give out a hymn, and we would sing. Abe was about fifteen years of age. He preached, and we would do the crying. Sometimes he would join in the chorus of tears.[26]

It is recorded that on occasion, following a Sunday service, young Abraham would jump up on a tree stump and, for his young friends, mimic the preachers' overwrought style. Old-time residents remembered that "on Monday mornings he would mount a stump, and deliver, with a wonderful approach to exactness, the sermon he had heard the day before."[27] Referring to these early days, Lincoln later wrote how "the preachers bellowed and spat and whined, and cultivated an artificial 'holy tone' and denounced the Methodists and blasphemed the Presbyterians and painted a hell whose horror even in the backwoods was an atrocity."[28]

Although there was probably a certain amount of youthful cynicism in these tree-stump stunts, it might have also been an expression of young Abraham's budding search for divine truth manifest through his fascination with public speaking and oratory, the preachers being the only public speakers he was probably able to observe. It also illustrates that Abraham's experiences with the religious contentions on the then western frontier appear to be similar to those experienced by young Joseph in rural upstate New York.

William E. Barton wrote, "Although disdainful of Christianity in its cruder, frontier forms, Lincoln seems to have been open to, even seeking, an account of faith that rang true on grounds of reason and justice."[29] Later in his life, Lincoln wrote, "I planted myself upon the truth and the truth only, so far as I knew it or could be brought to know it."[30] Referring to his early search for doctrinal consistency in divine truth, Lincoln said:

> Those days of trouble found me tossed amid a sea of questionings. They piled big upon me. . . . Through all I groped my way until I found a stronger and higher grasp of thought, one that reached beyond this life with a clearness and satisfaction I had never known before. The Scriptures unfolded before me with a deeper and more logical appeal, through these new experiences, than anything else I could find to turn to, or even before had found in them. I do not claim that all my doubts were removed then, or since that time have been swept away. They are not.
>
> Probably it is to be my lot to go on in a twilight, feeling and reasoning my way through life, as questioning, doubting Thomas did. But in my poor, maimed way, I bear with me as I go on a seeking spirit of desire for a faith that was with him of olden time, who, in his need, as I in mine, exclaimed, "Help thou my unbelief." . . . I doubt the possibility, or propriety, of settling the religion of Jesus Christ in the models of man-made creeds and dogmas. . . . I cannot without mental reservations assent to long and complicated creeds and catechisms.[31]

## COMMON BELIEFS

Through the personal records of Lincoln and those who knew him, we learn that certain doctrines troubled him. He could find no peace in the doctrine regarding the endlessness of God's punishment that was propounded by nearly all the Protestant and the Catholic churches—the belief that the benevolent Father would cause the punishments of His wayward children to go on forever. These tenets of eternal damnation and endless torment were ubiquitous in the hellfire-and-damnation sermons given throughout the country. They were most certainly heard by young Joseph Smith as well. On the doctrine of infinite punishment, William Barton summarizes, "This dogma Lincoln denied upon two grounds, as these letters affirm. First, the justice and mercy of God; and secondly, the fact that according to the Biblical scheme of redemption, whatever right the human race had possessed to immortality and lost through sin, had been restored in Christ."[32] In a rare religious conversation with friends in 1859, shortly before Lincoln's run for the presidency, Isaac Cogdal recorded Lincoln's emphatic sentiments:

> He did not nor could not believe in the endless punishment of any one of the human race. He understood punishment for sin to be a Bible doctrine; that the punishment was parental in its object, aim, and design, and intended for the good of the offender; hence it must cease when justice is satisfied. He added that all that was lost by the transgression of Adam was made good by the atonement: all that was lost by the fall was made good by the sacrifice.[33]

Lincoln was also reported to have said, "Christ's atoning death meant that punishment in the afterlife not only would fit the crime but also would be rehabilitative, designed to prepare the offender for eternal happiness."[34] His interpretation of this doctrine did not set well with the ministers or acquaintances of his day, and it served as added evidence in their minds that Lincoln was indeed an infidel.

On this, William J. Wolf commented:

> This is hardly the statement of an "infidel" position. It reveals rather a mind dissatisfied with the sectarian theology of his community probing deep into the Bible on its own.
> . . . The unchanging affirmations for him in this process were man's need of salvation in terms of Adam's fall, God's loving purpose behind the infliction of punishment, and Christ's atoning work through his sacrificial death.[35]

On this subject, Wolf concludes, "Lincoln's conviction that God would restore the whole of creation as the outcome of Christ's Atonement would have been in itself a bar to membership in the Springfield church he attended."[36]

Lincoln's belief that all men could be saved once just punishments for sins were exacted was shared by Joseph Smith and his followers, and they too were derided for it. The third Article of Faith of The Church of Jesus Christ of Latter-day Saints states, "We believe that through the Atonement of Christ, all mankind may be saved, by obedience to the laws and ordinances of the Gospel" (Articles of Faith 1:3). As far as we know, Lincoln was unaware of this belief among the Mormons who were then congregating several hundred miles north and east in Kirtland, Ohio. He was essentially alone on the Illinois western frontier with his personal view of a just God who would certainly bring judgment for unrepented sins, but also of a God filled with a mercy and love for his children—a God that would eventually bestow the blessed gift of eternal life once the demands of justice had been fulfilled.

It was not in Lincoln's nature to be critical of anything or anyone, but he did harbor other differences with the churches of his day. These he would only occasionally and guardedly express. His dissatisfaction with the these religions was that they "neglected this fundamental love of God and of neighbor by too much introverted attention upon correctness in theological opinion."[37] He also "took a dim view of preachers who used the pulpit for politics and said he preferred those who preached 'the gospel.'"[38] When Lincoln would express his doubts regarding certain Protestant beliefs, he would sometimes add that he never denied the truth of the scriptures. Lincoln's uncommon depth of biblical knowledge and understanding led him to perceive and reject the man-made abstracts often present in the religious frontier squabbles of his day. We can infer from these statements and many others throughout his life that Lincoln's unwillingness to join any church was based on his unsuccessful search for a church that taught and practiced the pure doctrines and heavenly truths as he perceived them. Where Lincoln could find no peace in doctrines of the Protestant religions, the Bible became his source of inspiration.

As much as he loved the Bible, as a young man, Lincoln sometimes pointed out inconsistencies found therein. This confirmed the view that he was an infidel. Here, Latter-day Saint doctrine again harmonized with Lincoln's. While Latter-day Saints believe in the integrity of the word written by the holy prophets, they also believe that in the various translations over the centuries, changes occurred to the original texts. Research with the Bible translations has confirmed that numerous passages are clearly mistranslated and that some of these changes were made intentionally. Bart D. Ehrman writes an exhaustive treatment on these Biblical losses in *The Orthodox Corruption of Scripture.* He describes in great detail the translation process of the ancient biblical texts by scribes of the early Christian centuries. Ehrman states, "My thesis can be stated simply: scribes occasionally altered the words of their sacred texts to make them more patently orthodox and to prevent their misuse by Christians who espoused aberrant views."[39]

He continues:

> The New Testament manuscripts were not produced impersonally by machines capable of flawless reproduction. They were copied by hand, by living, breathing human beings who were deeply rooted in the conditions and controversies of their day. Did the scribes' polemical contexts influence the way they transcribed their sacred Scriptures? The burden of the present study is that they did, that theological disputes, specifically disputes over Christology, prompted Christian scribes to alter the words of Scripture in order to make them more serviceable for the polemical task. Scribes modified their manuscripts to make them more patently "orthodox" and less susceptible to "abuse" by the opponents of orthodoxy.[40]

The eighth Article of Faith for The Church of Jesus Christ of Latter-day Saints states, "We believe the Bible to be the word of God as far as it is translated correctly; we also believe the Book of Mormon to be the word of God" (Articles of Faith 1:8).

Lincoln's knowledge of the Bible was expansive. While discussing the poor turnout at the Ohio convention nominating John C. Fremont for President in May 1854, Lincoln reached for his Bible and "turned quickly to 1 Samuel 22:2 and read about David in the Cave of Adullam: 'And every one that was in distress, and every one that was in debt, and every one that was discontented, gathered themselves unto him; and he became a captain over them: and there were with him about four hundred men'" (1 Samuel 22:2).[41] That such an obscure passage of the Old Testament could be recalled so easily is a witness of Lincoln's grasp of and deep respect for the Bible.

Those close to Lincoln would frequently hear his ordinary daily speech salted with Biblical quotes and references, reflecting the depth of his immersion in Holy Writ. On another occasion, Lincoln told a friend, "I decided a long time ago that it was less difficult to believe that the Bible was what it claimed to be than to disbelieve it. It is a good book for us to obey—it contains the Ten Commandments, the Golden Rule, and many other rules which ought to be followed. No man was ever the worse for living according to the directions of the Bible."[42]

As President, Lincoln would refer to God in his speeches, his conversations, and his writing more than any other President before or after him. He was the first and only American president to publicly call for the intervention of the Holy Spirit: "I invite the people of the United States to . . . invoke the influence of his Holy Spirit to subdue the anger which has produced and so long sustained a needless and cruel rebellion."[43] Lincoln seemed to always be reaching for and operating from a higher spiritual plane than those around him. In one of his debates with Stephen A. Douglas over slavery in America, he said, responding to an accusation made by Douglas:

> My friend has said to me that I am a poor hand to quote Scripture. I will try it again, however. It is said in one of the admonitions of the Lord, "As your Father in Heaven is perfect, be ye also perfect." The Savior, I suppose, did not expect that any human creature could be perfect as the Father in Heaven; but He said, "As your Father in Heaven is perfect, be ye also perfect." He set up that standard, and he [Jesus] who did most towards reaching that standard, attained the highest degree of moral perfection. So I say in relation to the principle that all men are created equal, let it be as nearly reached as we can.[44]

In the course of human existence, there have quite probably been men and women who have approached this perfection of character that Jesus called for. But it is unlikely that there are more documented accounts of a human striving for such Christlike perfection than there are of Abraham Lincoln. As these pages will chronicle, it is abundantly evident that Lincoln achieved a remarkable level of purity and virtue over the course of his life.

In 1820, fourteen-year-old Joseph Smith related his heavenly vision to his family, who, remarkably, believed him. Armed with this familial support, he went to a trusted minister to seek his guidance. To the young boy's surprise, the minister responded with contempt and told Joseph that what he had described was from the devil and that "visions and revelations had ceased with the apostles." (Joseph Smith—History 1:21). To the bewilderment of the teenager, the minister noised the account to others in the small community. The contentious religious zeal already present immediately turned against Joseph and his family. Joseph recorded:

> I soon found, however, that my telling the story had excited a great deal of prejudice against me among the professors of religion, and was the cause great persecution, which continued to increase; and though I was an obscure boy, only between fourteen and fifteen years of age, and my circumstances in life such as to make a boy of no consequence in the world, yet men of high standing would take notice sufficient to excite the public mind against me, and create bitter persecution; and this was common among all the sects—all united to persecute me." (Joseph Smith—History 1:22).

Three years later, at the age of seventeen, Joseph related that while praying to God he had another heavenly manifestation. He maintained that a heavenly being appeared in his room, called Joseph by name, and instructed him on numerous biblical scriptures and doctrines. This being told the teenager that God would restore the church that Jesus had organized during his earthly ministry through him.[45] It would be based on the original organization of apostles, prophets, evangelists, pastors, and teachers delineated in Ephesians 4:11, and unlike most other churches, all members in this new church were to be called upon to contribute in various manners according to their several abilities with the head never saying to the foot, "I have no need of you" as described in I Corinthians 12:21. The messenger informed Joseph that an ancient record was deposited in a nearby hillside and instructed him to go there. The next day Joseph confided this bewildering experience with his father, who believed his son's account and charged him to "not to fail in attending strictly to the instruction which he had received from the heavenly messenger."[46] Remembering the directions given by the angel, Joseph repaired to the hillside and easily found the place described.

Then using a branch for a lever, he moved a rock with rounded corners to find that it covered a stone box. Inside was a book-like set of metal plates appearing to be made of gold, bound by three rings, as well as two stones that would serve as interpreters and an ancient breastplate. At that moment the messenger appeared again and forbade Joseph from removing the contents. Rather, he was to return each year on that date, September 22, to view again the plates and receive more instructions. After four years, he would be permitted to remove the plates and begin translating the record, as Joseph described it, "by the gift and power of God."[47]

Joseph's mother, Lucy Mack Smith, remembered:

> The ensuing evening, when the family were altogether, Joseph made known to them all that he had communicated to his father in the field, and also of his finding the record, as well as what passed between him and the angel while he was at the place where the plates were deposited.
>
> . . . He charged us not to mention out of the family that which he was about to say to us, as the world was so wicked that when they came to a knowledge of these things they would try to take our lives; and that when we should obtain the plates, our names would be cast out as evil by all people.
>
> From this time forth, Joseph continued to receive instructions from the Lord, and we continued to get the children together every evening for the purpose of listening while he gave us a relation of the same. I presume our family presented an aspect as singular as any that ever lived upon the face of the earth—all seated in a circle, father, mother, sons and daughters, and giving the most profound attention to a boy, eighteen years of age, who had never read the Bible through in his life . . . This caused us greatly to rejoice, the sweetest union and happiness pervaded our house, and tranquility reigned in our midst.
>
> During our evening conversations, Joseph would occasionally give us the most amusing recitals that could be imagined. He would describe the ancient inhabitants of this continent, their dress, mode of traveling . . . their cities, their buildings, with every particular; their mode of warfare; and also their religious worship. This he would do with as much ease, seemingly, as if he had spent his whole life among them.[48]

Even Joseph's older brothers believed these unusual accounts and vowed to protect and support him in what they perceived to be a great and marvelous work. Joseph's oldest brother, Alvin, would die of an illness just two months later. On his death bed, he admonished Joseph "to do everything that lies in your power to obtain the Record," and to "be faithful in receiving instruction, and in keeping every commandment that is given you."[49] Hyrum, Joseph's other older brother, would be gunned down with Joseph in the jail at Carthage, Illinois, after living his entire adult life standing at his younger brother's side. Hyrum, Alvin, and all of Joseph's family believed that Joseph's work was authored by God Himself. Many others would come to believe it as well, but most Americans of Joseph's day would not.

## Chapter One Endnotes

1. The Lincoln Presidential Museum, Springfield, IL.

2. "Heber J. Grant: Quotes on Freedom, America, Constitution, Liberty, Etc. . . ." last modified February 25, 2014, http://www.latterdayconservative.com/quotes/heber-j-grant/.

3. William J. Wolf, *The Almost Chosen People: A Study of the Religion of Abraham Lincoln* (Garden City, NY: Doubleday, 1959), 24–25.

4. Abraham Lincoln, "Second Inaugural Address," (March 4, 1865).

5. John Wesley Hill, *Abraham Lincoln: Man of God* (New York: G. P. Putnam's Sons, 1920), 152.

6. Ibid., 98.

7. Wolf, *The Almost Chosen People*, 24–25.

8. Ibid., 13.

9. Ibid., 22.

10. Ibid., 24.

11. Thomas Freiling, ed., *Abraham Lincoln's Daily Treasure: Moments of Faith with America's Favorite President* (Grand Rapids, MI: Fleming H. Revell, 2002), 253.

12. One of their articles of faith reads: "We believe in the same organization that existed in the Primitive Church, namely, apostles, prophets, pastors, teachers, evangelists, and so forth." (Articles of Faith 1:6)

13. Hill, *Abraham Lincoln*, 129.

14. Philip L. Ostergard, *The Inspired Wisdom of Abraham Lincoln: How Faith Shaped an American President—and Changed the Course of a Nation* (Carol Stream, IL: Tyndale House Publishers, 2008), 95.

15. William E. Barton, *The Soul of Abraham Lincoln* (New York: George H. Doran Company, 1920; repr.,University of Illinois Press, 2005), 300.

16. Freiling, *Abraham Lincoln's Daily Treasure*, 8.

17. Ibid., 11.

18. Susan Hill Lindley, *You Have Stept Out of Your Place: a History of Women and Religion in America* (Westminster John Knox Press, 1996), 59.

19. Wolf, *The Almost Chosen People*, 40.

20. Ibid., 42.

21. Barton, *The Soul of Abraham Lincoln*, 257.

22. Wolf, *The Almost Chosen People*, 30.

23. Ibid., 41.

24. Ibid., 57.

25. Ibid., 35.

26. Ibid., 38.

27. Ibid.

28. Barton, *The Soul of Abraham Lincoln*, 48.

29. Ibid, xxiv.

30. Freiling, *Abraham Lincoln's Daily Treasure*, 235.

31. Wolf, *The Almost Chosen People*, 50–51.

32. Barton, *The Soul of Abraham Lincoln*, 137.

33. Wolf, *The Almost Chosen People*, 104.

34. Barton, *The Soul of Abraham Lincoln*, xxiv.

35. Wolf, *The Almost Chosen People*, 47.

36. Ibid., 104.

37. Ibid., 92.

38. Ibid.

39. Bart D. Ehrman, *The Orthodox Corruption of Scripture: The Effect of Early Christological Controversies on the Text of the New Testament* (New York,: Oxford University Press, 1993), xi.

40. Ibid., 3–4.

41. Wolf, *The Almost Chosen People*, 133.

42. Ibid., 136.

43. Abraham Lincoln, *State Papers, 1861–1865* (New York: Current Literature Publishing, 1907), 159.

44. Wolf, *The Almost Chosen People*, 98.

45. Lucy Mack Smith, *History of Joseph Smith by His Mother* (Salt Lake City, UT: Bookcraft, 1901), 74–75.

46. Ibid., 80.

47. "Introduction" in *The Book of Mormon: Another Testament of Jesus Christ*, trans. Joseph Smith, Jr.

48. Smith, *History of Joseph Smith*, 81–83.

49. Ibid., 87.

# Chapter Two

# "A STRANGE NEW SECT"

Outside of Joseph's family, there was one important resident of Palmyra who believed Joseph's extraordinary accounts. His name was Martin Harris. He employed Joseph Smith Sr. and his sons on his large, prosperous farm. Harris looked forward with anticipation to the day when Joseph would be allowed to take possession of the plates. Around the time that Joseph was to receive the plates, someone, either Harris or a member of his family, disclosed the account of the gold plates, igniting wild rumors of a golden bible.[1]

At that time, Josiah Stowell and Joseph Knight, farmers from southern New York, were in Palmyra buying grain and heard the rumors. Josiah was deeply intrigued. Sometime earlier, a document had fallen into his hands that purportedly contained information about an abandoned Spanish silver mine somewhere in northern Pennsylvania. He hoped that Joseph could employ some supernatural ability to find the mine and came to the Smith home intent on hiring Joseph to do so. Joseph assured Stowell that he had no such powers and declined the offer for employment, but Stowell was persistent and offered a generous wage. With the persecutions mounting in Palmyra, the thought of leaving the area had some appeal. Joseph relented on the condition that his father, who was in need of additional income, could accompany him. Stowell agreed, and Joseph and his father left the area in late 1825 to join Stowell's other hired hands to search for the mine.

After a month of searching, Joseph and his father convinced Stowell to abandon the search. Stowell yielded, but, admiring the Smiths' integrity and character, he hired them for other work on his farm. Joseph's father would later return to Palmyra, but Joseph remained in South Bainbridge, near Joseph Knight's farm, gristmill, and carding machine.[2] Knight's son Newell grew particularly fond of Joseph and said this of him:

> The business in which my father was engaged often required him to have hired help, and among the many he from time to time employed was a young man by the name of Joseph Smith, Jun., to whom I was particularly attached. His noble deportment, his faithfulness and his kind address, could not fail to win the esteem of those who had the pleasure of his acquaintance. One thing I will mention, which seemed to be a peculiar characteristic with him in all his boyish sports and amusements; I never knew any one to gain advantage over him, and yet he was always kind and kept the good-will of his playmates.[3]

There are numerous accounts of Joseph's fun-loving nature and his delight in engaging in wrestling and other manly activities of the day. He, like Lincoln, was often described as athletic and strong yet uncommonly fair, and Joseph was never known to have met his equal in popular games of strength such as stick pulling and leg wrestling.

Like so many in that day, Newell was an avid reader of the Bible. He wrote, "I found by reading and searching the Bible, that there would be a great falling away from the gospel as preached and established by Jesus and His apostles, that in the last days God would set His hand again to restore that which was lost."[4] With such a perception, it is not surprising that Newell would find Joseph's account to be of interest. Newell continues:

> During this time we were frequently visited by my young friend, Joseph Smith, who would entertain us with accounts of the

wonderful things which had happened to him. It was evident to me that great things were about to be accomplished through him—that the Lord was about to use him as an instrument in His hands to bring to pass the great and mighty work of the last days. This chosen instrument told us of God's manifestations to him, of the discovery and receiving of the plates from which the Book of Mormon was translated, of his persecutions for the gospel's sake, and many other items of his eventful life. So honest and plain were all his statements that there was no room for any misgivings with me on the subject.[5]

It must have been heartening to Joseph to find that the Knight and Stowell families believed his report.

## EMMA

There was a compelling reason for Joseph to stay in South Bainbridge. During his month working for Stowell, Joseph Smith boarded with the Isaac Hale family in Harmony, Pennsylvania, and there met his future wife, Isaac's daughter Emma. Emma was struck by the handsome, muscular six-foot-two boarder. She'd grown up in Harmony and received a good education. With her brothers, she became skilled at canoeing and horseback riding. Emma Hale was about eighteen months older than Joseph. She was described by those who knew her as beautiful and intelligent, and it was said that she possessed an excellent singing voice. Joseph continued to call on Emma. He asked Isaac Hale's permission to marry her twice in 1826, and both times he was denied. It is quite certain that by this point in their relationship Joseph would have disclosed his unusual past to Emma, and it is clear that it did little to extinguish her feelings for him. Like Joseph's family, Emma embraced his message.

In January 1827, Emma accompanied Joseph on horseback to Josiah Stowell's home. After discussing their mutual disappointment at being unable to marry, Stowell convinced the pair to marry the next day. Joseph had already confided his interest in marrying Emma to his parents in Manchester, and they had readily approved. Emma later recalled that she had no intention of marrying when she left home, but preferring to marry Joseph to any other man that she knew, she consented.[6]

Stowell led them to Squire Tarbill's home, and there they were married. Instead of returning to Harmony, they went north to Manchester to live with the Smiths, where Joseph helped on the family farm through the summer. Emma's parents were heartsick and angry over the elopement. On the other side, Lucy Mack Smith was immediately taken by her new dark-eyed, raven-haired daughter-in-law. The two women would be close through the rest of their lives as they stood by their persecuted son and husband.

On September 22, 1827, exactly four years from the date that Joseph first viewed the plates hidden in the hillside, Josiah Stowell and Joseph Knight had business again in Palmyra. It appears that they timed their visit to see if Joseph would indeed obtain the plates. At near midnight, all had retired except Joseph's mother, Lucy, who, without questioning the men, nervously watched as Emma quietly "passed through the room with her bonnet and riding dress,"[7] then out the door with her husband. They boarded Joseph Knight's horse-drawn wagon and rode off without saying where they were going or why they were leaving at such a late hour. They rode to the base of the nearby hill, where Emma remained alone in the dark night while Joseph ascended. After a long time, Joseph finally returned without the plates. He informed Emma that he had indeed obtained the plates but had secreted them in a hollow birch log some three miles from the house.

Back at the house, Lucy was so filled with anxiety that she could not sleep. She spent much of her sleepless night in prayer for her son. Morning arrived, but Joseph and Emma had not, adding to Lucy's consternation. At breakfast, Joseph Sr. called for Joseph Jr., apparently unaware that Joseph had left the night before. Lucy successfully changed the subject without informing him of their son's midnight departure. Soon Joseph Knight entered the home, alarmed that his horse and wagon were gone. Lucy assured him that they would both soon be found but again said nothing about Joseph taking them.

Shortly thereafter, Joseph and Emma arrived. Lucy recounted, "I trembled so with fear lest all might be lost in consequence of some failure in keeping the commandments of God that I was under the necessity of leaving the room in order to conceal my feelings."[8] Upon leaving the room, she met Joseph, who sensed her alarm and assured her that all was well. He said nothing of the plates; he only asked where he might acquire a small chest with a lock. The following day, Joseph Sr. overheard a group of men plotting how they were going to find "Joe Smith's gold Bible"[9] by employing a conjuror to divine the place where Joseph had secreted them. Emma borrowed a horse and rode to the place where Joseph was working to warn him of the threat; Joseph returned with Emma but calmly assured her that the plates were safe. After eating his supper, he sent his youngest brother, Don Carlos, to Hyrum's home to ask Hyrum to bring the chest. Joseph left in the night to retrieve the plates, having been instructed by the messenger that no one else was to see them at that time.

Joseph's mother records the following:

> Joseph, on coming to [the plates], took them from their secret place, and, wrapping them in his linen frock, placed them under his arm and started for home.
>
> . . . Traveling some distance . . . as he was jumping over a log, a man sprang up from behind it and gave him a heavy blow with a gun. Joseph turned around and knocked him down, then ran at the top of his speed. About half a mile farther he was attacked again in the same manner as before; he knocked the man down in like manner as the former and ran on again; and before he reached home he was assaulted the third time. In striking the last one, he dislocated his thumb, which, however, he did not notice until he came within sight of the house, when he threw himself down in the corner of the fence in order to recover his breath. As soon as he was able, he arose and came to the house. He was still altogether speechless from fright and the fatigue of running.[10]

After gathering himself, he asked his father, Stowell, and Knight to go out to see if they could find the men who had accosted him. When Hyrum arrived with the chest, Joseph placed the wrapped object inside and locked it. He recounted his harrowing night to his family, Stowell, and Knight. Then he showed them his thumb, saying, "I must stop talking, father, and get you to put my thumb in place, for it is very painful."[11]

Joseph hid the chest and its contents under the hearthstones of the Smith family home. Soon after, two groups of men rummaged in and around the house looking for the plates but did not find them. The persecution became so intolerable that Joseph and Emma decided to leave Palmyra and return to Harmony.

Joseph and Emma hid the plates in a barrel of beans and struck out for Harmony to face Emma's parents. Upon their arrival, Joseph received the anticipated scolding from Isaac Hale. He accused Joseph of stealing his daughter and marrying her and said that he would much rather have followed her to her grave. But the Hales could not conceal their relief at seeing their daughter again and at observing her contentment with being Joseph's wife. They offered Joseph and Emma an unoccupied cabin a short distance from their own, where Joseph and Emma, with great relief, settled in.

It was here that Joseph commenced the translation of the record. Joseph read the words through the interpreters and Emma wrote them. Emma would sit for hour upon hour while her husband translated the writing on the plates, and she would write word for word and sentence by sentence with little or no hesitation. She recalled that when Joseph would come upon a proper name that he could not pronounce, he would promptly spell it for her and would even know, somehow, when she had written it incorrectly and would correct her spelling from the other side of the table without seeing the manuscript.[12]

Emma, like everyone else, was not allowed to view the plates, but she would daily see the covered object in her home, and she later commented on how she often moved the heavy object from place to place. In Emma's later years, her son Joseph Smith III interviewed her regarding the plates and their translation:

> Question. Had he not a book or manuscript from which he read, or dictated to you?
>
> Answer. He had neither manuscript nor book to read from.
>
> . . . Question. Are you sure that he had the plates at the time you were writing for him?
>
> Answer. The plates often lay on the table without any attempt at concealment, wrapped in a small linen tablecloth, which I had given him to fold them in. I once felt of the plates, as they thus lay on the table, tracing their outline and shape. They seemed to be pliable like thick paper, and would rustle with a metallic sound when the edges

were moved by the thumb, as one does sometimes thumb the edges of a book.

. . . Question. Could not father have dictated the Book of Mormon to you . . . after having first written it, or having first read it out of some book?

Answer. Joseph Smith [and for the first time she used his name direct, having usually used the words, "your father" or "my husband"] could neither write nor dictate a coherent and well-worded letter, let alone dictate a book like the Book of Mormon. And, though I was an active participant in the scenes that transpired, and was present during the translation of the plates, and had cognizance of things as they transpired, it is marvelous to me, "a marvel and a wonder," as much so as to anyone else.

Question. I should suppose that you would have uncovered the plates and examined them?

Answer. I did not attempt to handle the plates, other than I have told you, nor uncovered them to look at them. I was satisfied that it was the work of God, and therefore did not feel it to be necessary to do so . . .

Question. Mother, what is your belief about the authenticity, or origin, of the Book of Mormon?

Answer. My belief is that the Book of Mormon is of divine authenticity—I have not the slightest doubt of it. I am satisfied that no man could have dictated the writing of the manuscripts unless he was inspired; for, when acting as his scribe, your father would dictate to me hour after hour; and when returning after meals, or after interruptions, he could at once begin where he had left off, without either seeing the manuscript or having any portion of it read to him. This was a usual thing for him to do. It would have been improbable that a learned man could do this; and, for one so ignorant and unlearned as he was, it was simply impossible.[13]

Earlier, Martin Harris had given Joseph and Emma fifty dollars, and Joseph Knight sent food and provisions upon which the Smiths supported themselves during the translation period. This assistance allowed Joseph to concentrate his efforts on translating. After a few weeks, Harris arrived from Palmyra to assist Emma as scribe. Harris's arrival was particularly welcome to Emma, who was enduring a difficult pregnancy with her first child. Harris's involvement allowed her to manage the affairs of the home and meals while the work of translation continued uninterrupted. On June 15, 1828, Emma gave birth to her and Joseph's first child, a son that they named Alvin after Joseph's oldest brother. The infant died shortly after his birth. The delivery nearly took the Emma's life as well, leaving the young couple grief stricken for several days. With Emma still recovering, Joseph and his in-laws buried Alvin in a cemetery near their home.

It would be three years later before Emma would give birth again. Joseph and Emma Smith's seventeen-year marriage produced eleven children (including adopted twins), six of whom did not survive infancy. The surviving five grew up as the children of a persecuted and controversial father who was frequently called away from them. They later felt the dreadful loss of his murder while still young.

## A PIECE OF FLOATING DRIFTWOOD

In March of 1830, while Joseph Smith was making preparations for the organization of The Church of Jesus Christ of Latter-day Saints on April 6, Abraham Lincoln was helping his father, Thomas Lincoln, and stepmother, Sarah, move the family to Macon County, Illinois. There they experienced another outbreak of the milk-sick, a mysterious sickness associated with contaminated milk (now known to be caused by cattle eating the toxic white snakeroot plant).[14] The malady had taken the life of nine-year-old Abraham's mother, Nancy. When it surfaced on Pigeon Creek, and Thomas wasn't about to have more of that. He sold the place and headed northwest.

Abe stayed with Thomas and Sarah until April 1831 to help them establish their home and farm. Then, at age twenty-two, he struck out on his own. He and two friends were hired to build a flatboat, load it with live hogs and barrels of bacon, corn, and wheat, and guide it to New Orleans. Abe had done this once before at age seventeen. The flatboat launched on the Sangamon River in central Illinois and headed for the Mississippi, but it became lodged on the sawmill dam at the village of New Salem and began taking on water. Abe and his friends labored furiously to free the boat and save their cargo. Before long, many in the village arrived to observe the spectacle.

The men struggled unsuccessfully to free the craft. Then, oddly, the tall one named Lincoln began boring a hole in the bow of the boat. He directed his coworkers to unloaded the cargo at the rear. The New Salem villagers puzzled at his strange operation but soon saw that this procedure was causing the boat's stern to rise. When the water poured out through the hole that Abe had bored, the whole craft slowly lifted and floated over the dam. The townsfolk were impressed at Abe's ingenuity, as was the relieved owner of the flatboat and cargo, Denton Offutt, who made plans then and there to further employ the innovative Abe Lincoln upon his return from New Orleans.

Young Lincoln was enthralled by the bustling city of New Orleans except for the numerous slave pens, high-walled enclosures where slaves waited their day at the slave markets to be callously displayed, inspected, and sold to the highest bidder. On his first New Orleans flatboat trip as a teenager, Abe and his friends had happened upon the slave market while an auction was taking place. He watched in horror as families were systematically disassembled, mothers being sold to one plantation owner, fathers to another, and children to still another, likely to never again be reunited.

Solomon Northup, a slave who was sold at a New Orleans slave market some years later, described the auction of a young boy named Randall at the slave market. The scene was probably similar to the one Lincoln observed:

> The little fellow was made to jump, and run across the floor, and perform many other feats, exhibiting his activity and condition. All the time the trade was going on, Eliza [his mother] was crying aloud, and wringing her hands. She besought the man not to buy him, unless he also bought herself and Emily. She promised, in that case, to be the most faithful slave that ever lived. The man answered that he could not afford it, and then Eliza burst into a paroxysm of grief, weeping plaintively. Freeman [the auctioneer whom Solomon Northrup described as a man known to be very amiable and pious-hearted] turned round to her, savagely, with his whip in his uplifted hand, ordering her to stop her noise, or he would flog her. He would not have such work—such snivelling; and unless she ceased that minute, he would take her to the yard and give her a hundred lashes. Yes, he would take the nonsense out of her pretty quick—if he didn't,

might he be d—d. Eliza shrunk before him, and tried to wipe away her tears, but it was all in vain. She wanted to be with her children, she said, the little time she had to live. All the frowns and threats of Freeman, could not wholly silence the afflicted mother. She kept on begging and beseeching them, most piteously not to separate the three. Over and over again she told them how she loved her boy. A great many times she repeated her former promises—how very faithful and obedient she would be; how hard she would labor day and night, to the last moment of her life, if he would only buy them all together. But it was of no avail; the man could not afford it. The bargain was agreed upon, and Randall must go alone. Then Eliza ran to him; embraced him passionately; kissed him again and again; told him to remember her—all the while her tears falling in the boy's face like rain.

Freeman d—d her, calling her a blubbering, bawling wench, and ordered her to go to her place, and behave herself; and be somebody. He swore he wouldn't stand such stuff but a little longer. He would soon give her something to cry about, if she was not mighty careful, and *that* she might depend upon.

The planter from Baton Rouge, with his new purchases, was ready to depart.

"Don't cry, mama. I will be a good boy. Don't cry," said Randall, looking back, as they passed out of the door.

What has become of the lad, God knows. It was a mournful scene indeed. I would have cried myself if I had dared.[15]

It is likely that young Abe could not help but notice that the white auctioneers and buyers seemed unaffected by the awful transactions. Leaning over to his companions, Abraham said, "Let's get away from this. If ever I get a chance to hit that thing [slavery] I'll hit it hard."[16] Some three decades later, Lincoln would find himself landing the blow that would end slavery forever in the United States.

Indeed, federal and state lawmakers' success in defining slaves as property in the years following the formulation of our Constitution made tragic scenes like young Randall being torn from his mother's loving arms commonplace and perfectly legal. During the Constitutional Convention of 1787 in Philadelphia, some of the original founding fathers threatened to leave the Convention should the Constitution interfere with slavery. This forced the compromise delineated in Article 1, Section 1, Clause 3 of the Constitution. Known as the three-fifths compromise, it set the formula for allocating seats in the House of Representatives, which were based on population. Specifically, slaves would count as three-fifths of a person for the purposes of representation—even though they we ineligible to vote.

In his later years, Lincoln would lament this unfortunate imbalance and its damaging effect on America when he said:

> Maine and South Carolina have exactly the same number of senators, of House members, and of electoral votes in choosing a president. Equal power. But Maine has more than twice as many white citizens as South Carolina; the "equality" is brought about by adding three-fifths of South Carolina's slave population. "The slaves do not vote; they are only counted and so used, as to swell the influence of the white people's vote." . . . Equal power for the state with fewer than half the voters means that "each white man in South Carolina is more than the double of any man in Maine. . . . The South Carolinian is more than double of any one of us in this crowd."[17]

Lincoln returned to New Salem to receive his meager pay for the flatboat venture, and, having nowhere else to go, he accepted Offutt's offer to cut wood for the sawmill. He told his newfound friends in New Salem that he was just "a piece of floating driftwood"[18] and would remain there until he had somewhere else to go. Lincoln lived the next six years of his life in the tiny settlement. The hamlet had about one hundred residents when he arrived, approximately the same population as Chicago in 1831. It was, however, the largest community in which Lincoln had ever resided. After a few months of cutting timber, Abe became Offutt's store clerk until Offutt sold the unprofitable business. For Abe, this job was preferable to cutting wood or farming, and he was happy for that. Although he was known as a hard and reliable worker, employment in the small store provided him with nearly everything he could want in that stage of his life: a roof over his head, food, a wage (albeit meager), conversation, and, most importantly to him, the opportunity to read.

It was here that people grew acquainted with Abe's uncompromising honesty and integrity. He was known to walk miles to return a few pennies of incorrect change he had mistakenly withheld or to deliver a small under-measurement of tea. Though New Salem reached its population zenith with only some twenty-five families, it became the commerce center for the settlers in the surrounding area, and the new, affable and awkward drifter relished every opportunity to strike up conversation with everyone except the young ladies. Lincoln was painfully shy around them.

Lincoln seemed very self-conscious of his appearance. He would often joke about it. Years later, when Stephen A. Douglas accused Lincoln of being two-faced, Abraham simply joked that if he had two faces, did Douglas really think he would choose to wear this one? At New Salem, Abe Lincoln quickly became a part of the small community. He joked at social gatherings, pitched in at house-raisings, mourned with friends at burials and funerals, attended Sunday worship services, and fully engaged in any conversation he could find.

## The Unwelcomed New Sect

Soon after Joseph Smith's 1830 organization of his new religion, rumors regarding the Mormons began to spread. Lincoln doubtlessly heard at least some of them; he once commented to a friend on the "strange, new sect." Articles about the tiny yet rapidly growing church were appearing in the Sangamo Journal printed in nearby Springfield, Illinois. As a young man, Abe Lincoln relished the opportunity to read any newspaper he could find, and it is likely that the Sangamo Journal was the most widely read paper in New Salem. Lincoln probably read most of the articles that follow—this first one appearing just a year and a half after the Church's organization.

# Sangamo Journal.

Springfield, Illinois, Sat., November 10, 1831. Vol. I. No. 1

The fact that a sect of fanatics, calling themselves Mormonites, have sprung up and extended themselves in the western part of New

York and the eastern part of Ohio, is partially known to our read-ers. The origin, character and numbers of this sect have not yet been noticed in the Gazette, and, it seems proper now to notice them.

The ostensible founder of this fanaticism is a man of the name of Joseph Smith, an indolent, ignorant, careless shiftless fellow in the commencement of life. He prayed, preached, and made converts. He "put money in his purse," and in consequence of a divine revelation, removed with his converts [from New York] to the neighborhood of Painesville, Ohio. Here his converts increased rapidly, and recently a company of about one hundred immigrated from that place to some promised land upon the Missouri, taking with [them?] their common means, their religious instructors, and their Mormon Bibles.

Even from this isolated frontier village, Abraham Lincoln came to learn much about the Mormons. While Joseph Smith was gather-ing converts to the newly formed Church of Jesus Christ of Latter-day Saints, young Abraham, along with much of America, followed its turbulent beginnings through a plethora of newspaper accounts. In fact, by the 1840s, it was a rare American who did not know at least something, accurate or not, about this new and unpopular religion. Unfortunately for Lincoln and for the rest of the United States, what they knew of this unwelcome sect came primarily through negative newspaper accounts. Some of what was printed was true, some was not.

Considering the Baptist, Methodist, Campbellite, and other Prot-estant sects so prominent in America at that time, it is not surprising that many Americans would disagree with Mormon doctrine. What is surprising is the venomous and often violent opposition that surfaced against the new church and its followers. As the name suggests, The Church of Jesus Christ of Latter-day Saints taught (and still teaches) that Jesus Christ is the Son of God and Savior of the world, that He gave His life for the sins of mankind, and that He was resurrected. They believed His teachings in the Bible. They believed in repen-tance, forgiveness, the healing of the sick through faith and anointing as prescribed in the New Testament, the gift of tongues, baptism by immersion, and the gift of the Holy Ghost. These beliefs hardly seem grounds for the malicious persecution that followed them.

But it rankled many that Joseph Smith claimed to receive rev-elations from God like the prophets of the Bible. Opponents of

Mormonism also revolted against the thought of another book claiming to be scripture on the same level as the Bible. The Book of Mormon purports to contain teachings of Jesus Christ given through ancient prophets in the Americas, Mormon being the one who compiled the ancient record. The Latter-day Saints (the Mormons referred to themselves as saints, as did the New Testament apostles when they referred to their followers) did not claim that their new book supplanted or negated the Bible, but rather that it complemented Biblical teachings. Such a notion, however, was repulsive and blasphemous to many Christians.

Adding to the opposition's alarm was the fast-rising number of people who listened to Mormon doctrine or read the Book of Mormon and then left their Protestant congregations for the new religion. The anti-Mormons also rankled at the numerous reports by eyewitnesses and recipients of healings through prayer and the laying on of hands by Mormon leaders. Such things were regarded as heresy.

Few Protestants today can relate the origins of their religions, and few consider it a matter of importance. Conversely, Latter-day Saints then and now solemnly and frequently witness their conviction that their Church's inauspicious beginnings with a prophet, apostles, angels, revelations, and translations of ancient records, are the true workings of the Almighty God in the latter days. For the early Latter-day Saints, such testimonies and convictions occasionally gained a convert, but more often they formed embittered enemies, and even though an astonishing number were accepting this message and being baptized into the Church, their foes grew at a much faster and more ominous rate.

The appearance of this new sect on the American continent, just a few decades following the formation of the Baptist, Methodist, and Presbyterian denominations in England, came at a time when religion was on the mind of nearly every American. As a result of the high religious fervor of the Second Great Awakening, it was a rare American who had not aligned him or herself with one of the various and frequently conflicting religions. Those who had not were, in the public mind, infidels—Abraham Lincoln and Joseph Smith included.

# Chapter Two Endnotes

1. Lucy Mack Smith, *History of Joseph Smith by His Mother* (Salt Lake City, UT: Bookcraft, 1901), 104–5.

2. Newell Knight, "Newel Knight's Journal," in *Autobiography (1800–1846): Classic Experiences and Adventures* (Salt Lake City, UT: Bookcraft, 1969), http://www.boap.org/LDS/Early-Saints/NKnight.html.

3. Ibid.

4. Ibid.

5. Ibid.

6. George Q. Cannon, *Life of Joseph Smith the Prophet* (Salt Lake City, UT: Deseret Book, 1972), 43.

7. Smith, *History of Joseph Smith*, 102.

8. Ibid., 103–4.

9. Ibid., 105.

10. Ibid., 108.

11. Ibid., 109.

12. "Emma Smith Bidamon," on Moroni's Latter-day Saint Page, last modified 19 November, 2011, http://www.moroni10.com/witnesses/EmmaSmith.html.

13. Ibid.

14. "Milk Sickness," http://en.wikipedia.org/wiki/Milk_sickness, accessed March 31, 2014.

15. Solomon Northup, *Twelve Years A Slave* (Auburn, NY: Derby and Miller, 1853), 29.

16. Lloyd Ostendorf, *Abraham Lincoln: the Boy, the Man* (Springfield, IL: Wagner, 1962), 55.

17. William Lee Miller, *Lincoln's Virtues: An Ethical Biography* (2002; repr., New York: Vintage Books, 2003), 259.

18. David Herbert Donald, *Lincoln* (New York: Touchstone, 1995), 38.

*Chapter Three*

# PEACEABLY IF THEY COULD, FORCIBLY IF THEY MUST

Within a year of the new church's organization, Joseph Smith told his members that he had received a revelation from God informing him that war was in America's near future and that the Saints, for their safety, should gather to the western frontier of America:

> Ye hear of wars in foreign lands; but, behold, I say unto you, they are nigh, even at your doors, and not many years hence ye shall hear of wars in your own lands.
>
> Wherefore I, the Lord, have said, gather ye out from the eastern lands, assemble ye yourselves together ye elders of my church; go ye forth into the western countries, call upon the inhabitants to repent, and inasmuch as they do repent, build up churches unto me." (D&C 45:63–64).

In the coming years, the Mormon prophet would receive numerous other revelations, most of which were complied in a book entitled the *Doctrine and Covenants*. In early 1831, fleeing relentless opposition, Joseph Smith and his small flock of followers left upstate New York and made their first westward move to Kirtland, Ohio (as noted earlier in the *Sangamo Journal* article). Mormon missionaries had baptized more than one hundred new converts in that area, many of whom were former members of the Campbellite movement then flourishing on the western frontier.

Through subsequent revelations, Joseph announced to his followers that another gathering place would be near Independence, Missouri, at that time the western boundary of the United States. In the summer of 1831, a group of twenty-eight Latter-day Saints (significantly fewer than the one hundred inaccurately reported in Springfield's *Sangamo Journal*) led by Joseph Smith traveled from Kirtland, Ohio, to Jackson County, Missouri. This small band divided up and traveled different routes, sharing their gospel message and gaining converts along the way. Joseph traveled through Cincinnati, across southern Illinois to St. Louis, and then on to Independence. While in Cincinnati, Joseph arranged to meet Walter Scott, a cofounder with Alexander Campbell of the Campbellite sect. Joseph eagerly shared his message with Scott, but Scott and Campbell were already soured by the unsettling number of their followers leaving Campbellite congregations to join with the Mormons in the Kirtland area. Two of their former ministers, in fact, were traveling with Joseph to Independence. Instead of collaborating as Joseph had hoped, Campbell and Scott defiantly rejected his message. They would later assail Joseph Smith's character and the Book of Mormon in their periodicals and sermons.[1]

Upon arriving to their destination in western Missouri, the travelers met up with four Mormon missionaries who had gone before them to preach their message to the Shawnee and Delaware Indians living west of Independence. Their intent was to inform these Native Americans that the Book of Mormon was a record written by their ancestors with a message that was of value to them as well as to whites. The chief was intrigued by this white man's religion that venerated the much maligned Native American, so he invited them to return in the spring to tell them more. Other Christian missionaries already working with these tribes were indignant at the Mormons' intrusion and appealed to the Indian agents to have them banned from preaching to the Indians. The agents quickly complied with the request, and the Mormons were banished from the reservation, preventing their promised spring-time meeting with the tribal elders.

At Independence, after surveying the area and selecting a parcel of land upon which to build a temple, Joseph Smith held a public meeting that was attended by local settlers, some Indians, and a few free blacks. The local settlers were curious as to why the notorious Mormon prophet would be in their remote frontier location, and they came from miles around to hear him. In his address, Joseph shared his gospel message, the Mormons' plans to settle the area, and their hope that they could live in peace with the Missouri settlers, which caused consternation to some in the audience. Within a week of this meeting, the first group of Mormons arrived, including the Joseph and Newell Knight families and others from the South Bainbridge and Colesville area of New York. Aging Josiah Stowell did not make the pilgrimage, but some years later a reporter came to the Colesville area and interviewed locals about their recollection of the Mormon prophet. Stowell was interviewed, and he expressed a strong witness of his continued belief in Joseph Smith and the Book of Mormon. The Colesville saints, led by Newell Knight, purchased land some twelve miles west of Independence, becoming some of the first settlers of what would become Kansas City.

Before returning to Ohio, Joseph appointed a few from his traveling party to remain. Edward Partridge was to open a store and, as agent for the Church, purchase land for the arrival of more Saints. W. W. Phelps was appointed to establish a printing office and Joseph hoped that a newspaper would help smooth the transition for the non-Mormon settlers.[2] While some locals in the area were untroubled at the arrival of the Mormons, others were suspicious of their intentions. Joseph also appointed W. W. Phelps to open a proselyting mission in Missouri in July 1831. Shortly thereafter, Phelps preached a sermon wherein he specifically referred with deference to some Negroes who were among his first audience, adding to the uneasiness of the locals.

## The Divisive Influence of Slavery

The territory of Missouri applied for statehood in 1818. To their surprise, Northern politicians tried to restrict slavery in Missouri as a condition of their admittance to the Union. After a bitter political battle, the Missouri Compromise of 1820 was passed, allowing Missouri into the Union as a slave state. At the time, most Missouri settlers were pro-slavery Southerners, and they became deeply resentful of this northern intrusion, which heightened their suspicion of outsiders. The arrival of the mostly northern and antislavery band of Mormons seemed another intrusion. This, and the fact that Indians and Negroes were welcomed to Mormon public meetings, became fuel for the flames of unrest and violence that were to follow. The Mormons were later accused of inciting the Indians to violence and of inviting Negroes into their church. There is no evidence of the former accusation being true, but ample evidence that the latter was.

As editor of the *Morning and Evening Star*, W. W. Phelps hoped the paper would be an organ of goodwill in the Missouri communities. Unfortunately, the result was just the opposite. In the summer of 1833, Phelps wrote a piece on blacks, both free and slave, that created a firestorm in Jackson County. Phelps was probably aware of some early black converts to his religion as well as some southern slave-owning converts who, may have wanted to settle in Missouri along with their slaves.[3] His article was well intentioned. It reminded Mormon slave-owners and free blacks that Missouri had been designated a slave state by the government. He went on to refer to the developing abolition movement as one of the wonderful events of the age. Some old settlers misread this article. Few in Missouri besides the Mormons would agree with Phelps on abolition. Many locals interpreted both messages to be an invitation for blacks, free and slave, to migrate to Missouri to become Mormons and gain emancipation. Although relatively few old settlers owned slaves, most had no intention of freeing them and viewed this Mormon position as seditious. Many states were enacting laws such as Missouri's, which stated:

> If any negro or mulatto came into the state of Missouri without a certificate from the court . . . evidencing that he was a citizen of

such state, such negro or mulatto could be commanded by the justice to leave the state; and if the colored person so ordered did not leave the state within thirty days . . . the court was authorized to sentence such person to receive ten lashes on his or her bare back, and then order him or her to depart from the state.[4]

Phelps quickly tried to explain his intentions in an extra edition of the paper, but the damage was done. Within five months, the Mormons would find themselves forcibly driven from Jackson County.

The fact that the Mormons were willing to preach their gospel to blacks was not unusual. Many contemporary protestant preachers also sought to bring Christianity to blacks. What was unusual was the fact that the Mormons were willing to include blacks in their congregations. They even went as far as ordaining them officers in the priesthood. This gave blacks the authority to preside in meetings—over white members, a condition that the white Mormons seemed generally willing to accept. A few faithful black men were ordained as elders, and some of these participated in the Mormons' most sacred temple rites along with whites.

Most black converts to protestant religions were encouraged to form their own black congregations In mixed congregations, blacks were to sit in a designated section of the chapel. Neither of these conditions were embraced by the Mormons. The blacks intermingled with the white members in their worship services and participated, by and large, as equals. This too was troubling to some of the old settlers of Jackson County.

There are two probable sources of this Mormon tolerance and inclusion of blacks and Native Americans in their communities and congregations. First, the Book of Mormon instilled in its readers an almost celebratory status for the Native Americans that was uncommon in that era. The Book of Mormon chronicles the journey of a group of Israelites who were guided by the hand of God to cross the ocean to the Americas. The record stresses that the American Indians were heirs of God's promises to covenant Israelites. It also contains messages like this one, which states that Christ:

> Inviteth them all to come unto him and partake of his goodness;

and he denieth none that come unto him, black and white, bond and free, male and female; and he remembereth the heathen; and all are alike unto God, both Jew and Gentile. (2 Nephi 26:33)

The other source was Joseph Smith himself. He taught his followers that "it is not right that any man should be in bondage one to another" (D&C 101:79) and that their "everlasting gospel" was intended for "every nation, kindred, tongue, and people" (D&C 77:8). In March 1832, while the Saints were settling in Missouri, Joseph said of slavery, "it makes my blood boil"[5]—a position very similar to Lincoln's, who said, "I am naturally anti-slavery. If slavery is not wrong, nothing is wrong. I can not remember when I did not so think, and feel."[6]

## MOBS

On April 30, 1831, Emma Smith gave birth to twins Thaddeus and Louisa in Kirtland, Ohio. They, like their brother Alvin before them, lived only three hours, leaving the couple again in deep sadness at their loss. Three days later, Julia Murdock, a family friend, gave birth to twins, also a girl and a boy, but Julia died from complications in the delivery. John Murdock, the father of the twins, was deeply worried over his ability to care for the infants, and he approached Joseph and Emma with the prospect of them adopting his twins. They accepted the infants with deep gratitude, naming them Joseph and Julia Murdock.

While the number of Mormons was growing in Ohio and Missouri, some dissatisfied followers left the Church and became its bitter enemies and persecutors. On a cold March night in 1832 following Joseph's return to Ohio, he and Emma were caring for their ten-month-old twins, who were ill with severe cases of the measles. An angry mob of between one and four dozen men broke into their home, carried Joseph a quarter mile into the woods. There they beat him, choked him to near unconsciousness, tore off his clothes, and then, as Joseph recorded, "one man fell on me and scratched my body like a mad cat, and then muttered out: 'That's the way the Holy Ghost falls on folks.'"[7] One tried to force poison into his mouth but only succeeded in breaking one of Joseph's front teeth with the vial.

As a result of the broken tooth, Joseph spoke for the rest of his life with a slight lisp. They then smeared hot tar and feathers on his face and body.

In the mob were Simonds Ryder and Ezra Booth, former ministers who had converted to the Mormon sect and then shortly thereafter became dissatisfied and left. Their interest in the Mormons began when they heard that the notorious Mormon prophet had relocated to their region. Booth traveled to the Mormon settlement of Kirtland with John and Elsa Johnson, members of his Methodist congregation, to meet the newly arrived Joseph Smith. The following is an account of the event that led to his conversion as recorded by a non-Mormon source:

> Mr. and Mrs. Johnson . . . visited Smith at his home in Kirtland, in 1831. Mrs. Johnson had been afflicted for some time with a lame arm, and was not at the time of the visit able to lift her hand to her head. The party visited Smith partly out of curiosity, and partly to see for themselves what there might be in the new doctrine. During the interview the conversation turned on the subject of supernatural gifts, such as were conferred in the days of the apostles. Some one said, "Here is Mrs. Johnson with a lame arm; has God given any power to man now on the earth to cure her?" A few moments later, when the conversation had turned in another direction, Smith rose, and walking across the room, taking Mrs. Johnson by the hand, said in the most solemn and impressive manner: "Woman, in the name of the Lord Jesus Christ I command thee to be whole," and immediately left the room. The company were awe-stricken at the infinite presumption of the man, and the calm assurance with which he spoke. The sudden mental and moral shock—I know not how better to explain the well-attested fact—electrified the rheumatic arm—Mrs. Johnson at once lifted it up with ease, and on her return home the next day she was able to do her washing without difficulty or pain.[8]

Ezra Booth was so impressed with this healing that he investigated the new religion further and forsook his Methodist congregation to join the Church, as did the Johnsons. A few weeks later, Ezra Booth accompanied Joseph on the aforementioned nine-hundred-mile trek to Missouri. He became disillusioned when, likely along with other reasons, God did not grant him power to "smite men and make them believe."[9] When his frequent demands to see further miracles went unheeded, he became an outspoken and violent opponent of the Mormons. Joseph concluded his account of his midnight attack with:

> My friends spent the night in scraping and removing the tar, and washing and cleansing my body; so that by morning I was ready to be clothed again. This being Sabbath morning, the people assembled for meeting at the usual hour of worship, and among those came also the mobbers, viz.: Simonds Rider, a Campbellite preacher and leader of the mob; one McClentic, son of a Campbellite minister; and Pelatiah Allen, Esq., who gave the mob a barrel of whiskey to raise their spirits; and many others. With my flesh all scarified and defaced, I preached to the congregation as usual, and in the afternoon of the same day baptized three individuals.[10]

Sadly, the twins' condition worsened, probably from exposure to the cold on the night of the attack. The twin named Joseph died five days later. After just five years of marriage, Emma had been the mother of five, all dying in infancy except Julia. John Murdock learned the news upon returning from a mission. Murdock remained a faithful friend to the Smiths and would follow them throughout their many expulsions, enduring countless persecutions for his faith. He always remained close to Julia, the surviving twin.

## THE DISTURBANCE IN GATHERING

The number of Saints settling in Missouri exploded to more than eight hundred by the following summer. Not surprisingly, this staggering influx of Mormons greatly alarmed the non-Mormon settlers already in Missouri, and trouble ensued. The following year, some four or five hundred more new Mormon converts, again mostly from the Northeast, settled the area. Most of the Missouri-bound Latter-day Saints passed through Illinois, some through Springfield itself. The residents of Illinois, including, most likely, young Abe Lincoln, followed the unfolding drama in their neighboring state with rapt interest.

# Sangamo Journal.

Vol. I. Springfield, Illinois, January 5, 1832 No. 9.

The Mormon delusion.—By information from the west, some are falling off, as well as others uniting with Joe Smith, the head man from Palmyra. One who has lately left them by the name of Henry [*sic*—probably Ezra] Booth, of Portage county, Ohio, is publishing in the Ohio Star an expose of their diabolical pretensions and impositions. They pretend an ability, as in ancient times, to speak with tongues; and that Smith is able to hold converse with celestial spirits whenever he pleases. One of them pretends to have received a commission to preach the gospel, directly from heaven on a piece of parchment; another to have received his on the palm of his hand; and witnesses are found to attest to these lies. Visions are in great repute. One who has seen the New Jerusalem, and passed through its apartments, &c. . . . Such are some of their absurdities which this young man is exposing.

N. Y. Baptist Register.

Articles such as this blanketed the nation. They left much of America wagging their heads in disgust and many Latter-day Saints scratching their heads in bewilderment at the rejection and rancor.

## LINCOLN QUIETLY OBSERVES THE TURMOIL

To the dismay of much of America, people continued to embrace the Mormon faith. This engendered rancorous denunciations on the part of many, particularly ministers and preachers, of Mormon beliefs that were dissimilar to their own. Such was the turmoil experienced and described by fourteen-year-old Joseph Smith in New York while his own immediate family was divided in their congregational choices, some joining with one congregation and others with another. Young Abe Lincoln had a similar experience over the tumultuous division and competition among the various religious persuasions in Indiana and later in Illinois.

There were no fewer than 137 articles on the Mormons published in Springfield's *Sangamo Journal* from the years 1831 to 1848. Some were written with tedious detail and hyperbole. Lincoln, an avid newspaper reader, would certainly have read most of them. The sensational topic was likely a frequent conversational topic among New Salem and Springfield residents. Yet we have no clear record of Lincoln's impressions regarding either the Mormons in Missouri or those passing through his state.

# Sangamo Journal.

Vol. II. Springfield, Illinois, July 5, 1832 No. 35.

> The Mormons.—A band of thirty or forty pilgrims of this delectable sect, men women and children, passed through this county a few days since, on their way to the "promised land," in Jackson county, Missouri.—It appears that the "promised land" is continually receiv[ing] emigrants of this description.

While mostly peaceable, the Mormons were immediately different from the locals in Missouri. Mormon historian B. H. Roberts, exposing a hint of righteousness indignation that may have contributed to the tensions, wrote,"The Saints could not join the Missourians in their way of life—in Sabbath-breaking, profanity, horse-racing, idleness, drunkenness, and debauchery." Roberts also pointed out that the local pro-slavery settlers were more than alarmed to know that these saints were coming "from the Northern and New England States, and the hatred that existed at that time between the people of the slave-holding and free states, was manifested toward the saints by their 'southern' neighbors."[11]

Unsurprisingly, the Mormons' assertion that God had declared Jackson County to be a place of inheritance for them did not sit well with the old settlers. Trouble was inevitable. The mushrooming number of new Mormon converts and their willingness to leave their homes and farms to unite with the other saints in Missouri and Ohio created an unprecedented sociological, political, and religious dilemma for the Joseph Smith and his followers.

By the spring of 1832, signs of the approaching storm appeared. Rocks were thrown at a few Mormon homes, frightening the families inside. By the fall, a number of Mormon-owned haystacks were burned, and bullets were fired at some Mormon homes. About this same time, the Reverend Finis Ewing, head of the Independence Presbyterian Church, published the following statement: "The 'Mormons' are the common enemies of mankind and ought to be destroyed."[12] The Reverend Pixley went house to house encouraging a general uprising against the alarming number of Mormons in the area.

## THE BLACK HAWK WAR

While trouble was brewing for the Mormons in Missouri, Illinois had its own crisis. A large group of Sauk and Fox Indians were unhappy with being relocated west of the Mississippi years earlier by government agents and had crossed back into northern Illinois to reclaim their original homeland. Exaggerated reports of burned-out settlements and murdered settlers prompted local militias to organize with the purpose of driving the Native Americans back across the Mississippi. A sense of duty and adventure led Lincoln and his young friends to willingly conscript for the thirty-day campaign. When it came time to elect their captain, twenty-three year-old Abe received the surprise of his young life when a large majority of his company selected him to serve as their captain. He served under Major Lewis Bidamon, the man Emma Smith would marry following Joseph's martyrdom.

On May 15, 1832, Lincoln's company was ordered to Stillman's Run. According to letters from General Samuel Whiteside, brigade commander at the time, Lincoln and his men arrived at sunset to find twelve militiamen dead, scalped, and mangled from a battle with a war party the day before. Lincoln and his men solemnly buried the deceased and then remained at Stillman's Run in an attempt to draw out the war party again, but the Indians had left the area and no confrontation took place.

At the end of his thirty-day commitment, Lincoln and a few others re-enlisted as privates for an additional sixty days. He saw no action against the Indians, but the militia experience gave new acquaintances outside of New Salem, most notably with Orville Browning and John Todd Stuart, who would become common friends with Joseph Smith in the coming years. Lincoln also acquired a lasting respect and loyalty from the men that he captained for his raw, capable, and fair-minded leadership of the company.

Years later Lincoln made a tongue-in-cheek remark concerning his Black Hawk War service during an 1848 speech before the US Congress. Lincoln was stumping for the Whig presidential Candidate, General Zachary Taylor. The Democratic nominee, Lewis Cass, had just addressed the assembly. As touted by his Democratic supporters, Cass was a hero from the War of 1812 who gained renown for having broken his sword over his knee in disgust at the news of the surrender of Fort Detroit to the British during the war. To the delight of the Whigs on the House floor, Lincoln compared Cass's military experience to his own in a facetious courtroom-like analysis:

> [Cass] *in*vaded Canada without resistance, and he *out*vaded it without pursuit. As he did both under orders, I suppose there was, to him, neither credit or discredit in them . . . he was volunteer aid to Gen. Harrison on the day of the battle of the Thames; and, as you [the partisan Democrats] said in 1840 [when Harrison ran for president] Harrison was picking huckleberries two miles off while the battle was fought, I suppose it is a just conclusion with you, to say Cass was aiding Harrison to pick huckleberries.[13]
>
> By the way, Mr. Speaker, did you know I am a military hero? Yes, sir; in the days of the Black Hawk War, I fought, bled, and came away . . . I was not at Stillman's defeat, but I was about as near it, as Cass was to Hull's surrender; and like him, I saw the place very soon afterwards. It is quite certain I did not break my sword, for I had none to break; but I bent a musket pretty badly on one occasion. If Cass broke his sword, the idea is, he broke it in de[s]peration; I bent the musket by accident. If Gen. Cass went in advance of me picking huckleberries, I guess I surpassed him in charges upon the wild onions. If he saw any live, fighting indians, it was more than I

did; but I had a good many bloody struggles with the mosquitoes; and although I never fainted from loss of blood, I can truly say I was often very hungry.[14]

## LINCOLN ENTERS THE WORLD OF POLITICS

At the end of his military service, Lincoln returned to New Salem, where his neighbors continued to marvel at the young, gangly bachelor who would not drink alcohol, smoke, chew tobacco, or gamble, and who was the strongest wrestler, fastest runner, and quickest wit in the area. Lincoln's reputation of unwavering honesty grew while operating his struggling store. Prior to leaving with the militia, prominent men in the community who recognized young Abe's unique intelligence and integrity encouraged him to run for a seat in the Illinois state legislature. His late return from militia duty cut into his time to develop an effective campaign. Considering the fact that he was mostly unknown outside of his New Salem community, Lincoln did relatively well in the election. He expressed his unique character in a handbill he wrote for his first political campaign that summer:

> Every man is said to have his peculiar ambition. Whether it be true or not, I can say, for one, that I have no other so great as that of being truly esteemed of my fellow-men by rendering myself worthy of their esteem.[15]

Despite his popularity, Lincoln awoke on the morning of August 7, 1832, to learn that he had been defeated in his first run for a seat in the legislature. In the surrounding county, where he was relatively unknown, he garnered few votes. But in the precinct that included New Salem, the vote for him was nearly unanimous. But the spark was kindled. He would run in the subsequent race and win in 1834.

Upon his return from the militia, Lincoln also embarked on his first business venture. Two established New Salem businessmen offered Lincoln and William Berry (one of Lincoln's corporals in the militia) an opportunity to purchase their store. Lincoln had no money for the purchase, but with his reputation for honesty already well established, they sold them the store on Lincoln's signature.

These more experienced merchants could probably see what young Lincoln and Berry could not—that the little village was declining and could not support the store. Lincoln's first business venture faltered. Berry drank too heavily, and Lincoln was too interested in his books and too generous to excel financially. Shortly thereafter, Berry unexpectedly passed away, leaving Lincoln with the failing store and a burdensome debt—both his own and Berry's. People began leaving New Salem for more prosperous settlements, forcing property values sharply down. Lincoln was soon forced to sell the store and its goods for pennies on the dollar to two brothers who eventually left town and disappeared, never paying Lincoln what they owned him.

As a young man, Bill Green clerked in the Berry & Lincoln store and lived in the back of the store with Lincoln. Several years later, a group of listeners told Bill that he was the best storyteller they had ever heard. He responded by saying that there was one even better who:

> Used to keep a grocery whar I live. He kin make a cat laugh. I've seen the whole neighborhood turn out to hear him tell stories. . . . He's a great big feller, with a big mouth, and he kinder acts it all out, smilin' and laffin'. I never seed a real clown, but he'd make one. But I've seen him when he was the solumest man in ten states. When he kem back from runnin' a flatboat to New Orleans, ef anybody said anything about nig—rs he would git so solum, an' tell about a nig—r auction he seed in New Orleans—how they sold a fambly, the man to one planter and his wife to another an' passeled the childern out among the highes' bidders, an' he thought it was awful. I've seen him turn pale . . . when talkin' about this auction, and seem to take sick to his stomick, and then begin to cuss and take on . . . I never once heerd him swar excep' when talkin' o' that nig—r auction.

The listeners asked Green for the name of this curious fellow. Green replied, "He's as good a feller as ever lived; but he's kinder common—sorter jes' like everybody, no better no worse, jes' a good feller." Then Green told them the youth's name was "Abe Linkern" and continued:

> He is the curi'est feller I ever seed! He could ask more questions

than a Philadelphia lawyer could answer. Thar never kem a man inter the neighborhood, but [Abe]'d find out jes' the things he knowed. He'd make friends with him by tellin' him stories an' then he'd pump him. I've seen him pump a down-East Yankee 'bout Boston till he knowed more 'bout Boston, an' Plymouth Rock, and Bunker Hill than the Boston feller hisself. When he heerd of a grammar-book he walked six miles to git it, an' when he got through with it he knowed more grammar than the schoolmaster.[16]

While other sources confirm Bill Green's assessment of young Abe, it should be noted that there is no evidence that Lincoln ever used the disrespectful term for the black race as was so freely used by Green and many others in his day.

After selling his store, Lincoln went to work as New Salem's part-time postmaster, where he read the various newspapers that were mailed through the Post Office. The job provided less income than Abe needed, so he took on extra jobs and boarded with families or at the tavern. The tavern owner, Henry Onstott, said of Abe, "Lincoln never drank liquor of any kind and never chewed or smoked. We never heard him swear, though Judge Weldon said . . . that once in his life when he was excited he said, 'By Jing!'"[17] Abe was soon offered the opportunity to become the deputy county surveyor. He surprised many by learning the trade in just six months through an intense self-guided study of the craft. As he traveled the county as a surveyor, his circle of friends widened—as did his political options.

## UNREST IN MISSOURI

In April 1833, some four hundred old settlers assembled in Independence to address the Mormon problem, but they could not agree on a plan of action. Later, following W. W. Phelps's incendiary July article on blacks, a "Secret Constitution"[18] circulated, delineating the grievances against the Mormons and "binding all who signed it to assist in 'removing the Mormons.'"[19] The document declared that the Mormons were idle, lazy, and vicious and that they claimed to receive revelations directly from God, to heal the sick by the laying on of hands, to speak in unknown tongues, and perform all "the wonder-working miracles wrought by the inspired apostles and prophets of God."[20] The document went on to say that these practices were "derogatory of God and religion, and subversive of human reason."[21] The Mormons' affinity toward the Indians and their anti-slavery sentiments were also cited. In the resolution, the signers pledged to rid their country of the Mormons "peaceably if they could, forcibly if they must."[22] Their eradication efforts would take on the tenor of a holy crusade to clear their communities of the Mormons.

Young Abe Lincoln would likely have read the following:

# Sangamo Journal.

Vol. II. Springfield, Illinois, August 17, 1833. No. 93.

From the Western Monitor.

MORMONISM.

At a meeting of the citizens of Jackson county, Missouri, called for the purpose of adopting measures to rid themselves of the set of Fanatics called Mormons, held at Independence on the 20th day of July, 1833, which meeting was composed of gentlemen from every part of the county, there being present between four and five hundred persons.

The evil is one that no one could have foreseen, and is therefore unprovided for by the laws, and the delays incident to legislation, would put the mischief beyond remedy.

But little more than two years ago, some two or three of this people made their appearance in the Upper Missouri, and they now number some 1200 souls in this county, and each successive autumn and spring pours forth its swarms among us, with a gradual falling of the character of those who compose them; until it seems that those communities from which they come, were flooding us with the very dregs of their composition. Elevated as they mostly are, but little above the condition of our blacks, either in regard to property or education, they have become a subject of much anxiety on that part, serious and well grounded complaints having been already made of their corrupting influence on our slaves.

. . . it requires no gift of prophecy to tell that the day is not far distant when the civil government of the county will be in their hands. When the Sheriff, the Justices, and the County Judges will be Mormons, or persons wishing to court their favor from motives of interest or ambition.

Of their pretended revelations from Heaven—their personal intercourse with God and his Angels—the maladies they pretend to heal by the laying on of hands—and the contemptible gibberish with which they habitually profane the sabbath, and which they dignify with the appellation of unknown tongues, we have nothing to say, vengeance belongs to God alone. But as to the other matters set forth in this paper, we feel called on by every consideration of self preservation, good society, public morals, and the fair prospects, that if not blasted in the germ, await this young and beautiful county, at once to declare, and we do hereby most solemnly declare,

1. That no Mormon shall in future move and settle in this country.

2. That those now here, who shall give a definite pledge of their intention within a reasonable time to remove out of the county . . .

3. That the editor of the "Star" be required forthwith to close his office, and discontinue the business of printing in this county . . .

4. That the Mormon leaders here, are required to use their influence in preventing any further emigration of their distant brethren to this county . . .

The violence against the unwelcome newcomers soon escalated to driving logs through windows, ransacking homes, damaging crops, scattering livestock, whipping Mormon men (the ever-efficient disciplinary tool for slaves), all of which was traumatizing to the Mormon women and children. Two Mormon leaders were captured and threatened with violence if they would not renounce their religion. They would not, and for that they were tarred and feathered while taunts were heard from the crowd like, "Call upon your God to deliver you—pretty Jesus you worship!"[23] Mormon Bishop Edward Partridge recorded:

I was taken from my house by the mob, George Simpson being their leader, who escorted me about a half a mile, to the court house, on the public square in Independence; and then and there, a few rods from the said court house, surrounded by hundreds of the mob, I was stripped of my hat, coat and vest and daubed with tar from head to foot, and then had a quantity of feathers put upon me; and all this because I would not agree to leave the county, and my home where I had lived two years.[24]

Before tarring and feathering me I was permitted to speak. I told them that the Saints had suffered persecution in all ages of the world; that I had done nothing which ought to offend anyone; that if they abused me, they would abuse an innocent person; that I was willing to suffer for the sake of Christ; but, to leave the country, I was not then willing to consent to it. . . .

Until after I had spoken, I knew not what they intended to do with me, whether to kill me, to whip me, or what else I knew not. I bore my abuse with so much resignation and meekness, that it appeared to astound the multitude, who permitted me to retire in silence, many looking very solemn, their sympathies having been touched as I thought; and as to myself, I was so filled with the Spirit and love of God, that I had no hatred towards my persecutors or anyone else.[25]

Charles Allen was next stripped and tarred and feathered, because he would not agree to leave the county, or deny the Book of Mormon. Others were brought up to be served likewise or whipped.[26]

In spite of the persecutions taking place in Missouri, other Mormons from the east were journeying through Lincoln's Illinois toward the unrest.

---

# Sangamo Journal.

---

Vol. II. Springfield, Illinois, November 2, 1833. No. 104.

---

Companies of Mormons continue to pass through this State for "Mount Zion." One would suppose that the late events at Zion would cool the zeal of the new converts. But it is not so. It is given out that one of the prophets, some two years since, foretold the destruction of Zion, and the fulfilment of his prediction is regarded as conclusive evidence of the Divine character of the new religion. One of the Mormons on being required to point out another prophecy and its fulfilment, stated that about one year ago a Mormon prophet visited Cincinnati, and foretold the destruction of that city; and he had lately seen a person direct from Cincinnati, who informed him that the cholera and small pox had carried off nearly all the inhabitants of that city!!

# Sangamo Journal.

Vol. II. Springfield, Illinois, Sat., November 16, 1833. No. 106.

### CIVIL WAR IN MISSOURI.

The St. Louis Republican of Tuesday contains an account of a series of affrays in Jackson County, Missouri, between citizens of that County and the Mormons, in which between twenty and thirty citizens and several Mormons were KILLED. The Mormons, according to the account, acted only on the defensive. At the date of the last accounts there was a tremendous excitement in the county. No one could calculate the issue of it. Among the persons killed were some of the most respectable citizens.

The Mormon leaders made numerous appeals to local civil authorities for protection but received little. There is evidence that some of the local civic leaders were directly involved in the persecutions. B. H. Roberts records:

> The outrages of this day were the more reprehensible because of the character of the leaders of the mob. In the main they were the county officers—the county judge, the constables, clerks of the court and justices of the peace; while Lilburn W. Boggs, the lieutenant-governor, the second officer in the state, was there quietly looking on and secretly aiding every measure of the mob—who, walking among the ruins of the printing office and the house of W. W. Phelps, remarked to some of the saints, "You now know what our Jackson [county] boys can do, and you must leave the country!"[27]

Not all of the old settlers were behind the violence, but any demonstration of sympathy for or assistance to the Mormons was answered with threats and harassment. Unable to secure protection from local authorities, the Mormons took their appeals for protection directly to Governor Daniel Dunklin, who expressed sympathy and issued orders to restore the peace, which were essentially ignored. By the fall of 1833, it was apparent that the rising population of Mormons would lead to a strong political majority and, eventually, Mormon elected officials with their anti-slavery slant. This was a deeply troubling prospect to the old settlers.

Drastic and violent action followed. In early November, some five hundred armed and angry men began a systematic raid of the dispersed Mormon settlements. In the process, they ran more than twelve hundred Mormon men, women, and children from their homes, sending them scattering in the cold. Desperate to protect their homes and families, a group of armed Mormon men banded together. Skirmishes ensued in which two old settlers and one Mormon were killed and one other Mormon seriously wounded—far fewer than that reported in the *Sangamo Journal*. The account of the wounded Mormon, Philo Dibble, was recorded by a Mormon leader, Parley Pratt, and collaborated in other sources:

> In the battle brother Philo Dibble, of Ohio, was shot in the body through his waistband; the ball remained in him. He bled much inwardly, and, in a day or two his bowels were so filled with blood and so inflamed that he was about to die. . . . At length Elder Newel Knight administered to him, by the laying on of hands, in the name of Jesus; his hands had scarcely touched his head when he felt an operation penetrating his whole system as if it had been a purifying fire. He immediately discharged several quarts of blood and corruption, among which was the ball with which he had been wounded. He was instantly healed, and went to work chopping wood.[28]

Philo Dibble lived to be eighty-nine years old. He confirmed this account throughout his life, except that he said the ball had remained lodged in his back. The protrusion could be seen and felt until the day he died in Springville, Utah.[29]

W. W. Phelps's printing press and home were demolished, as was the Mormon mercantile establishment of Whitney & Gilbert. Terrified women and children were seen everywhere running to the woods for safety, some returning to find home and possessions burned to the ground.

# Sangamo Journal.

Vol. II. Springfield, Illinois, Sat., Dec 7, 1833 No. 106.

Straightway came the Mormons, headed by a fanatic, who is a disgrace to the creation of God. In their doctrine, they [claimed] as an inheritance the whole of Jackson county. By fraudulent and false statements, they were gathering together the scum of the earth— were offering inducements to the free negroes, every where to come up and join them, and had succeeded in alienating many of the Indians who surrounded them. That the people, among whom they had settled, should feel disposed to rid themselves of such a pest, we think is extremely natural; and that they would have fared better, in any other country, we are very much disposed to doubt.

The homeless Mormons who wandered south into Van Buren County were quickly run off. The bulk of the Mormons were literally driven north under deplorable conditions:

All through this day and the day following (the 6th and 7th of November,) women and children were fleeing in every direction from the presence of the merciless mob. One company of one hundred and ninety—all women and children, except three decrepit old men—were driven thirty miles across a burnt prairie. The ground was thinly crusted with sleet, and the trail of these exiles was easily followed by the blood which flowed from their lacerated feet! This company and others who joined them erected some log cabins for temporary shelter, and not knowing the limits of Jackson County, built them within the borders thereof. Subsequently, in the month of January, 1834, parties of the mob again drove these people, and burned their wretched cabins, leaving them to wander without shelter in the most severe winter months. Many of them were taken suddenly ill and died.[30]

Such was the case with expectant mother Keziah Higbee, who,

"in the most delicate condition, lay on the banks of the river all night, while the rain descended in torrents, and under these circumstances was delivered of a male child; but the mother died a premature death through the exposure."[31]

Those who ventured farther north in the cold, rain, and snow fortunately met with compassionate settlers in Clay County, who offered kind assistance to the desperate Mormon families. Clay County swelled with the battered Latter-day Saints, and rudimentary temporary shelters soon dotted the landscape.

Hope for redress came in the February 1834 term of the circuit court in Independence. The state did file charges against a number of Jackson County citizens for the violence and unlawful removal of the Mormons from their homes. Twelve Mormons were subpoenaed as witnesses for the State, and on February 23, 1834, they were escorted across the Missouri River to Independence under the protection of the Liberty Blues, a militia unit led by Captain David R. Atchison, one of a small number of old settlers who were repulsed by the violence. Trouble was anticipated, so an additional two hundred militiamen were called up to guard against any disruption of the court proceedings.[32]

Upon their arrival, the witnesses were quartered in the Flourney Hotel, where they were cordially met by the circuit attorney and the state attorney general, who had been sent by the governor to "investigate as far as possible, the Jackson outrage."[33] Only minutes after their arrival, "Captain Atchison informed the witnesses that he had received an order from Judge Ryland that the services of his company were no longer needed in Jackson County. So the witnesses for the State were marched out of town to the tune of Yankee Doodle—quick time."[34] The Mormons were abruptly denied their day in court, and the trial was dismissed by Judge Ryland.

The depth of the religious conviction of the early Mormons is an intriguing phenomenon. Few of these persecuted Mormons had practiced their religion for more than two years; many of them were converts of but a few months. The congregations of the dominant Baptist and Methodist religions were always at their disposal, requiring little of the sacrifice that their new faith seemed to unceasingly require. Accepting the Mormon faith and the ridicule that was so often packaged with it and then accepting the call to assemble in Ohio and Missouri reflects an uncommon degree of commitment.

Surely the outspoken disregard for the Mormon beliefs by neighbors and friends would be influential in the new converts' decision to leave their communities and join with the other saints. There they could find acceptance among fellow believers and, they supposed, safety. But why they would endure such extreme persecution for their newfound beliefs is somewhat a marvel. A simple retraction of their allegiance to the Church and realignment with any of the other Protestant religions would have ended their suffering. The local churches would have welcomed these misguided souls back into their congregations as they did Ezra Booth and Simonds Ryder. Remarkably, the majority of Mormons chose to endure their affliction rather than turn from their new faith.

# Chapter Three Endnotes

1. B. H. Roberts, *The Missouri Persecutions* (Salt Lake City, UT: Bookcraft, 1965), 39–40.

2. Joseph Smith, et al., *Doctrine and Covenants of The Church of Jesus Christ of Latter-day Saints, Containing Revelations Given to Joseph Smith, the Prophet with Some Additions by His Successors in the Presidency of the Church*, Sections 57:11, 58:24.

3. B. H. Roberts, *The Missouri Persecutions* and *History of the Church*.

4. B. H. Roberts, *History of the Church*, (Salt Lake City, UT: Deseret Book), vol. II, xxii

5. B. H. Roberts, *History of the Church of Jesus Christ of Latter-day Saints: An Introduction and Notes*, 2nd ed.; rev. ed., (Salt Lake City, UT: Deseret Book, 1966), vol. 4, 544.

6. Ronald C. White, Jr., *The Eloquent President: A Portrait of Lincoln through his Words* (New York: Random House, 2005), 260.

7. George Q. Cannon, *Life of Joseph Smith the Prophet* (Salt Lake City, UT: Deseret Book, 1972), 134.

8. B. H. Roberts, *History of the Church of Jesus Christ of Latter-day Saints: An Introduction and Notes*, 2nd ed.; rev. ed., (Salt Lake City, UT: Deseret Book, 1967), vol. 1, 215–216.

9. B. H. Roberts, *The Missouri Persecutions* (Salt Lake City, UT: Bookcraft, 1965), 57.

10. Ibid., 59–60.

11. Ibid., 72.

12. Ibid., 73.

13. Abraham Lincoln, "Speech in the US House of Representatives on the Presidential Question," on July 27, 1848 in *Collected Works of Abraham Lincoln* (Ann Arbor, MI: University of Michigan Digital Library Production Services, 2001), 509, http://quod.lib.umich.edu/l/lincoln/lincoln1/1:516?rgn=div1;view=fulltext.

14. Benjamin J. Thomas, *Lincoln's New Salem*, rev. ed. (1954; repr.,Carbondale, IL: Southern Illinois University Press, 1987), 83.

15. Wilma Frances Minor, "Lincoln the Lover," *The Atlantic Monthly*, January 1, 1929, http://www.theatlantic.com/magazine/archive/1929/01/lincoln-the-lover/304445/.

16. Carl Sandburg, *Abraham Lincoln: The Prairie Years* ( New York: Harcourt Brace, 1926), 299–300.

17. William E. Barton, *The Soul of Abraham Lincoln* (New York: George H. Doran Company, 1920; repr.,University of Illinois Press, 2005), 55.

18. Roberts, *The Missouri Persecutions*, 74.

19. Ibid.

20. Ibid.

21. Ibid.

22. Ibid.

23. Ibid., 86.

24. Roberts, *History of the Church*, vol. 1, 390–391.

25. Ibid., 391

26. Ibid.

27. Roberts, T*he Missouri Persecutions*, 87.

28. Parley Pratt, ed., *The Autobiography of Parley Pratt*, 7th ed. (1938; repr., Salt Lake City, UT: Deseret Book, 1968) 99–100.

29. "Life History of Philo Dibble in a Condensed Form, 1806–1895," last modified April 1, 2014, http://familytreemaker.genealogy.com/users/d/i/b/George-A-Dibble-III/FILE/0004page.html.

30. Roberts, *The Missouri Persecutions*, 107.

31. Ibid., 108.

32. Roberts, *The Missouri Persecutions*, 118–19.

33. Ibid., 119.

34. Ibid.

*Chapter Four*

# THE MORMON WAR

When word of the suffering Jackson County Saints reached
Joseph Smith in Ohio, he was reportedly overcome with grief,
bursting into tears and sobbing.[1] He prepared a petition to Governor
Daniel Dunklin of Missouri asking for the formation of a militia to
protect the twelve hundred freezing and homeless Latter-day Saints
as they returned to their homes. The Mormon leaders in Missouri
did the same, but their petition included specific details of the illegal
forced expulsion and detailed their losses and the names of many
of the perpetrators. Governor Dunklin, facing a precarious political
dilemma, responded that without permission from Washington, the
laws of his state did not authorize him to form a military force in
Jackson County and that he could do nothing else for them; he also
expressed fear that the presence of a Mormon-protecting militia in
Jackson County would incite a war.[2] He might have been right.

At this news, Joseph Smith petitioned the President of the
United States. The Andrew Jackson administration responded by
saying that the President could not call out a military force to aid in
the execution of the state laws unless requested by constituted state
authorities. This implied a possible willingness to respond. With this
new information, the Mormons pled again with Governor Dunklin
to appeal to Washington, but no appeal for help was ever issued by

the state of Missouri. Instead, Dunklin passed the problem to his legislature, ordering that a special committee be organized to investigate the matter.[3] The Mormons submitted their detailed petition to the state legislature, again imploring them for help in returning safely to their homes. Remarkably, the legislature, the governor, and the federal government did nothing, and the saints languished the remaining winter months in temporary shelters.

With this disappointing response from all levels of government, Joseph Smith called a council of church leaders in Ohio to discuss the matter. It was resolved that a group of two or three hundred men would assemble and march to Missouri with the intent of forming a treaty of peace and aiding the saints in returning to their homes. Emissaries were sent out to various eastern congregations to recruit volunteers, but the response was disappointing.

One of the few who responded was a recent convert, twenty-seven-year-old Wilford Woodruff of Connecticut. He settled his business affairs and walked to Kirtland, where, having no place to live, he was invited to board at the Prophet's home while preparations were made for the journey. Woodruff would become the fourth president of The Church of Jesus Christ of Latter-day Saints in 1889. Thirty-two year old Brigham Young also volunteered for the march, and he would succeed Joseph Smith as the president and prophet of the Church following Joseph's murder in 1844.

On May 1, 1834, a disappointed yet determined Joseph Smith and only twenty men embarked on the over nine-hundred-mile march to Missouri. Three days later, eighty additional volunteers joined them. By the time they reached the Salt River in Missouri, their rescue force had grown to 207 men, eleven women, eleven children, and twenty-five baggage wagons, some of which were loaded with clothing and provisions for the displaced families in Missouri.

Wagons and westward-headed settlers were a common sight on the frontier, but this large body of men traveling without their families appeared very much like a military force. This provoked considerable curiosity and suspicion along their journey. From an early point they noticed men following them that they suspected were spies seeking to learn of their purpose and destination. Knowing this, Joseph took measures to conceal their destination, identity, and purpose in order to avoid problems along the way. Much of their journey was made along the National Road, the main east-west thoroughfare for travelers at that time, which led them to Indianapolis. Before passing through, Joseph ordered most of the men to ride concealed in the wagons and then had the wagons roll into the town staggered and separated. He assigned a dozen men to walk through the town separately and mingle with the locals to hear their reactions to the passing militia. They succeeded in laying low and crossed the White River at the National Road ferry outside the town without difficulties.

As they approached Springfield, Illinois, a local Mormon, Eleazer Miller, joined the group with three fresh horses. Joseph Smith recorded, "This reinforcement was very seasonable, as many of our horses were afflicted, as they very frequently are in changing country, climate and food."[4] On May 30, Joseph sent Almon Babbitt and Fredrick G. Williams into Springfield ahead of the company to once again determine the mind of the people regarding their curious band and to purchase gunpowder. The Springfield residents had heard of the approaching company, yet they expressed no real alarm, so the camp cautiously passed through without incident. Joseph Smith's journal continues: "We passed through Springfield; our appearance excited considerable curiosity, and a great many questions were asked. The spies who had followed us so long pursued us very closely, changing their dress and horses several times a day."[5] The company camped three miles west of the town at Spring Creek when the scouts Babbitt and Williams returned with two kegs of powder and a confirming report that while the Springfield residents were curious of the group, none felt threatened by them and they expressed no intention to hinder their march.

The campsite at Spring Creek placed Joseph Smith some ten miles from New Salem, where Lincoln was living. It is unlikely that young Abe had any idea of his proximity that night to the notorious Mormon prophet of whom he had read so much in the *Sangamo Journal.*

While at Spring Creek, another Springfield-area Mormon visited the camp. He declined Joseph's urging to join their rescue mission, but he gave Joseph a much-needed hundred dollars to support their journey. He informed Joseph that he had recently overheard some men talk of how they had been following Zion's Camp for three hundred miles with the intent of taking some advantage of the party.

Camp members Almon Babbitt and Wilford Woodruff may have been impressed with Springfield because they later returned to live there for a short time. In 1844, Babbitt, a lawyer, was elected to serve in the Illinois state legislature, and during these times he and Woodruff may have become acquainted with Lincoln.

Jackson County residents were warned of the approaching force when the postmaster near Kirtland wrote to his counterpart in Independence that the Mormons were marching for Missouri to retake their homes and farms by the force of arms. The Missourians responded by setting sentries, drilling a defending militia, dispatching scouts to monitor the approach of the Mormon force, and burning a reported 207 empty Mormon cabins in the county to ensure that there would be nothing for the Mormons to return to.

Zion's Camp, as it was called, hadn't gone far before they became convinced that their march was known to the Missourians. A Missourian entered their camp and swore that he knew their destination was Jackson County and then warned them that they would never cross the Mississippi River alive. They crossed the river without incident, however. Once in Missouri, Joseph sent envoys to Governor Daniel Dunklin to inform him of their arrival in his state and their peaceful intentions, and to inquire whether he and his government intended to help restore the Saints to their deeded properties. In reply, Dunklin encouraged them to appeal through the courts. This course they had already taken to no avail because so many local justices, officials, and lawyers were complicit in the Mormons' unlawful removal.

From the beginning, Joseph Smith had repeatedly affirmed that his aim was not violence but only the safe return of his followers to their homes. They had pinned their hopes on Governor Dunklin's intercession, and in this they were deeply disappointed. After hearing Governor Dunklin's reply, they commenced a cautious march toward Jackson County. On their way, while camped at Fishing River, Joseph Smith expressed to some that he had a premonition of danger. Shortly thereafter, five men rode into the camp cursing and exclaiming that the Mormons would see hell by morning. They boasted that at that moment some four hundred men from several counties were in the process of crossing the Missouri River to destroy the Mormons.

As this was happening, a large black cloud formed in the west and quickly moved eastward. It soon became a violent storm that nearly prevented the return of the ferry carrying the Missouri militiamen across the river. The storm's intensity caused Zion's Camp to abandon their tents and run for shelter in a nearby Baptist church. Wilford Woodruff recorded this incident in his journal, noting that once inside the church, Joseph Smith exclaimed, "Boys, there is some meaning to this. God is in this storm."[6] Another camp member recorded that "during this time the whole canopy of the wide horizon was in one complete blaze with terrifying claps of thunder."[7] It was impossible for anyone to sleep, so the group sang hymns and waited out the storm on the church pews. The storm thwarted the Missourians' river crossing, soaked their ammunition, and scattered their horses as the men ran for shelter.

In the end, there was no battle, no killing, and no resolution for the Saints. Bewildered by the burned-out Mormon homes, Joseph and his camp members met and worshipped in somber disillusionment with the displaced Saints in Clay County and then resolved to return to Ohio. Aside from the strong message of support for their beleaguered brethren in Missouri and a strengthened solidarity among most of the camp's members, the endeavor ended in disappointment for the Mormons and triumph for the Missourians. Some from Zion's Camp remained in Missouri, and the rest made the return march back to their homes and families, probably passing through Springfield again.

## ALEXANDER DONIPHAN

The citizens of Clay County Missouri magnanimously received the twelve hundred cold, homeless Mormons who fled to their county from the Jackson County mob. They did what they could to provide sustenance and shelter during the winter months for the destitute Mormon families, but as the months rolled on, they too began to worry over the Mormons' vast numbers and the social, religious, and political challenges they brought with them. Eventually, people began to speak against Mormon settlement in their county.

Tempers flared at a meeting that was held with Jackson County representative Samuel Owens, who warned the assembly that he and his fellow Missourians were willing to fight to retain every inch of the Mormons' Jackson County property. At the same meeting, a Baptist minister declared that the Mormons had been in Clay County long enough and had to clear out or be cleared out. The moderator of the meeting, a Mr. Turnham, responded, "Let us be republicans; let us honor our country, and not disgrace it like Jackson county. For God's sake don't disfranchise or drive away the Mormons. They are better citizens than many of the old inhabitants."[8]

After the Mormon hot potato was tossed from Governor Dunklin back to the local courts, Joseph Smith and other Mormon leaders called upon a young, fair-minded Jackson County lawyer to represent them the local courts one last time. Young Alexander Doniphan was disappointed at the actions of his fellow Jackson County neighbors toward the Mormons, and he was one of the few who wasn't afraid to express it. Doniphan gave a valiant representation of their losses but gained nothing from the determined Mormon opponents.

While serving in the Missouri General Assembly some months later in 1836, Doniphan proposed a peaceful solution to the Mormon problem in Clay County. He sponsored a bill that called for the creation of two new Missouri counties, Daviess and Caldwell, one of which he proposed to be a settlement location for them. The General Assembly recognized the advisability of Doniphan's solution and passed a bill designating Caldwell County for exclusive occupation by the Mormons and as a general recompense for their losses in Jackson County. The Mormons were pleased with the General Assembly's reasonable settlement location, but they were disappointed at having to relocate once again. Heartened by finally having a sanctioned settlement, they accepted the solution. Within a year, the new Mormon town of Far West became one of the largest communities in the state. Within two years, the open prairie of Caldwell County became a bustling Mormon city of about five thousand residents with two hotels, a printing office, blacksmith shops, stores, and some hundred and fifty hastily constructed homes.

When Abraham Lincoln met Doniphan in February 1861, Lincoln probably recognized a number of similarities they shared: they were both six feet, four inches tall, gifted lawyers, and Whigs. Like Lincoln, Doniphan was opposed to slavery and secession and maintained a reverence for the Constitutional right of religious expression—as reflected by his courageous defense of the Mormons. When Doniphan was invited to Washington by President-elect Lincoln to represent Missouri in a Peace Conference, Lincoln, noting the tall stature they shared, quipped that Doniphan was the only man that he had met whose appearance came up to his expectations.

It is likely that President Lincoln was aware of Doniphan's courageous defense of the Mormons, yet there is no way to tell whether this had anything to do with Lincoln's invitation. To this day, Alexander Doniphan remains one of the most heroic figures in Missouri state history. A ten-foot statue of Doniphan stands on the Ray County Courthouse grounds, placed there in 1918 in honor of Doniphan's military gallantry in the Mexican War and his attributes as a citizen, lawyer, and orator.

## OPPORTUNITIES

Shortly after his militia duty, Lincoln was elated with the opportunity to become the assistant surveyor for Sangamon County. The county surveyor at that time was John Calhoun, who had taken part in the Black Hawk War with Lincoln and was impressed with Lincoln's intellect and integrity.

Calhoun gave Lincoln the required books on surveying, and in just six weeks Lincoln surprised him by saying he had learned the craft and was ready to go to work. Abe had studied day and night, seeming to focus on nothing else. His friends protested his dogged determination and the resultant decline in evenings spent entertained by Lincoln's wit and good nature. Calhoun put Lincoln to work at once. He surveyed privately owned tracts of land, laid out public roads, and tradition has it that in his first survey he used a grapevine until he could acquire a chain.

As early as 1832, Lincoln was drawing up legal documents for his newfound friends. He was not yet a lawyer, but even before coming to New Salem, he had studied law books. He even appeared from time to time in the court of the corpulent New Salem Justice of the Peace, Bowling Green, to plead cases. He owned a book of legal forms, using which he wrote out deeds, mortgages, and other documents for those who needed them. Lincoln rarely charged any fees even though he sorely needed additional income.[9]

Young Abe was intensely interested in the law and yearned for what appeared to be the impossible: the opportunity to become a lawyer. Attendance at law school required money, influential connections, or both, and Lincoln had neither. With his meager income and self-guided education, this dream seemed unreachable.

While living in Indiana, Lincoln gained access to the *Statutes of Indiana* and studied it from cover to cover. He also had occasional access to the books owned by lawyers such as Judge John Pitcher of Rockport, Indiana, and these he devoured as well. He had also come to know the Revised Laws of Illinois, of which he made use in the cases he presented before Bowling Green in New Salem. But to understand the law sufficiently to pass the bar exam, he would need what was commonly referred to as Blackstone's *Commentaries*, or *Commentaries on the Laws of England* by William Blackstone, the principles upon which United States law was based. This four-volume work was not available to Lincoln in New Salem.

To his utter surprise, Lincoln acquired Blackstone's *Commentaries* in a most unexpected way. A stranger migrating west purchased some supplies from Lincoln's store. Finding that he hadn't the room in his wagon for the new items, he took an old barrel from the wagon and asked Lincoln if he would buy it. Lincoln made a passing inspection of the contents of the barrel and determined that it contained little of value to him, but he obliged the man anyway by paying half a dollar for the barrel. The barrel sat in his store for some days before he emptied all of the contents. It was then that he discovered at the bottom a set of Blackstone's *Commentaries*. This fortuitous acquisition would break the poverty that had confined Lincoln and so many others on the American frontier. He immersed himself in the law books with his usual intensity, later declaring that never in his life was his mind so thoroughly absorbed.[10]

Kind friends aided Lincoln in repaying some of the debts from his failed store. His creditors were for the most part lenient, but one of them, Peter Van Bergen, brought suit against him when his note fell due and Lincoln was unable to pay. Van Bergen sued Lincoln for his horse, saddle, and surveying instruments, items Lincoln badly needed for surveying. Lincoln did not contest the suit, knowing full well that Van Bergen was entitled to the settlement. But a good friend, James Short, more familiarly known as Uncle Jimmy Short, heard of Abe's plight and purchased the items from Van Bergen. He then gave them back to Lincoln. Lincoln was deeply touched by the kindness, and years later, as President, he was able to return the favor. Upon hearing that Uncle Jimmy was living in California and had experienced some financial reversals, President Lincoln commissioned Short as an Indian agent with a full regular salary.[11]

In the midst of these financial difficulties, Lincoln was eager to make a second and more determined run for the State Legislature in 1834. Once again, his friends were ready to support him. The 258-dollar salary earned by state legislators would be largest sum of money he had ever possessed—and would make a nice dent in the debts he carried. In this campaign, Lincoln made fewer statements on political issues. He chose instead to ride throughout the county and meet face-to-face with the residents, many more of whom now knew him from his surveying work.

As with his other jobs, surveying gained Lincoln a reputation for accuracy and fairness. On one occasion, he approached a field where some thirty men were at work harvesting grain. He began speaking to the group when someone grumbled that he would cast no vote for any man that could not hold his own in the field. Lincoln replied, "Well, boys . . . if that is all, I am sure of your votes."[12] He then grabbed a harvesting cradle and with perfect ease led the harvesters on a full round of the field. The farm owner recalled, "The boys were satisfied, I don't think he lost a vote in the crowd."[13] The votes were cast on August 4, and the top four candidates elected. Lincoln, at age twenty-five, received 1,376 votes, second highest of the field of thirteen candidates. He borrowed money from Coleman Smoot to purchase the first suit he had ever owned so as to he make a decent appearance in the legislature. This was an important purchase—the lanky bachelor did not often impress with his appearance. One acquaintance described Lincoln as one of the most uncouth-looking young man he ever saw.

## THE CURSE OF SLAVERY

In the 1830s, a grassroots movement to end slavery developed in earnest, led by William Lloyd Garrison. Recognizing that the United States Constitution essentially allowed slavery, Garrison maintained that the framers of the government were men like all others, fallible and weak. While many of the delegates in the Constitutional Convention of 1787 hoped for a Constitutional end to slavery, others threatened to leave the convention should any interference with slavery take place. Had any of them walked out on the proceedings, there would have been no Constitution, no republic, and no government of the people, for the people, and by the people. Lincoln often referred to the compelling need for our nation's founders to compromise on the two-centuries-old institution of American slavery. They did so for the sake of completing the work of building the Constitution with the requisite number of delegates to gain ratification.

American slavery had the strength to derail the fragile Constitutional Convention—and it nearly did so. Contrary to Garrison's depiction of fallible framers, Abraham Lincoln and Joseph Smith independently revered the Founding Fathers, viewing them as heroic, God-inspired men—despite the gaping hole in the Constitution that allowed slavery. During this rising abolition crusade, the Mormon prophet taught his people that the Constitution and the men who framed it were raised up and inspired by God for that purpose.[14] Repairing that hole would be left to Lincoln some three decades later. Yet strong premonitions left Lincoln with the ominous and unrelenting impression that he was to become a major figure in the future of the nation.

Legislators from the Southern states implored their Northern neighbors to quash Garrison's divisive abolition movement. From Mississippi, Northern lawmakers received the supplication to "suppress by penal laws those who are plotting . . . to undermine, disturb or abolish our institutions of domestic slavery."[15] Many Northern states, Illinois included, responded in support of the Southern states' concerns. This occurred because the majority of the early settlers in Illinois had southern roots, and with them they brought the centuries-old tradition of slavery.

## THE YOUNG POLITICIAN

Most of Lincoln's constituents and friends in New Salem were Whigs, but the outlying settlements in his district were predominantly pro-slavery Democrats. On December 1, 1834, Lincoln boarded a southbound stage for Vandalia, the state capital of Illinois, to serve his first term as an Assemblyman in the Illinois state legislature. He roomed with his senior legislator and mentor, John Todd Stuart, the major of Lincoln's 1832 militia battalion. There, the new-suited Lincoln anxiously took his seat as the second-youngest Illinois State Legislator of 1834. He was exceptionally consistent with his attendance, and for the most part, he was an attentive yet mostly quiet participant in the proceedings. During the course of the six-week legislative session, Lincoln's superior writing ability was recognized, and he was asked to draw up bills for the other legislators. The affable Lincoln gladly obliged. It didn't take long for his colleagues to observe that this good-natured newcomer from New Salem always seemed good for a laugh.[16]

To the dismay of Vandalia's residents, a campaign was in motion in the legislature to move the Illinois state capital to Springfield. Lincoln was instrumental in passing this measure, which made the young assemblyman something of a hero in Springfield. It was during this legislative session that Lincoln met the twenty-two-year-old Stephen A. Douglas, who was serving as the prosecuting attorney for Morgan County and would be elected to the senate in the next term as a Democrat. Like Joseph Smith, Douglas was born in Vermont and moved to New York, where he lived some fifteen miles from the Smith home while he attended the academy in Canandaigua. Douglas would certainly have heard tales of the Mormon prophet, his gold bible, and his peculiar church. When Douglas's parents were unable to continue their financial support for his education, he moved west to Illinois and, like Lincoln, took only three years to establish himself and get elected to the state legislature.

Lincoln and Douglas were frequently on opposite sides of the day's political issues, but the well-known rivalry between Douglas and Lincoln occurred much later in their careers. In fact, the young bachelors, though political opponents in state government, respected one another and often socialized together.

In 1831, three years prior to Lincoln's first term, the legislature had passed a law requiring all free blacks to post a prohibitive one-thousand-dollar bond as a guarantee of good behavior while living in the state. This was done with the approval of the majority of the citizens because it effectively excluded free blacks from settling in Illinois. Similar "black laws," as they were called, were commonplace throughout America at that time.[17]

In 1837, to punctuate their solidarity with the slave states, Lincoln's second session of the Illinois legislature enthusiastically received a resolution from a joint committee of Whigs and Democrats stating that slavery continue as an accepted and supported institution in their state. Twenty-eight-year-old Lincoln listened intently as the legislature heard the resolution. With few exceptions, Illinoisans, along with the vast majority of Americans, had an overwhelming bias against blacks, both free and slave. This prejudice was well represented in the Illinois legislature on that cold January day. The resolution affirmed their "deep regard and affection for our brethren of the South,"[18] then continued by exclaiming, "that the purposes of the abolitionists are highly reprehensible. . . . Your committee cannot conceive . . . how any true friend of the black man can hope to benefit him through the instrumentality of abolition societies."[19]

The Speaker of the House called for a vote, and in alphabetical order the clerk called each legislator by name to cast his vote: Mr.

Able? —Aye. Mr. Aldrick? —Aye. Mr. Ball? —Aye. And so it contin-
ued to Lincoln's friend and political colleague John Dawson—Aye.
Mr. Douglas? —Aye. Then the vote came to Jesse Dubois, another
life-long friend of Lincoln's, who responded aye. Mr. Edwards? —
Aye. Ninian Edwards would soon become Lincoln's brother-in-law.
Assemblymen Elkins and Enloe, both friends of Lincoln, voted aye.
And another friend, Reverend John Hogan, submitted his aye vote.[20]

When the clerk came to the name of Assemblyman Lincoln, the
vote stood at thirty-two ayes and zero nays. What no one in that
room could possibly know was that the next man to vote would be
the sixteenth president of the United States, the president who would
frequently refer to himself as God's humble instrument, the president who would eradicate two and a half centuries of American slavery. For this nearly impossible feat, President Lincoln would refuse to
take credit, acknowledging instead the hand of the Almighty God:
"He, from Whom all blessings flow, must not be forgotten . . . no part
of the honor . . . is mine."[21]

By this stage of the voting process, the success of the resolution
was evident. To vote against such a solid majority could create future
difficulties for a dissenting legislator in such a pro-slavery state.

The clerk called, "Mr. Lincoln?" And he responded, "Nay."
Abraham Lincoln had begun his assault on slavery.

William Lee Miller observed, "When in a legislative body the
steady drone of expected votes is interrupted by an unexpected
vote, there may be a suppressed stir, a rustle of surprise, veiled
glances, an exchange of significantly raised eyebrows."[22] Such was
probably the case here. The young and inexperienced Lincoln, only
days into this term in the legislature, was the first to vote no. Five
others would follow with a nay vote, and the motion would carry
seventy-seven to six. The resolution was forwarded to the senate,
which included many additional Lincoln friends, where it was
passed unanimously—not a single dissenting vote.

Most Americans viewed Garrison's abolition crusade as
extreme and some referred to Garrison and his followers as Consti-
tution-wreckers and zealots. Yet it garnered support, primarily in
the North, just about as fast as it gained opponents in the South.

Garrison decried the horrible inhumanity of slavery, accusing slaveholders of:

> Plundering two millions of human beings of their liberty and the fruits of their toil—driving them into the fields like cattle—starving and lacerating their bodies—selling the husband from his wife, the wife from her husband, and children from their parents—spilling their blood—withholding the bible from their hands.[23]

Again, independently, both Lincoln and Joseph Smith agreed with Garrison's perception of the gross inhumanity of slavery yet disagreed with his abolition movement. Lincoln had to know that his vote would rankle some of his constituency, yet even with that, he demonstrated six weeks later that he was not finished with the issue. Three days before the house's March 6 adjournment, Lincoln and Dan Stone, one of the five who had joined with Lincoln in opposition to the resolution, filed a formal protest to ensure that their reasons for opposing the resolution would be heard and recorded. On March 3, Lincoln and Stone, upon being given the floor, announced:

> Resolutions upon the subject of domestic slavery having passed both branches of the General Assembly at its present session, the undersigned [Lincoln and Stone] hereby protest against the passage of the same.
>
> They believe that the institution of slavery is founded on both injustice and bad policy; but that the promulgation of abolition doctrines tends rather to increase than to abate its evils.
>
> . . . The difference between these opinions and those contained in the said resolutions, is their reason for entering this protest[24]

Lincoln, like the abolitionists, wanted to see the end of slavery. Yet he disagreed with their approach, believing that the abolition movement ran contrary to the Constitution's allowance for slavery. But with this protest and his nay vote, he recorded for history his first official swipe at the deplorable practice.

## FIRST LOVE

Lincoln's legislative protest was made with a deep and slow-healing wound in his heart. Yet another tragedy had struck his life some eighteen months earlier. He, like so many frontier Americans of that day, was well acquainted with grief. He already carried the sorrow of his mother's death when he was nine and yet more when Sarah Lincoln, his only sibling, had died giving birth to her first child when Abraham was sixteen. At age twenty-five, Lincoln had finally found the love of his life. Her name was Ann Rutledge. She was also from New Salem. He had lived in the Rutledge tavern some years earlier while Ann was being courted by and eventually became engaged to the successful John McNeil. After the engagement, McNeil returned to New York to bring his ailing parents west for the upcoming wedding but failed to return. Communications from him ended abruptly after the first few months of his absence, and just why was an agonizing ordeal for Ann.

Had he lost interest in their marriage? Had he become ill? Had death overtaken her betrothed? She had no information explaining his two-year absence. And it was to Lincoln, the local postmaster, that Ann hesitatingly approached for a letter from her lost fiancé, and it was Lincoln who gave her the sad news, time after time, that no mail had arrived for her from McNeil. Little is known of their courtship, but it is probable that is was during these sad conversations that Lincoln, in extending comfort to her, developed warm feelings for Ann Rutledge and she for him. We do know that as McNeil's absence protracted into the third year, Abraham and Ann were making plans to marry in the upcoming spring of 1836, after she fulfilled a lifelong dream to go to a neighboring town to attend school. But before any of their plans could be set in motion, Ann took sick, poisoned by their contaminated family well. Her attending doctor recommended against visitors, but she insisted on calling for Abraham. He rushed the seven miles to her home and spent some last anguished moments with her. She died shortly thereafter in August 1835. The depth of Lincoln's grief was profound:

> One stormy night Lincoln was sitting beside William Greene, his head bowed on his hand, while tears trickled through his fingers; his friend begged him to control his sorrow, to try to forget. "I cannot," moaned Lincoln; "the thought of the snow and rain on her grave fills me with indescribable grief."[25]

On September 9, 1836, after a year of combating his sorrow through his law books, Lincoln held a license authorizing him to practice law in all Illinois courts. The young state assemblyman was now a lawyer. A few months later, he left the dwindling village of New Salem to reside in the new Illinois capital of Springfield and become a law partner with John Todd Stuart. In 1837, Springfield boasted some fourteen hundred residents, including twelve lawyers (counting Lincoln) and six churches.

## MOBOCRACY IN AMERICA

Eight months after Lincoln's protest of the Illinois legislature's pro-slavery resolution, an event took place in Lincoln's home state that would rock the nation. Elijah Lovejoy, a New England Presbyterian minister and publisher who had joined the abolitionist movement, took his printing press and ideals to St. Louis, Missouri, and started an antislavery newspaper. His crusade was not well received, and he woke up one day to find that his press had been demolished and his printing office ransacked. This compelled him to purchase another printing press and move his family across the Mississippi River to Alton, Illinois, where he hoped his business would be safer.

That September, he circulated his first issue of the *Alton Observer*. It included an even more strident anti-slavery sentiment, advocating the immediate and unconditional emancipation of the slaves. Although not acquainted with Lincoln, Lovejoy was one of the small minority in Illinois who would have been pleased with his protest of the legislature's proslavery resolution in March. In July 1837, Lovejoy took his crusade even further by calling for the organization of an Illinois Antislavery Society. Upon hearing of his new undertaking, his old adversaries in St. Louis issued their own decree that something must be done to stop this antislavery lunacy across the river. In August, taking a lesson from the Jackson County rowdies who had destroyed the Mormons' printing press and office four years earlier, a mob attempted to assault Lovejoy. He was able to escape, but his press did not. He ordered yet another press with the help of friends sympathetic to his cause. This one arrived the next month on a Sunday.

So as not to dishonor the Sabbath, Reverend Lovejoy left the press on the dock to be recovered the next day. During the night, some proslavery Alton locals demolished that one and threw it in the Mississippi River.

This lawless violence gained the national eye, growing into much more than a local newsman's business misfortunes. It provoked a question that had largely been ignored in America: Was there to be freedom of expression and of the press as guaranteed by the Constitution? At that time in America, censorship of the press was ubiquitous. Antislavery publications were banned in the South, and some writers of pro-slavery books and articles were harassed in the North.

Reading of Lovejoy's plight, abolitionists in Ohio sent money for Lovejoy to purchase his fourth printing press. It arrived on November 6, 1837, and was rushed to the third floor of a stone warehouse. Anticipating trouble, Lovejoy secured permission from the Alton mayor to deputize a group of men to protect this press from destruction, and some sixty men stepped forward to defend it. The following day, twenty of these men gathered to stand watch on the building and to barricade the entrances. At around 10:00 p.m. that night, a large group of angry and mostly inebriated men gathered around the warehouse, intent on destroying yet another printing press. When their demand that the press be surrendered was denied, they pelted the warehouse with stones and bullets. Unable to gain access, the mob brought a ladder, set it against the warehouse, and set the roof afire; Lovejoy emerged from the warehouse to stop them and was immediately shot and killed in a hail of bullets.

Elijah Lovejoy's murder sent shock waves through the nation. Once again, unruly vigilante mobs were acting with impunity. Never had a white man lost his life so visibly in the cause of freeing the slaves. His martyrdom became a reverberating rallying cry for the abolitionist movement. The newspaper industry also stepped forward and immediately claimed Lovejoy as a martyr for the cause of freedom of the press. Lovejoy's death solidified both movements. Elijah's younger brother, Owen Lovejoy, carried on his brother's work and eventually become a conductor on the Underground Railroad, a US congressman, and a good friend and longtime supporter of Abraham Lincoln.

## Prophetic Warnings

Just three months after Reverend Lovejoy's murder, Lincoln was invited to speak to the Young Men's Lyceum group in Springfield. His speech made Lincoln one of the only Illinois leaders to publicly denounce Lovejoy's unpunished murder. Lincoln also mentioned the burning alive of a free black man in St. Louis a year earlier, the assembly of vigilante groups lawlessly driving citizens from their homes and businesses (as was done to the Mormons in Missouri and Ohio), and the blatant disregard for the constitutional freedoms of the press and of speech for which Elijah Lovejoy gave his life.

He further denounced "the ravages of mob law," and "the increasing disregard for law which pervades the country."[26] Despite standing before an audience by no means sympathetic to Elijah Lovejoy, twenty-eight-year-old Lincoln courageously warned:

> Whenever the vicious portion of the population shall be permitted to gather in bands of hundreds and thousands, and burn churches, ravage and rob provision-stores, throw printing presses into rivers, shoot editors, and hang and burn obnoxious persons at pleasure, and with impunity; depend upon it, this Government cannot last.[27]

It is a safe assumption that Lincoln's warning regarding their imperiled government left few hearers, if any, disconcerted. Rare was the American in 1838 that had doubts about the stability of their nation's government. But two facts regarding this idea are worthy of serious consideration. First, this theme of an endangered republic and government, given twenty-three years before Lincoln's presidency and the Civil War, is a theme that Lincoln never stopped addressing, even knowing full well that many regarded such rhetoric as unfounded and foolish. In his storied debates with Stephen A. Douglas for the Illinois Senate seat, Lincoln repeatedly admonished the people using a New Testament scripture that "a house divided against itself cannot stand," that "this government cannot endure, permanently half *slave* and half *free*."[28] Lincoln would repeat this theme numerous times in the years between this Lyceum speech and his assassination.

The other significant fact to consider is that Lincoln was not the only notable American who shared this foreboding for his nation's future. Five years prior to Lincoln's impassioned Lyceum address, on December 25, 1832, Joseph Smith sat pondering and praying on the subject of slavery and recorded this revelation:

> Verily, thus saith the Lord concerning the wars that will shortly come to pass, beginning at the rebellion of South Carolina, which will eventually terminate in the death and misery of many souls; and the time will come that war will be poured out upon all nations, beginning at this place. (D&C 87:1–2)

Joseph Smith was strikingly specific and accurate in pinpointing South Carolina as the flash point of the war. Current events likely precipitated Joseph's meditations on slavery and subsequent Civil War prophecy. A South Carolina convention had recently declared the tariff acts of 1828 and 1832 null, void, and not binding upon their state. They further stated that on February 1, 1833, South Carolina would secede from the Union if the government attempted to enforce these federal laws. In response to this threat, Congress passed the Force Act, authorizing the use of military force against any state that resisted the tariff acts. Just fifteen days before Joseph's declaration, President Andrew Jackson issued a proclamation to the people of South Carolina, threatening to send forty thousand US troops to the Palmetto State to ensure compliance. South Carolina withdrew its defiance and begrudgingly remained in the Union.

This 1832 precursor to the secession of 1860 certainly engendered some of Lincoln's forebodings as well. South Carolina's recalcitrance posed a dramatic dilemma for the nation. If one state could simply defy federal law and go as far as to exit the Union, then other states could certainly do the same over future disagreements. The end result could be a continent of weak and separate nation-states, each with their own diluted and weakened version of the original Constitution.

In response to newspaperman Horace Greeley's harsh public criticism of his presidency, Lincoln calmly replied with the following so as not to be misunderstood:

> I would save the Union. I would save it the shortest way under

the Constitution. The sooner the national authority can be restored, the nearer the Union will be "the Union as it was." My paramount object in this struggle is to save the Union, and is not either to save or destroy slavery.[29]

Joseph Smith's revelation further declares:

> For behold, the Southern States shall be divided against the Northern States, and the Southern States will call on other nations, even the nation of Great Britain, as it is called. (D&C 87:3)

The prediction that the South would appeal to Great Britain was again remarkably accurate. Great Britain's voracious appetite for the South's affordable and abundant cotton had fueled the South's burgeoning textile successes, and the Confederacy pinned their hopes on British support. In November 1861, they dispatched two emissaries to England to encourage their recognition and support. To the relief of President Lincoln and the North, England chose to remain neutral, avoid involvement, and smugly watch America defeat itself— something Britain had failed to do twice before.

As bold as the Great Britain component of the revelation was, the next declaration was, at the time, considered even less likely to come to pass:

> And it shall come to pass, after many days, slaves shall rise up against their masters, who shall be marshaled and disciplined for war. (D&C 87:4)

As absurd as talk of civil war was in 1832, even more ludicrous was the notion that black men could ever be successful in battle, let alone be viewed as worthy and capable of being called upon to fight for either cause. Yet the Mormon prophet boldly declared that after they would be marshaled and disciplined for war, the slaves would rise up against their masters.

President Lincoln's Emancipation Proclamation of 1863 brought slaves to Union regiments in droves. They left their plantation owners and then picked up arms against them, participating in operations in the southern states such as General William Sherman's destructive march to the sea from Atlanta. Lincoln explained his decision to arm the blacks for the sake of preserving the cause that his Caucasian

Army was losing in his second annual message to Congress, saying that "In giving freedom to the slave, we assure freedom to the free—honorable alike in what we give, and what we preserve. We shall nobly save, or meanly lose, the last best, hope of earth."[30]

Whenever the topic arose, Lincoln was quick to defend his conviction that the black soldier would be equal to any other. His decision to arm the blacks was both courageous and controversial. For two hundred and fifty years, black men were considered incapable of bearing arms; it was inconceivable to suggest that they could be called upon to defend white Americans in battle. There was no precedent for Lincoln's faith in their character, bravery, and resolve, but the 180,000 former slaves who fought to preserve the Union were resolute and able fighters who literally turned the tide of the war.

Their competence on the battlefield demolished the centuries-old prejudice that the blacks were incompetent by nature. Their valor as soldiers was positive proof of this fallacy, and this proof destroyed the fundamental rationale of two hundred fifty years of slavery.

It is curious see that Abraham Lincoln and Joseph Smith, infidels in the minds of many, would share this accurate vision of the nation's future. Joseph Smith prophesied, and Abraham Lincoln fulfilled those prophesies.

Joseph Smith's prophecy continues:

> And thus, with the sword and by bloodshed the inhabitants of the earth shall mourn; and . . . be made to feel the wrath, and indignation, and chastening hand of an Almighty God. (D&C 87:6)

During the early 1860s, the Mormons in Utah would think back often on Joseph Smith's 1832 prophecy on war. The states in the east were being ravaged. The Civil War took a staggering 750,000 American lives, leaving few families untouched by grief and loss. Yet the Mormons in Utah were safely insulated from this colossal tragedy. They saw the war as the Lord's wrathful, indignant, and chastening hand finally being raised to avenge them of their enemies.

Just why President Lincoln did not include the thousands of eligible Utah Mormon men in the various military drafts to replenish the Union Army was as unclear then, as it is now. Draftees were conscripted from Colorado and other western states and territories, but not from Utah.

Utah Mormons were virtually untouched by the losses and destruction of the war, and they were convinced that God was vexing the nation as he promised in the 1832 revelation.

Again, Lincoln and Joseph shared an uncommon perception—that the Civil War was a divine chastisement of America. While president, Abraham Lincoln issued twelve official proclamations to the American people, nine of which called for days of fasting and prayer to implore God's intervention in ending the war. In many of these proclamations, Lincoln, in a prophetic manner, unabashedly called the American people to repentance. In his first proclamation, issued August 12, 1861, he avowed:

> Whereas it is fit and becoming in all people at all times, to acknowledge and revere the supreme government of God, to bow in humble submission to his chastisements, to confess and deplore their sins and transgressions, in the full conviction that the fear of the Lord is the beginning of wisdom.[31]

In his Proclamation of a National Fast Day issued on March 30, 1863, he said:

> And whereas it is the duty of nations as well as of men to own their dependence upon the overruling power of God; to confess their sins and transgressions in humble sorrow, yet with assured hope that genuine repentance will lead to mercy and pardon; and to recognize the sublime truth, announced in the Holy scriptures and proven by all history, that those nations only are blessed whose God is the Lord.[32]

Joseph Smith prophetically declared that the Almighty God would vex the nation and that with the sword and by bloodshed He would cause that the inhabitants of the earth should mourn.[33] The disobedient would be made to feel God's wrath and indignation beginning with the great war on American soil that would be ignited in South Carolina. Once again, these unacquainted presidential prophets had an identical message for all who would hear.

## MORE MOBOCRACY

In 1838, a group of apostate Mormons, angry with Joseph Smith for the county's financial collapse during the nationwide panic of

1837, joined forces with anti-Mormon Ohioans. They forced Joseph Smith, the general Church leadership, and the rest of the Mormon faithful to flee Ohio for their lives. The Mormons hoped to find a safer environment in Caldwell County, Missouri, but they were sorely disappointed. The arrival of the notorious Church President and hundreds more Mormons only heightened the alarm of the Missourians. The Ohio Mormons joined the Missouri saints in Far West, the new headquarters for the church. These developments deeply troubled many of the non-Mormon settlers.

On March 12, 1839, Joseph Smith lamented:

> With my family I arrived at Far West, Caldwell county, after a journey of one thousand miles . . . enduring great affliction. . . . Soon after my arrival at that place, I was informed that a number of men living in Daviess county . . . had offered the sum of one thousand dollars for my scalp: persons to whom I was an entire stranger, and of whom I had no knowledge. In order to attain their end, the roads were frequently waylaid for me. At one time in particular, when watering my horse on Shoal Creek, I distinctly heard three or four guns snapped at me. . . . In consequence of such threats and abuse . . . my family were kept in a continual state of alarm, not knowing any morning what would befall me from day to day.[34]

On July 4, 1838, a local militia made up of Caldwell County Mormons and a small, radical Mormon group known as the Danites marched around the Liberty pole in Far West for an Independence Day celebration. The Danites were a splinter group of Mormons who pledged to defend their families from being driven again from their homes. Sidney Rigdon, Joseph Smith's first assistant, gave a speech recounting the persecutions they had endured thus far. Then, apparently emboldened by the presence of the Church leadership now in Missouri, and with the flight from Ohio fresh in his memory, he passionately declared that the Latter-day Saints would no longer be driven from their homes by persecution from without or dissension from within. He exclaimed:

> And that mob that comes on us to disturb us; it shall be between us and them a war of extermination, for we will follow them, til the last drop of their blood is spilled, or else they will have to exterminate

us: for we will carry the seat of war to their own houses, and their own families, and one party or the other shall be utterly destroyed.[35]

Rigdon's defiance was published in a pamphlet that gave heart to the Mormons. But his warning of a war of extermination served only to enflame the resolve of the non-Mormon settlers that the dangerous Mormons needed to be driven out.

Newly created Daviess County, immediately north of Caldwell County, was sparsely settled until the spring of 1838, when Latter-day Saints established a settlement called Adam-ondi-Ahman and began to quickly settle the county. In a matter of months, the Mormon population equaled or exceeded the non-Mormon population in Daviess County. When Alexander Doniphan had proposed the creation of Caldwell and Daviess Counties in the Missouri legislature, most non-Mormons understood that the Mormons had agreed to settle only Caldwell County. Doniphan later stated that the problems leading up to the Mormon war began when the Latter-day Saints began settling in Daviess County—outside of the agreement.

August 6, 1838, was the first Election Day for Daviess County. Days earlier, the two major candidates for office, Colonel William Peniston, a Whig, and Judge Josiah Morin, a Democrat, each visited Adam-ondi-Ahman to campaign for the Mormon vote. Afterward, Peniston concluded that the Mormons intended to vote as a bloc for Morin and conspired to use force to prevent them from voting. When the Election Day arrived, Peniston made a speech in the county seat of Gallatin, claiming that "suffer such men as these [Mormons] to vote, you will soon lose your suffrage."[36]

When a group of about thirty Latter-day Saints approached the polling place, they encountered a crowd of about two hundred non-Mormons who had assembled to intimidate the Mormons from voting. One account of the confrontation states that a Missourian in the crowd named Dick Weldon shouted that in Clay County, the Mormons, like the Negroes, had not been allowed to vote.

A Mormon named Samuel Brown began an argument with Weldon that escalated until Brown struck Weldon. Some of the Mormons tried to restrain Brown, but others immediately jumped into the fray. It was reported that when the brawl began, a Mormon named John Lowe Butler shouted a Danite rallying cry, "Oh yes, you Danites, here is a job for us!"[37] This prompted the other Mormons in this splinter group to rush forward and join the fight. Although outnumbered, they managed to drive away Peniston's intimidators. Rumors spread that there were casualties in the conflict, prompting Joseph Smith to ride to Adam-ondi-Ahman to assess the situation. Discovering that there was no truth to the rumors, he returned to Far West.

Conditions worsened as the year went on. In September, Joseph heard that the Saints in DeWitt County were being harassed by a mob, and he rushed to their aid. He wrote:

> I arrived there . . . and found the account which I heard was correct. Our people were surrounded by a mob, and their provisions nearly exhausted.
>
> Being now almost destitute of provisions, and having suffered great distress, and some of the brethren having died in consequence of their privations and suffering—I had then the pain of beholding some of my fellow-creatures perish in a strange land, from the cruelty of a mob—and seeing no prospect of relief, the brethren agreed to leave that place and seek a shelter elsewhere, after having their houses burnt down, their cattle driven away, and much of their property destroyed. . . . In our journey several of our friends died and had to be interred without a coffin, and under such circumstances, this was extremely distressing.[38]

Joseph appealed to Governor Lilburn W. Boggs for protection, to which the governor replied that the quarrel was between the Mormons and the mob and that they might fight it out. In 1834, then Lieutenant Governor Boggs had condoned the expulsion of the Mormons from Jackson County. He was elected Governor of Missouri in 1836 and found that his temporary solution of removing the Mormons from Jackson County had only grown to much larger proportions in Caldwell and Daviess counties. But as Mormon numbers multiplied, so did non-Mormon settlers in Caldwell and surrounding counties, resulting in mounting tension between the groups.

It was clear that the Mormons could again appeal to no one for intervention and safety. With winter approaching, another forced expulsion was becoming more and more imminent. After passively leaving New York, Ohio, Jackson County, and Clay County, Joseph Smith alerted his followers that this time they would need to defend themselves and their homes. Soon after, the mostly Mormon Caldwell County militia led by Colonel George Hinkle, a trusted Mormon, sallied out to confront the threatening bands of Missourians. The Missourians eluded the Caldwell County militia, but the Mormons burned some buildings in Gallatin and the surrounding area, hoping it would discourage further oppression. It didn't. Word of the burnings served as justification for more dramatic action by Governor Boggs.

The Northern Missouri troubles escalated to such a degree that Governor Boggs ordered militias to be mustered from neighboring counties. Many of these militia members had only expulsion and violence on their minds, which increased the dread of the Latter-day Saints. Rumors of Danite threats of reprisals caused some non-Mormon families in Daviess County to leave their homes in search of safety. When word came that three Mormon men had been taken from their homes, Judge Elias Higbee ordered Colonel Hinkle to pursue the mob and recover the prisoners. The next morning, October 25, a battle commenced in which three Mormons were killed, including highly respected Apostle David W. Patton. One Missouri militiaman was also killed, and others on both sides were wounded.

A frantic message was rushed to Governor Boggs, stating that some sixty militiamen had been slaughtered and dozens others taken prisoner and that the Mormons were on their way to sack and burn the town of Richmond. In reality, no prisoners were taken, and no assault on Richmond took place, although rumors had circulated that the Danites intended to do so.[39]

Shortly after this report was made to Governor Boggs, he issued an executive order calling for the removal or extermination of the Mormons from Missouri, perhaps mimicking Sidney Rigdon's words of a war of extermination. Issued on October 27, 1838, Boggs's order stated that due to:

> Open and avowed defiance of the laws, and of having made war
> upon the people of this state . . . the Mormons must be treated as

enemies, and must be exterminated or driven from the state if necessary for the public peace—their outrages are beyond all description.[40]

---

# Sangamo Journal.

---

Vol. VIII. No. 4. Springfield, Illinois, November 17, 1838.
Whole 368.

---

MORMON WAR.

The St. Louis Republican of the 15 inst. contains the following particulars of another outrage committed on the Mormons. It is
taken from the Jeffersonian, printed at Jefferson City.

We likewise learn that another engagement has taken place in
Caldwell County, in which 36 Mormons were killed on the ground,
without any loss on the part of our citizens. This report was brought
to this office (unofficially) on Wednesday, by a Mr. Herriman; who
says the Mormons were attacked by a company of Rangers of about
50 in number, while guarding a mill which they had seized and partially destroyed. The Mormon force is stated to have been about the
number killed.

Three days after the Governor's extermination order, an organized militia of around 240 men on horseback led by Colonel William Jennings, the Sheriff of Caldwell County, surrounded the small
village of Haun's Mill. Sheriff Jennings fired a shot, sending the
inhabitants running in all directions. The Mormon men sent their
women and children across the creek and into the brush for safety,
then took refuge in the blacksmith's shop. The militia fired some one
hundred rounds at the blacksmith shop, then charged into the village and surrounded the shop.

Thomas McBride, a seventy-eight-year-old veteran of the American Revolution, approached the mob, offered them his gun, and
pleaded, "Spare my life, I am a Revolutionary soldier."[41] But Mr.
Rogers of Daviess County summarily shot him and then "fell upon

him and hacked him to pieces with an old corn cutter."[42] The militia dismounted, and, seeing that no one fired at them from the blacksmith shop, they placed their guns through the spaces in the logs and shot at the unarmed men and boys until all appeared to be dead or mortally wounded. Upon entering the carnage inside, they poured more balls into the those still alive to ensure that their deed was complete. They found one survivor, ten-year-old Sardius Smith. The boy was unharmed and hiding under the blacksmith bellows near his father's corpse. A Mr. Glaze dragged him from his hiding place, put his musket to the head of the trembling boy, and shot the top of his head off, killing him instantly. Glaze was heard later to boast that, "Nits will make lice, and if he [Sardius] had lived he would have become a Mormon."[43]

It is difficult to imagine such a scene transpiring in America, but it did. One of the survivors was Amanda Smith. She, with her husband Warren and their five children, had left Kirtland, Ohio, with the same traveling party as the Mulliners and the Stringhams. It is quite certain that Amanda Smith, Katherine Mulliner, and Polly Stringham became friends after traveling such a long and arduous journey.[44] But when they reached Springfield, the Smiths chose to forge forward on to Missouri rather than stop and settle like the Mulliners and Stringhams. The Smiths had the misfortune of arriving at the Haun's Mill settlement in Missouri on the day of the massacre. Two days earlier they had been taken prisoners by an armed militia that had confiscated all their weapons, then set them free. In Amanda's claim for redress, she wrote that upon arrival at Haun's Mill:

> My husband pitched his tent by a blacksmith's shop.
>
> Brother David Evans made a treaty with the mob that they would not molest us. He came just before the massacre and called the company together and they knelt in prayer.
>
> I sat in my tent. Looking up I suddenly saw the mob coming— the same that took away our weapons. . . .
>
> Before I could get to the blacksmith's shop door to alarm the brethren . . . the bullets were whistling amongst them.
>
> . . . Yet though we were women, with tender children, in flight for our lives, the demons poured volley after volley to kill us.
>
> A number of bullets entered my clothing, but I was not wounded.

. . . When the firing had ceased I went back to the scene of the massacre, for there were my husband and three sons, of whose fate I as yet knew nothing.

. . . Emerging from the blacksmith's shop was my eldest son, bearing on his shoulders his little brother Alma.

"Oh! My Alma is dead!" I cried, in anguish.

"No, mother; I think Alma is not dead. But father and brother Sardius are killed!"

What an answer was this to appall me! My husband and son murdered; another little son [age seven] seemingly mortally wounded; and perhaps before the dreadful night should pass the murderers would return and complete their work!

But I could not weep then. The fountain of tears was dry; the heart overburdened with its calamity, and all the mother's sense absorbed in its anxiety for the precious boy which God alone could save by his miraculous aid.

The entire hip joint of my wounded boy had been shot away. Flesh, hip, bone, joint and all had been ploughed out from the muzzle of the gun which the ruffian placed at the child's hip through the logs of the shop and deliberately fired.

We laid little Alma on a bed in our tent and I examined the wound. It was a ghastly sight. I knew not what to do. It was night now.

There were none left from that terrible scene, throughout that long, dark night, but about a half a dozen bereaved and lamenting women, and the children. . . .

The women were sobbing, in the greatest anguish of spirit; the children were crying loudly with fear and grief at the loss of fathers and brothers; the dogs howled over their dead masters and the cattle were terrified with the scent of the blood of the murdered.

Yet was I there, all the long, dreadful night, with my dead and my wounded, and none but God as our physician and help.

Oh my Heavenly Father, I cried, what shall I do? Thou seest my poor wounded boy and knowest my inexperience. Oh Heavenly Father direct me what to do!

And then I was directed as by a voice speaking to me.

The ashes of our fire was still smouldering. We had been burning the bark of the shag-bark hickory. I was directed to take those ashes and make a lye and put a cloth saturated with it right into the wound. It hurt, but little Alma was too near dead to heed it much. Again and again I saturated the cloth and put it into the hole from which the hip joint had been ploughed, and each time mashed flesh and splinters of bone came away with the cloth; and the wound became as white as chicken flesh.

. . . I again prayed to the Lord and was again instructed as distinctly as though a physician had been standing by speaking to me.

Near by was a slippery-elm tree. From this I was told to make a slippery-elm poultice and fill the wound with it.

. . . the poultice was made, and the wound, which took fully a quarter of a yard of linen to cover, so large was it, was properly dressed.

It was then that I found vent to my feelings in tears, and resigned myself to the anguish of the hour. And all that night we, a few poor, stricken women, were thus left there with our dead and wounded.

. . . The crawling of my boys under the bellows in the blacksmith's shop where the tragedy occurred, is an incident familiar to all our people. Alma's hip was shot away while thus hiding. Sardius was discovered after the massacre by the monsters who came in to despoil the bodies. The eldest, Willard, was not discovered. In cold blood, one, Glaze, of Carroll county, presented a rifle near the head of Sardius and literally blew off the upper part of it, leaving the skull empty and dry while the brains and hair of the murdered boy were scattered around and on the walls.[45]

I now leave it with this Honorable Government to say what my damages may be, or what they would be willing to see their wives and children slaughtered for, as I have seen my husband, son and others.

I lost in property by the mob—to goods stolen, fifty dollars; one pocketbook, and fifty dollars cash notes; damage of horses and time, one hundred dollars; one gun, ten dollars; and in short, my all. Whole damages are more than the State of Missouri is worth.

Written by my own hand, this 18th day of April, 1839.

Amanda Smith[46]

But to return to Alma, and how the Lord helped me to save his life.

. . . "Alma, my child," I said, "you believe that the Lord made your hip?"

"Yes, mother."

"Well, the Lord can make something there in the place of your hip, don't you believe he can, Alma?"

"Do you think that the Lord can, mother?" inquired the child, in his simplicity.

"Yes, my son," I replied, "he has shown it all to me in a vision."

Then I laid him comfortably on his face, and said: "Now you lay like that, and don't move, and the Lord will make you another hip."

So Alma laid on his face for five weeks, until he was entirely recovered—a flexible gristle having grown in place of the missing joint and socket, which remains to this day a marvel to physicians.

. . . It is now nearly 40 years ago, but Alma has never been the least crippled during his life, and he has traveled quite a long period of the time as a missionary of the gospel and a living miracle of the power of God.[47]

Having already been thrice (including the Ohio expulsion) driven from their homes, the Mormons keenly felt the danger of yet another forced eviction. The Mormons assembling at Far West were soon confronted with an estimated two thousand militia men ordered to northern Missouri by Governor Boggs, many of them enflamed by his executive order to drive the Mormons out or exterminate them. It was a condition that is nearly beyond comprehension today and one that shocked Americans throughout the country as local newspaper accounts like the one below blanketed the nation.

# Sangamo Journal.

S. &. J. Francis. Springfield IL., November 10, 1838. Vol. 1. - No. 1.

### THE MORMONS

Annexed is the latest news (from the St. Louis Republican) on the same subject.—The remarks of the Republican on the Massacre of the Mormons, and the general character, of the wars, meet our own view of the matter.

Further from the Mormons:—The account of a bloody butchery of thirty two Mormons, on Splown's [Shoal] Creek is fully confirmed:—Two children were killed, we presume, by accident. Considerable plunder—such as beds, hats, &c. were taken from the slaughtered.—Not one of the assailants was killed or hurt.

About the time of the surrender, several Mormon houses were burnt in Chariton; and one Mormon who refused to leave killed.

At Far West, after the surrender, a Mormon had his brains dashed out by a man who accused the Mormons of burning his house in Daviess.

We copy the above paragraph from the Gazette of Saturday evening. We understand, that the company engaged in the attack at Splown's Creek, was not attached to any division of the army, but was fighting on its own hook. The men were principally from Chariton county and amongst the number was at least one member of the Legislature. The enemy had approached within eighty yards of the Mormons before they were apprized of their approach. The Mormons had their families with them, and to preserve their lives, the men separated from them and took refuge in a blacksmith's shop. Here they were murdered! It is said that the Mormons had arms, but it is a little singular that they should have used them so ineffectually as not to have touched one of the assailants. The latter, in some instances, placed their guns between the logs of the house and deliberately fired on the victims within,—These reports are founded upon statements of persons engaged in the attack; and bad as they are, are not likely to be overcharged. Will the actors in the tragedy be suffered, by the courts of that district, to go unpunished?

The disposition of the captured Mormons presents a case of great difficulty. They are generally poor—at least they have but little money and few means besides their stock and crops to preserve them from starvation. As it is, we suspect, their means are very much abridged. The presence of several thousand troops in their vicinity must have reduced them greatly. The proposition—so it is given out—is to remove them from the State. Who will advance the funds of wherewith to consummate such a measure? and where shall they be sent? Their numbers exceed five thousand men, women and children! Are these 5000 people—without any means and literally beggars—to be thrust upon the charity of Illinois, Iowa, or Wis.?

The question of which state would receive eight to twelve thousand cold and homeless Mormons likely rested heavy on Lincoln's mind as he read this article. He was then serving his fourth year in the Illinois State Legislature. The atrocities in Missouri frequently chronicled in Springfield's *Sangamo Journal* would likely have captured young Lincoln's attention after his Young Men's Lyceum speech on the dangers of lawless and mobocratic violence to democracy. Although fifty-five of the 240-member militia had been identified by name as participants in the massacre, none was prosecuted.

The day following the killings at Haun's Mill, Colonel Hinkle secretly negotiated a peace settlement with Colonel Lucas of the Missouri Militia, which included the surrender of Church leaders to the custody of Colonel Lucas. Hinkle believed he was following instructions and saving the Latter-day Saints from being massacred (it is possible that this clandestine exchange did save lives), but most Mormons viewed Hinkle's action as treacherous and deceitful, and they excommunicated him the following spring.

Joseph Smith and four of his trusted associates, including his brother Hyrum, were unwittingly enticed to participate in a negotiation meeting with the Colonel Lucas. Upon their arrival, they were promptly arrested and taken into custody.

That night, Colonel Lucas held an illegal court-martial of Joseph Smith and his captured companions even though military leaders could not legally try civilians. He found them guilty and ordered their execution in the town square of Far West the following day. Fortunately for Joseph and his friends, Lucas gave the execution order to Alexander Doniphan, who was leading one of the militia groups. Doniphan again came to the aid of the Mormons, flatly refusing to obey the order and decrying its illegal nature: "It is cold-blooded murder. I will not obey your order. . . . If you execute these men, I will hold you responsible before an earthly tribunal, so help me God."[48] He then exclaimed that he would defend the prisoners with his own life until proper legal proceedings could take place. Doniphan's resistance must have weakened Colonel Lucas's resolve. Lucas rescinded the execution order and ordered the prisoners' incarceration in Richmond to await a hearing. A hearing did take place. Of this hearing, one Clay County historian later wrote:

> The entire proceedings in the case were disgraceful in the extreme. There never was a handful of evidence that the accused were

guilty of the crimes with which they were charged. Those who were tried were defended by General Doniphan and James S. Rollins.[49]

Joseph and his fellow prisoners identified forty men in Far West who could testify in their behalf. A local minister and ardent persecutor of the saints rode to Far West with fifty men and escorted the forty witnesses to Richmond, then promptly had them all arrested, preventing them from testifying. Doniphan was so enraged that he stood and exclaimed:

> It is a dammed shame to treat these defendants in this manner. They are not allowed to put one witness on the stand; while the witnesses they have sent for have been captured by force of arms and thrust in the "bull pen," to prevent their testifying.[50]

A month later, after an irregular court of inquiry in Richmond, Joseph and his group were imprisoned in the jail at Liberty, Missouri, where they languished in cold and unsanitary conditions for four months while prosecutors searched unsuccessfully for evidence to try them on charges of treason and murder. Fully aware that many in Missouri sought to take his life, Joseph wrote to Emma, saying, "If I do not meet you again in this life, may God grant that we may meet in heaven. I cannot express my feelings; my heart is full. Farewell, O my kind and affectionate Emma. I am yours forever."[51]

With the Mormon leaders captured and Governor Boggs's order to drive the Mormons from the state, militiamen laid the town of Far West to ruin and ran the Mormons once again from their homes, farms, and businesses. Some eight to twelve thousand Mormons living in a four-county area were evicted, once again in the dead of winter. Homes were burned, livestock was shot, men were murdered, and a number of young Mormon women were raped, some to the point of death. As before, not a single person was prosecuted for these crimes.

People throughout America followed the sad Missouri saga. Surprisingly, public sentiment toward the Mormons began to shift from widespread derision to general support. The actions of Governor Boggs and the marauding militias were decried with abhorrence.

# Sangamo Journal.

Vol. VIII. No. 13 Springfield, Illinois, January 19, 1839. Whole. 377.

## THE MORMONS.

The present condition of the Mormons is set forth in the following article from the "Backwoodsman;"—

"The difficulties of this unfortunate sect are not yet at an end. Hundreds of them, driven from their homes, are without shelter and wandering in the woods. The Legislature in Misouri has granted $2000 for their relief.

"It has been long known that the authors of this war upon the Mormons, bad as their sect was, were actuated only by selfish motives. The following letter from the Editor of the Mo. Republican now at Jefferson City will explain their object:

"We have many reports here in relation to the conduct of some of the citizens of Daviess and other Counties, at the recent land sale at Lexington. Where the Mormons had made settlements and improvements, it is said, those citizens have purchased then for speculation. It is said that the town of "Adam on Diamond," a Mormon town in Daviess, in which there are several houses—a very valuable site for a town—was purchased at these sales for a dollar and a quarter an acre. It is further said, that there is a company formed, embracing a number of persons, for the purpose of speculating in the lands of those people."

It can hardly be expected that an editor in Mo. will come out fully and give the whole story to this base affair. Enough, however is disclosed to cover that part of the State with lasting disgrace. Can men women and children be driven from their homes to "bide the pettings of pitiless storm" of winter, many of them shot like wild beasts, for the purpose of obtaining their lands without incurring public indignation?

## CHAPTER FOUR ENDNOTES

1.  Lucy Mack Smith, *History of Joseph Smith* (Salt Lake City, UT: Bookcraft, 1901), 225.

2.  B. H. Roberts, *The Missouri Persecutions* ( Salt Lake City, UT: Bookcraft, 1965), 126–27.

3.  Ibid.

4.  Joseph Smith, his journal, dated Friday, May 30, 1834.

5.  Ibid.

6.  B. H. Roberts, *History of the Church of Jesus Christ of Latter-day Saints: An Introduction and Notes* (Salt Lake City, UT: Deseret News, 1968) vol. 2, 104.

7.  Journal of Moses Martin, LDS Historical Department, Salt Lake City, n.p.; spelling standardized; see also History of the Church, 2:104–5.

8.  Roberts, *History of the Church*, vol.2, 97–98.

9.  Carl Sandburg, "Abraham Lincoln The Prairie Years and the War Years," in Reader's Digest, illustrated ed. (New York: Harcourt Brace Jovanovich, 1970), 44.

10. "The Life of Abraham Lincoln," by Henry Ketcham, last modified June 6, 2009, http://www.authorama.com/life-of-abraham-lincoln-10.html.

11. Sandburg, "Abraham Lincoln: the Prairie Years," 627.

12. Benjamin Thomas, *Lincoln's New Salem* (1954; repr., Carbondale, IL: Southern Illinois University Press, 1987), 114.

13. Ibid.

14. Joseph Smith, et al., *Doctrine and Covenants of the Church of Jesus Christ of Latter-day Saints*, Section 101:80.

15. William Lee Miller, *Lincoln's Virtues: An Ethical Biography* (2002; repr., New York: Vintage Books, 2003), 117.

16. Ron L Andersen, *Abraham Lincoln: God's Humble Instrument*, (Salt Lake City, UT: Millennial Mind Publishing, 2009), 38.

17. William Lee Miller, *Lincoln's Virtues: An Ethical Biography* (2002; repr., New York: Vintage Books, 2003) 117.

18. Ibid.

19. Ibid.

20. Ibid., 116–20.

21. Roy Basler, ed., *Collected Works of Abraham Lincoln*, (New Brunswick, NJ: Rutgers University Press, 1953), vol.8, 399–400.

22. Miller, *Lincoln's Virtues*, 119.

23. William Lloyd Garrison, "'On the Constitution and the Union': An excerpt from

'The Great Crisis!'", *The Liberator* 2, no. 52 (December 29, 1832) http://fair-use.org/the-liberator/1832/12/29/on-the-constitution-and-the-union.

24. Miller, *Lincoln's Virutes*, 122.

25. Ida M. Tarbell, *The Life of Abraham Lincoln* (New York: McClure, Phillips, 1900; New York: Cosimo, 2008). vol. 1, 120.

26. Abraham Lincoln, "Lyceum Address" (address, the Young Men's Lyceum of Springfield, IL, January 27, 1838), http://www.abrahamlincolnonline.org/lincoln/speeches/lyceum.htm.

27. Ibid.

28. Ibid.

29. Ronald C. White, Jr., *The Eloquent President: A Portrait of Lincoln through his Words* (New York: Random House, 2005), 125.

30. Ibid., 170; Abraham Lincoln, "Annual Message to Congress," Washington, DC, December 1, 1862.

31. Ron L. Anderson, *Abraham Lincoln: God's Humble Instrument* (Salt Lake City, UT: Millenial Mind Publishing, 2009), 117.

32. Ibid., 356.

33. Doctrine and Covenants, Sections 101:89, 87:6.

34. B. H. Roberts, *History of the Church of Jesus Christ of Latter-day Saints*, rev ed. (Salt Lake City, UT: Deseret Book, 1974). vol. 3, 368.

35. Sidney Rigdon, "Oration Delivered by Mr. S. Rigdon" (Far West, Caldwell County, MO, July 4, 1838), http://www.sidneyrigdon.com/rigd1838.htm#pg12

36. "Gallatin Election Day Battle," *Wikipedia*, last modified February 6. 2014, http://en.wikipedia.org/wiki/1838_Mormon_War#Gallatin_Election_Day_Battle.

37. Ibid.

38. Joseph Smith, his journal, 102.

39. B. H. Roberts, *The Missouri Persecutions* (Salt Lake City, UT: Bookcraft, 1965), 225.

40. Governor Lilburn W. Boggs to General John B. Clark, 27 October 1838, Missouri Executive Order Number 44, www.quaqua.org/extermination.htm.

41. B. H. Roberts, *The Missouri Persecutions* (Salt Lake City, UT: Bookcraft, 1965), 235.

42. Ibid.

43. Church Educational System, Church History in the Fulness of Times Student Manual, 2nd ed. (1989; repr., Salt Lake City, UT: The Church of Jesus Christ of Latter-day Saints, 2003), 203, www.ldsces.org/inst_manuals/chft/chft-16-20.htm.

44. B. H. Roberts, *History of the Church of Jesus Christ of Latter-day Saints: An Introduction and*

*Note* (Salt Lake City, UT: Deseret Book, 1973), 91–93.

45. Edward W. Tullidge, *The Women of Mormondom* (New York, 1877), 121–27.

46. B. H. Roberts, *History of the Church of Jesus Christ of Latter-day Saints: An Introduction and Notes* (Salt Lake City, UT: Deseret News, 1968) vol. 3, 325.

47. Tullidge, *The Women of Mormondom*, 127–28, paragraphing altered.

48. Roberts, *History of the Church*, 190–91.

49. History of Clay County as published in St Louis by the National Historical Company, 1885.

50. Roberts, *The Missouri Persecutions*, 259.

51. Carol Cornwall Madsen, "'My Dear and Beloved Companion': The letters of Joseph and Emma Smith," *Ensign*, September 2008.

*Chapter Five*

# "I GET PLAIN
# SCARED . . . WHEN I LOOK A
# FEW YEARS AHEAD"

## PREMONITIONS

On a late summer Sunday in 1837, Lincoln jumped into a band-wagon with six other lawyers and two doctors. They headed for a New Salem camp meeting where one of the most notable of Illinois traveling preachers, Dr. Peter Akers, would be preaching. This sermon was sure to be heated. Akers was going to address the evils of slavery, a theme that would kindle the ire of most of his listeners, and this rowdy Illinois crowd was more than ready to express their displeasure toward any orator whose theme was not to their liking.

Young Lincoln could scarcely be in an informal setting without someone calling for him to entertain them with his stories, and on this hot August day, he did not disappoint. As the wagon rolled toward New Salem, he cracked jokes and spun yarns about the wagon, the horses, lawyers, doctors, and anything else that caught his attention during the fifteen-mile excursion. When they arrived, they found, as expected, a large crowd gathered to hear the renowned Methodist preacher expound on a sermon titled "The Dominion of Jesus Christ."[1] Dr. Akers characterized himself as a student of biblical prophesies, and his message was that Jesus Christ would certainly come again to earth, but not until the curse of slavery was eradicated from the nation's fabric. For three hours he quoted biblical scripture and noted prophecies and their fulfillment, setting many a devout believer at unease for embracing both faith in God and the evils of slavery.

Interestingly, during the course of his sermon, Dr. Akers made some prophesies of his own. The first was that slavery would be stamped out through a bloody American civil war, a far-fetched notion in 1837. He did not stop there. He exclaimed over the din of a growing number of hecklers, "I am not a prophet nor the son of a prophet, but a student of the prophets. As I read prophecy, American slavery will come to an end in some near decade, I think in the sixties."[2] T. Walter Johnson's biography of Dr. Akers further states:

> After discussing the subject of slavery at some length he approached the pulpit stand with a gravity which hushed the audience to a breathless stillness, placed his long fore finger upon the page of the open Bible, and with all the solemnity of a Jeremiah, said "I cannot give you the exact date but in the latter part of 1860 or the early part of 1861 there will arise in this nation the greatest internecine war known to the history of the world. It will be brother against brother, family against family, and thousands of hearth stones will be made desolate. But thru this bloody baptism we must pass for the deliverance of the slave from bondage."[3]

He then punctuated his revelation by saying that some of those present would live to see his prophecies fulfilled.

Dr. Akers was surprisingly accurate in his predictions. There was, of course, a civil war in America. It commenced in early 1861, and many in the audience were still living to see it, including Lincoln. But what made his three accurate prophecies even more astonishing was his fourth declaration. As the crowd began to surge toward him in angry disapproval, he exclaimed at the top of his voice, "Who can tell but that the man who shall lead us through this strife may be standing in this presence!"[4] A stunned Abraham Lincoln stood just thirty feet away.

Aker's impassioned sermon did not disappoint. Lincoln's friends had much to debate on their return to Springfield. The group had gone some distance before they realized that Lincoln, who had always been a ready entrant into any discussion, had been unusually silent and solemn. Indeed, he seemed almost unwilling to share his impressions of the sermon. One by one, the traveling companions took note of Lincoln's deep absorption in his own thoughts. At length he was called upon to report his impressions. His hesitation to respond was sensed by all, which only increased their determination to hear his thoughts.

After a long pause he said, "I never thought such power could be given to mortal man. Those words were from beyond the speaker. The Doctor has persuaded me that American slavery will go down with the crash of a civil war."[5] Then he was silent for a few more moments, and his friends remained so as well, detecting that Lincoln had even more solemn impressions to reveal.

Lincoln continued, "And do you know that all the time he was describing the overthrow of slavery in war and blood, it seemed to me that somehow or other, I was inseparably mixed up with it all, and so strong and deep was the impression, and so strange, that I cannot shake it off. I do not understand why it should be so."[6]

That night Lincoln had difficulty sleeping, and when he arrived late to his law office the next morning, his partner, John Todd Stuart, informed Lincoln without looking up that someone had come by to see him. Then, glancing up at Lincoln's haggard face, Stuart exclaimed, "Why, Lincoln, what's the matter with you?" To which Lincoln recounted the sermon from the day before and its relentless impression on him. He concluded by telling his law partner, "I am utterly unable to shake from myself the conviction that I shall be involved in that tragedy."[7]

## ANOTHER COURTSHIP

At about this same time in Lincoln's life, his friend Mrs. Elizabeth Abell proposed to send for her sister from Kentucky, playfully insisting that Lincoln commit to marry her. Lincoln had met this sister, Mary Owens, three years earlier. With no marriage prospects on the horizon, he agreed to do so. Mary Owens did make the trip to visit her sister in Springfield, and a meeting for the two was arranged. Mary came from a wealthy family and was well educated and refined. All of this made Lincoln uncomfortable; he was keenly self-conscious that he had very few material comforts to offer a wife.

The large debt he'd incurred from his failed business some three years earlier was still dogging him, and most of the money he had earned to that date had gone to paying his creditors. Every cent would eventually be repaid, but it took several years to fulfill these obligations. In that meeting with Miss Owens, Lincoln found that over the last three years Mary had gained some weight and lost some teeth—and that his interest in her had waned. Lincoln wrote a letter on the subject to Orville Browning, a friend from Quincy, Illinois, who was elected to the state senate in 1836. Lincoln and Browning had both served in the Black Hawk War four years earlier, were members of the minority Illinois Whig party, and abhorred the practice of slavery. Their association would span the next three decades. In his letter to Browning and his wife Eliza, Lincoln described his consternation:

> I was not all pleased with her. But what could I do? I had told her sister that I would take her for better or for worse; and I made a point of honor and conscience in all things, to stick to my word, especially if others had been induced to act on it, which in this case, I doubted not they had, for I was now fairly convinced, that no other man on earth would have her, and hence the conclusion that they were bent on holding me to my bargain.[8]

After a number of days, Mary returned to Kentucky, and over the next year she and the old bachelor exchanged letters while Lincoln procrastinated "the evil day."[9] At length he proposed that they marry in a letter, and to his surprise, she declined. He explained to Mrs. Browning:

> My vanity was deeply wounded . . . that she whom I had taught myself to believe no body else would have, had actually rejected me . . . I have now come to the conclusion never again to think of

marrying; and for this reason; I can never be satisfied with anyone who would be block-head enough to have me.[10]

## "Something of Ill-Omen, Amongst Us"

Early in Lincoln's legal career, he occasionally traveled to western Illinois to visit Orville and Eliza Browning in Quincy, a small town on the eastern bank of the Mississippi. The Browning home was small, so when Lincoln visited, Orville arranged for Lincoln to lodge with his more prosperous older cousin Jonathan Browning, who owned a larger home nearby. Jonathan was a respected gunsmith, inventor, and justice of the peace. He taught his craft to his son, John Moses Browning, who later became the founder of the Browning Rifle Company. While living in Quincy, Jonathan invented one of the first American repeating rifles.

Jonathan often related to his children and grandchildren an exchange between him and Lincoln during one of these overnight stays. This conversation is a treasure that demonstrates Lincoln's engaging affability, his links with the Mormons, an intriguingly deep foreboding for his country, and his looming role in those then future trials. Taking place at about the same time Lincoln gave his Lyceum speech, the conversation exhibits the same concern for his country.

There were certainly individuals in the mid-1830s who brooded over the country's direction, but they were few, and even fewer of these felt that a national calamity was in their future. Yet young Lincoln became convinced through Dr. Peter Akers that not only would "slavery go down with the crash of a civil war,"[11] but that he would be a major figure in the crisis. History would go on to prove that the premonitions of Lincoln, Joseph, and Akers were accurate, but given Lincoln's poverty and isolation, the likelihood of him being even a minor player in our national history was more than remote. Yet Lincoln was profoundly troubled by his premonitions of his future. Why was he troubling himself over the national condition? How could he see himself directly involved at a high level in an upcoming civil war? We know today what he did not know at that time: that he would go on to inspire a profound national course correction, not only politically but morally and spiritually as well.

In the coming years, both Orville and Jonathan Browning would develop intriguing connections with the Mormons who would flood into the Quincy area after Missouri Governor Boggs's extermination order in 1838. These developments would have been of keen interest to Lincoln and his fellow state legislators, and there can be little doubt that Orville and Jonathan would have recounted them in great and firsthand detail to their lanky friend. Jonathan Browning's family record narrates the following:

> "Judge," he [Lincoln] said, one thing leading to another, "somebody told me that a youngster in the neighborhood broke his arm yesterday and you set it. Do you fix anything that breaks—plow, gun, bone?" He smiled broadly.
>
> Jonathan grinned back. "Well, a doctor would have charged a dollar for the job, but I couldn't charge a neighbor for setting a bone any more than for helping him pull his wagon out of a mudhole. Fact is, I nearly turned doctor one time. When I was learning to read, and poking all around the countryside to find a book or two to practice on, I picked up a doctor book. Traded a gun for it that I'd fixed up. Fact is, that's the way I got my first Bible—traded a gun for it."
>
> Mr. Lincoln slapped his leg, and the chair snapped upright. "Now, hold on, Judge! Give me a minute to figure that one out. I want to laugh, but I don't quite see the point. It's tangled up in my mind with the saying about turning swords into plowshares, or is it pruning hooks?"
>
> "Plowshares," Jonathan answered, "Isaiah."
>
> "Well that's what you did in a way, turned a gun into a Bible. But the other fellow—he canceled you out by turning a Bible into a gun. Looks like the trade left the world just about where it was."
>
> The two men enjoyed a chuckle.
>
> "Well," Jonathan said after a moment, "there was something else funny about that trade. To tell the truth, the mainspring in that old gun was pretty weak, and the stock . . ."
>
> Lincoln interrupted with an upraised hand. "Judge Browning!" he rebuked, in an exaggerated courtroom manner. You mean that you cheated in a trade for a Bible—a *Bible*!"
>
> "Not exactly," Jonathan replied, his face as sober as Abraham's. "When I got to looking through that Bible at home, I found about half the New Testament was missing."

After a hearty laugh, Jonathan rose.

"Mr. Lincoln," he said, "I hate to end a pleasant evening like this, but you'll be wanting some sleep, I reckon. I'll light a candle for you. There's a water bucket and dipper, and your bed is right through this door. I hope you'll find it comfortable."

Mr. Lincoln stepped to the corner and took the dipper from its nail. "I hope your little patient is comfortable tonight."

"He'll be strutting around in a day or two with his arm in a sling. Nice, clean break."

"It's a fine life you're leading here, judge," Lincoln said thoughtfully, "mending anything that breaks. Looks funny at first glimpse to see a man welding a broken gun part for a farmer one day and next day setting a bone for the farmer's son. But the two jobs are somewhat alike."

"No difference," Jonathan smiled, "except that the bonesetting's a lot easier. Nature does most of that welding. But if it's two pieces of iron, you've got to blow up the forge and pound. Nature won't help with that."

Lincoln nodded soberly. "Hammer and hammer," he repeated, swinging the dipper to and fro. "I can't weld, but I've seen it done. Heat and hammer, heat and hammer. Whatever man makes, man breaks. And then somebody must mend. Judge Browning, there's a lot of mending to be done in these United States—a lot of mending!

" . . . I've knocked about a good deal—even made a couple of trips down the River on a flatboat, clear to New Orleans. And wherever I go, I hear sounds of little things breaking, and I see big things bending dangerously near to it. You see the signs all around you, hear the sounds. Fact is, I'm so worried that I have nightmares, and not all of them when I'm asleep. I get plain scared to death when I look a few years ahead."

For a long time he seemed to be doing just that, trying to look into the future. Jonathan nodded politely, but he was puzzled and worried too. He wondered if his guest was going into one of those moody spells Orville had mentioned. But with another swing of the dipper the shaggy giant continued.

"Judge Browning, the United States ought to become the greatest country on earth. But what if the hotheads break it in two, right down the middle? That would be a welding job! It would need the fires of the inferno for the forge. And where is the anvil? Where is the hammer? Where is the blacksmith?"

. . . Again an apologetic smile touched the rugged face. "It was the talk of your bonesetting and welding that started me off, Judge; maybe I'm just seeing stumps and gnarled limbs in the dark, and imagining bears. Hope so."

He took a drink of water, accepted the lighted candle, and stepped toward his room.

"Good night, Judge Browning, and many thanks for your hospitality."

"Good night, Mr. Lincoln."[12]

Some thirty years later in Utah, Jonathan would say, "That's about the way it happened. . . Two frontiersmen yarning. Only I'm just beginning to realize that I was listening to prophesy."[13]

Probably the most intriguing elements of this conversation are Lincoln's deep preoccupation with the country's ominous future and his unrelenting intuition that he would be embroiled in it.

## A NEAR MEETING

This account touches on a number of significant elements in Lincoln's remarkable life. First, it's not known when this visit with Browning took place, but historians have Lincoln in Carthage, Illinois, on April 22–25, 1839, defending William Fraim, who was charged with stabbing a fellow steamboat laborer to death during a drunken brawl. It is very likely that Lincoln would have traveled through Quincy on his journey to the trial in Carthage to visit and lodge with the Brownings. Court records show that Fraim was found guilty and sentenced on the day following the trial, Tuesday the 23. On Thursday, April 25, Lincoln argued unsuccessfully to set aside the sentence.

There is no record of Lincoln's whereabouts on Wednesday, April 24. Some speculate that the curious state legislator may have ridden ten miles west of Carthage to Commerce to see the place where, in about three weeks, thousands of Mormons would migrate to establish their new homes and businesses. The Brownings would have known that the area around Commerce was being considered as a location for the Mormons' new settlement, and they could have reported this common knowledge to Lincoln.

On March 22, 1839, one month before Lincoln's arrival in

Carthage, the local newspaper there posted an invitation for builders to bid on the construction of a new jail. While in Carthage, Lincoln, as the trial lawyer, would probably have been apprised of the plans for the new jail. Construction began on the Carthage Jail in December of that year. Five years later, Joseph Smith and his brother Hyrum were gunned down in that jail by a lawless mob while awaiting trial.

If Lincoln took the Quincy route to Carthage, he would have found Quincy teeming with thousands of Mormon refugees from Missouri. Assemblyman Lincoln would certainly have known of their arrival through newspaper accounts, and he may have been interested in how he and the legislature would now handle this mass migration to his state. Justice of the Peace Jonathan Browning and State Senator Orville Browning would have been reliable sources of information on how the remarkable residents of Quincy (and quite likely the Brownings themselves) opened their homes to the cold and homeless Missouri exiles. In fact, if Lincoln left Quincy on April 21st for the Carthage trial on the 22, he would have missed the arrival of Joseph Smith into Quincy by just one day. Records show that Smith reached Quincy on April 22, 1839 after being allowed to escape from his incarceration in Missouri. Years later, Jonathan's daughter Asenath would convey to her children, the visit of Joseph Smith to the Browning home in Quincy.

As noted earlier, Jonathan Browning recounted his Lincoln story some thirty years later in Utah. This begs the question: What led him to Utah? Sometime, probably after Lincoln's visit to Jonathan's home, a Mormon exile entered the Browning gunshop and engaged Browning in a conversation about his religion. Encouraged by Jonathan's interest, the refugee returned the next day with a copy of the Book of Mormon. Jonathan was moved by what he read, prompting him to consider the unthinkable: becoming a Mormon. He was baptized with his family into The Church of Jesus Christ of Latter-day Saints, placing him squarely on a path to bitter persecution. It is not known how Orville Browning felt about his cousin's conversion, but it certainly would have been salacious news to share with Lincoln.

While it is unlikely that Lincoln had heard of Joseph Smith's Civil War prophecy, it is possible. The early Mormon missionaries were very fond of including this prophecy in their sermons, and these missionaries often preached in Springfield. The Springfield Latter-day Saints would certainly have known of this prophecy and embraced it as a message from God, making it possible that some of the Mormons whom Lincoln knew, including Katherine Mulliner, the Groesbecks, and the Stringhams, shared it with Lincoln. While Lincoln was obviously not a Mormon, he was not a Methodist either. Yet Dr. Akers's prophesies had left an indelible foreboding in him. If he did hear of the Mormon prophecy, it would probably have added to his consternation.

## JAMES ADAMS

As mentioned earlier, Lincoln moved in April 1837 to Springfield to be the junior law partner with John Todd Stuart, a cousin of Lincoln's future wife, Mary Todd. Lincoln soon established a reputation in Springfield as a fine speaker and an unmatched storyteller who could entertain friends for hours.

One of the first court cases for the new Springfield lawyer caused a stir in the town that lasted for months. James Adams, a prominent Springfield resident, had served several years as the Probate Judge of Sangamo County and was twice a candidate for lieutenant governor. Lincoln would surely have known of Adams's unsuccessful run for Governor of Illinois in 1834, where he came in a distant third. Adams would later become the founder of the Springfield Lodge of Freemasonry and the Deputy Grand Master of the Freemasonry Lodge of Illinois.

At the passing of James Anderson and Andrew Sampson, family members of each accused Adams of illegally obtaining their adjoining property through fraudulent and forged deeds. They took their case to Lincoln, who agreed to represent them in court. One can only speculate as to why, but it is interesting that none of the dozens of more established Springfield attorneys took the case against the prominent judge. Possibly they recognized the volatile implications that Lincoln may not have seen. In any event, the case developed into a political battleground. Lincoln's friend Dr. Anson G. Henry, a Whig, was running against Adams, a Democrat, for the position of probate judge. Henry and an influential group of local Whigs employed Lincoln for his writing talent—and maybe his naiveté—as their scribe in an attempt to damage Adams's reputation and his campaign for re-election.

Through some notable research on Lincoln's part, he uncovered the fact that Adams had been accused of a very similar offense some two decades earlier in New York. Just before the court's verdict was rendered, Adams had gathered his belongings, bid his family good-bye, and quietly slipped away, never to return. His flight left many with the suspicion that he was, in fact, guilty of the crime. He eventually came a thousand miles west to Springfield. After establishing himself as the probate justice in Springfield, he hired some men to assist his family in moving there as well. They joined him almost three years after his rushed departure from New York.

Lincoln was incensed by what he believed to be a fraud committed by Adams against the survivors of Sampson and Anderson. Anson Henry was also indignant, but he was more motivated by a negative article in the *Illinois Republican* about his candidacy for the probate justice seat. Henry wanted a rebuttal from the *Sangamo Journal*, and the local Whig newspaper was eager to comply. Quite possibly at the prompting of Henry's group, Lincoln became the scribe of a ghost letter under the pen name of "Sampson's Ghost,"[14] and the group embarked upon a dramatic discrediting of Adams's character, capitalizing on Lincoln's New York discovery. The local Democratic newspaper (which we would consider ironically named), the *Springfield Republican*, joined the fray, and supporters of Adams rebutted the accusations, extolling Adam's stellar reputation in the community. Other letters to the editor and rebuttals followed as the newspapers dueled it out. In one letter accredited to Lincoln, Adams was accused to being "a forger, a whiner, a fool, and a liar."[15] Lincoln was rarely this critical of others. In fact, this public assault on Adams's character is so foreign to Lincoln's nature that this letter may reflect Henry's instigations more than Lincoln's actual feelings. It is possible that Lincoln was influenced by Anson Henry's group of Whigs and particularly by Anson Henry himself—the man was characterized by an acquaintance as having "a capacity for making two bitter enemies for each warm friend."[16] Or perhaps Lincoln's conviction that the widow and other survivors were heinously deceived by a person of trust led his idealistic young nature to carry the case to unprecedented proportions. At any rate, it is one of the few times in Lincoln's life where we may question his judgment.

The election arrived long before the case was resolved, and even though his reputation was damaged, Adams still won the election over Henry. After months of Adams resisting Lincoln's repeated newspaper appeals that Adams produce the documents that he claimed would prove his innocence, he came forth with the evidence. Adams's documents were curiously different from the original ones that Lincoln had observed, but they established him as the rightful owner of the two properties in question, and that ended the long dispute. Lincoln contended that segments of the document were written in Adams's handwriting and that his signature was added in fresh ink. But surprisingly, Lincoln could not prove the forgery, and Adams was exonerated. Lincoln's young career and reputation were damaged by the ugly affair, which left a residual tarnish on Adams as well.

It appears that Lincoln and Adams never mended their relationship. The two men mutually avoided each other until Adam's death six years later. If Lincoln ever had interest in joining the Masonic Lodge, which most gentlemen of influence did at that time, Adams and his high position with the Masons likely stood in the way. Fellow Democrat Stephen A. Douglas became a Mason in Judge Adams's Springfield Lodge Number Four, and the two became good friends and colleagues. If Lincoln ever could have met Joseph Smith during one of the prophet's three visits to Springfield in the next six years, it was likely James Adams that kept Lincoln at a distance from the enigmatic Mormon leader.

As noted earlier, Joseph Smith had announced to his followers that war should soon overtake the land. For that reason, the Mormons were to migrate west, far away from danger. In the midst of the Adams affair, Abraham Lincoln was invited to address a large group of local Springfield citizens, and he too warned his audience of impending dangers to the government and individual freedoms.

There is no real possibility that Lincoln and Joseph collaborated on the subject; it is very unlikely that the he and Joseph Smith had met at this early stage. Yet it is clear that they both accurately looked forward to dark days ahead at a time when division within the Union and civil war were far from the minds of most Americans.

On March 7, 1831, Joseph Smith recorded the following as a revelation from God:

> Ye hear of wars in foreign lands; but, behold, I say unto you, they are nigh, even at your doors, and not many years hence ye shall hear of wars in your own lands. (D&C 45:63)

As previously noted, a few weeks following the James Adams affair, on January 27, 1838, twenty-eight-year-old Abraham Lincoln was invited to address the Young Men's Lyceum of Springfield on his conviction that the American government was endangered. He began by reminding his audience of the favored state of Americans, who prospered under a government that offered more civil and religious liberty than any other nation in history. He then described his mounting and intriguingly accurate concern for what he viewed as an imperiled America:

> At what point then is the approach of danger to be expected? I answer, if it ever reach us, it must spring up amongst us. It cannot come from abroad. If destruction be our lot, we must ourselves be its author and finisher. As a nation of freemen, we must live through all time, or die by suicide.
>
> I hope I am over wary; but if I am not, there is, even now, something of ill-omen, amongst us. I mean the increasing disregard for law which pervades the country; the growing disposition to substitute the wild and furious passions, in lieu of the sober judgment of Courts; and the worse than savage mobs, for the executive ministers of justice. . . . Accounts of outrages committed by mobs, form the every-day news of the times. They have pervaded the country, from New England to Louisiana; . . . Alike, they spring up among the pleasure hunting masters of Southern slaves, and the order loving citizens of the land of steady habits.—Whatever, then, their cause may be, it is common to the whole country.
>
> Such are the effects of mob law; . . . becoming more and more frequent in this land so lately famed for love of law and order . . .

But all this even, is not the full extent of the evil.—By such examples, by instances of the perpetrators of such acts going unpunished, the lawless in spirit, are encouraged to become lawless in practice; and having been used to no restraint, . . . they thus become, absolutely unrestrained. . . . While, on the other hand, good men, men who love tranquility, who desire to abide by the laws, and enjoy their benefits, who would gladly spill their blood in the defense of their country; seeing their property destroyed; their families insulted, and their lives endangered; their persons injured; and seeing nothing in prospect that forebodes a change for the better; become tired of, and disgusted with, a Government that offers them no protection; . . . Thus, then, by the operation of this mobocractic spirit, which all must admit, is now abroad in the land, the strongest bulwark of any Government, and particularly of those constituted like ours, may effectually be broken down and destroyed.[17]

Young Lincoln concluded his message by referring to a biblical utterance, something Lincoln would do more than four hundred times during his presidency: "Upon these let the proud fabric of freedom rest, as the rock of its basis; and as truly as has been said of the only greater institution, *'the gates of hell shall not prevail against it'* (Matthew 16:18)."[18]

That Lincoln placed this nation and its government just below the "only greater institution," or God's kingdom, reflects his oft-stated belief that this government was a gift from the Almighty. His plea that the gates of hell not prevail against the government reflected his belief in the opposing powers of darkness, which in most Christian traditions have warred against God's goodness since the beginning of time. In the coming years, Lincoln would make many more references to the concepts of good versus evil and right against wrong. In fact, they are a common thread through many of his speeches and conversations.

In just a few years, Lincoln would watch his fellow Illinoisan, Joseph Smith, who used this gates of hell reference at least six times himself, declare his candidacy for the President of the United States. Joseph did this to ensure that the gates of hell would not prevail against God's work in the land he too considered chosen. Joseph was certain that a national war was on the horizon and he, like Lincoln, believed that the only hope of evading this calamity lay in a righteous people remembering God. In his December 1833 declaration, Joseph warned that should this nation not change its course, "then will the Lord arise and come forth out of his hiding place, and in his fury vex the nation" (D&C 101:89). Again and again, these two presidential prophets expressed their deep foreboding that forces of lawlessness were combining to thwart the works of God and extinguish the fragile experiment of government by the people.

## LINCOLN MEETS THE MORMONS

# Sangamo Journal.

Vol. VIII. No 7. Springfield, Illinois, December 8, 1838 Whole 371.

The Philadelphia US Gazette, says, "We perceive by the London papers received yesterday, that a number of Missionaries from the Mormons went on to England lately, and are there preaching their doctrines with some considerable success."

In the midst of all their trials, the Latter-day Saints continued undaunted in their determination to follow Jesus's directive to "go ye into all the world, and preach the gospel to every creature" (Mark 16:15). Many faithful men, upon receiving a calling from their prophet to be a missionary, would go two by two as instructed in the Bible, leaving their wives and children in the care of their fellow members. They became remarkably effective though untrained ministers of their restored gospel. In 1837, Joseph Smith called a handful of faithful believers to preach their gospel in Great Britain. They went, and in four years, some six thousand English, Scottish, and Welsh converts were garnered into the Latter-day Saint fold, many of whom heeded the call to gather with the Saints in Illinois.

One of the most successful of these missionaries was Wilford

Woodruff, a deeply devoted man in his thirties. He received this assignment while serving as a missionary in New England. He gathered his small flock of 53 believers and shepherded them in their quest to join the Saints in Missouri. Woodruff's life was threatened by angry New England locals, which hastened their departure.

It was an arduous journey fraught with breakdowns and delays, which caused them to stop short of Far West before the approaching winter. Woodruff's journal states:

> We had before us, at this late period, a gloomy land journey of two thousand miles, from Maine to Missouri. We continued to travel through rain, mud, cold, frost and snow, until we arrived in Rochester, Sangamon County, Illinois, December 19th, where I stopped and settled my family and company for the winter, being unable to proceed further.[19]

Rochester was some four miles east of Springfield, a community Woodruff had passed through while marching with the Zion's Camp four years earlier. It was here that he happened to meet some local Mormons, who informed him that the Illinois River could not be crossed because of ice and that the Saints in Far West had been violently driven from Missouri just weeks earlier. With this news, Woodruff's group chose to overwinter in the Springfield area alongside a number of Mormon families from Ohio. After seeing to the proper settling of his New England converts, Woodruff procured a home just outside of Springfield and lived there until the next spring. The New England company became quickly acquainted with the Springfield Mormons and joined them in their worship services. Once again, Lincoln likely became acquainted with some of them as they conducted commerce in and around Springfield.

One of the Springfield Mormons was Samuel Mulliner. He had married Katherine Nesbit in Scotland. Shortly thereafter, they moved to Toronto, Canada. One evening, Samuel heard a Mormon missionary preach on a Toronto street corner. Upon returning home to Katherine, he told her, "Katie, I have heard something good and sweet to me. I will listen again."[20] They both did, and he and Katherine embraced the new religion in 1837. The following spring, they, like so many others, sold their possessions to join the Saints in

Kirtland, Ohio. After only a few months in Ohio, persecutions there compelled them to flee from Kirtland with Joseph Smith.

Also journeying with the Mulliners was the George and Polly Stringham family. The Stringhams became acquainted with Joseph and Emma while in the Colesville, New York area and became some of the earliest converts to Joseph's fledgling religion. In spite of persecutions, the Stringhams were unwavering in their newfound faith. They opened their home for church meetings, and Joseph and Emma spent many nights lodging there as they ministered about the area. They too heeded the call to gather in Ohio and were driven out of Kirtland.

On the way to Missouri, an unknown illness coursed through the traveling party, claiming the lives of twelve small children, most under the age of three. Fortunately for the Mulliners and the Stringhams, their young children were spared. In late summer of 1838, they joined a small group of seventeen families that broke from the main party and settled in Springfield, Illinois. George Stringham and his two teenage sons launched a prosperous shingle-making business. Years later, the Stringham children often talked of seeing Abraham Lincoln, future President of the United States, conversing with their father in the shop doorway as he cut shingles.

The addition of Wilford Woodruff's New England Saints to the scattering of LDS families already in the Springfield area precipitated the organization of a branch, or congregation, of the Church on November 4, 1838. Samuel Mulliner officiated as a teacher in the Springfield branch. Not long after, the Springfield Stake[21] (an organizational level roughly equivalent to a Catholic diocese) was organized.

On March 8, 1839, the Mulliners (and probably the Stringhams) were in attendance at a Mormon conference in which saints gathered from surrounding communities to worship and be instructed. It was held in the brick chapel occupied by the Campbellite congregation in Springfield. As an Apostle, Wilford Woodruff was considered the presiding authority of the conference. He addressed the congregation, which probably numbered about two hundred, throughout the two-day conference. The gathering of so many Mormons in

Springfield was probably a topic of conversation among the locals, and it would have been an opportunity for Lincoln to acquaint himself with some of his new Mormon neighbors. There is no doubt that Lincoln was aware of this growing Mormon congregation—he referred to them in a letter early the following year—but there is no evidence that he took part in their gathering. The minutes of their meeting confirm a number of local Mormon families who participated in their conference: the families of Edwin Merriam, Jonathon Dunham, Joseph McCausland, D. Carter, James Higby, Br. Brewster, Arnold Stephens, Br. Stark, Stephen Mecham, Jonathon Fisher, Joshua Mecham, and Samuel Mulliner.

One condition that relentlessly dogged the Mormons wherever they congregated was the disapproval, derision, and persecution of neighbors. Springfield, however, was a notable exception, as evidenced by the local Campbellites offering their meetinghouse for the conference. While a considerable number of Mormons lived in and around Springfield, they appeared to have lived there in relative peace with the locals. The children of George and Polly Stringham, some of whom married and remained in Springfield for several years, confirmed this assessment. "During our sojourn in Springfield we were treated kindly by the people. Mormon girls and boys found ready employment; in fact, they were preferred for their honesty and good behavior."[22]

Soon after the Springfield conference, Samuel Mulliner was called to be a missionary himself. He was to be the first Mormon missionary to preach the gospel in his native Scotland. So in July 1839, shortly after Lincoln's return from Carthage, Samuel left his beloved Katie and his two young daughters in the care of the Mormon congregation in Springfield and "without purse, and scrip" (Luke 22:35), he and Katie raised money for his ocean voyage to Scotland. Katherine's family history, as compiled by her descendants, records:

> During this time Catharine . . . was providing for their two daughters in Springfield, Ill., by washing and ironing, and at the same time sending as much money as she could to Samuel. She was an expert ironer, and was in demand for ironing the stiff tucked shirt

fronts that were worn by the well dressed men of that time. In one of the letters she wrote to her husband she said that she was ironing shirts for a fine young lawyer in Springfield by the name of Abraham Lincoln.[23]

The young lawyer certainly needed someone to launder his shirts, as he was still a bachelor smarting over the death of his beloved fiancée, Ann Rutledge, and the rejection of Mary Owens. It is unknown why, out of all her numerous laundry customers, Katherine particularly mentioned Abraham Lincoln. Maybe Katherine was impressed that he was a prominent member of the Illinois Assembly. Lincoln had to enjoy Katherine's Scottish brogue, as he was often telling stories in the foreign accents of his characters.

Like all of the other Mormons, the Saints in Springfield were surely horrified with the *Sangamo Journal*'s report of the killings at Haun's Mill. One can only wonder if Katherine Mulliner would have shared her grief over Warren and Sardius Smith's murders with Lincoln during one of their frequent laundry handoffs.

But accounts abound of Lincoln's outgoing affability and kind regard for others endearing him to many. New Salem resident Caleb Carman recalled:

> He was liked by every person who knew him. While he boarded with me he made himself useful in every way that he could. If the water-bucket was empty he filled it; if wood was needed he chopped it; and was always cheerful and in a good humor.[24]

Of Lincoln's geniality during his New Salem days, William Gienapp wrote:

> Declining to judge people harshly, he made "great allowances for men's foibles," . . . and his conciliatory approach and obliging manner earned him additional friends. Thanks to his sociability and fondness for visiting, he soon "knew every man, woman and child for miles around."[25]

Given these firsthand observations it appears likely that Lincoln would have been acquainted with a number of these local Mormon families.

## RELIGIOUS OUTCASTS

We can only speculate, but it is possible that Lincoln would have had more than a passing interest in his launderer's maligned religion, the strength of the Mulliners's conviction to it, and Katherine's willingness to support her husband emotionally and financially while he was in Scotland serving as a mouthpiece for their beliefs without compensation. For the previous eight years, like most Americans, Lincoln had read dozens of newspaper accounts of the Mormons' many misfortunes and their remarkable resilience. It is probable that Katherine Mulliner, the Stringhams, and some in the Springfield Mormon congregation were the first Mormons that Lincoln came to know. The laundry exchanges provided frequent opportunities for conversation, and Lincoln was a ready conversationalist. He likely inquired about the well-being of her husband in Scotland, and it is equally probable that Katherine would have shared her husband's letters regarding his remarkable success in garnering converts. Did they discuss their common and divergent biblical beliefs? Did Katherine, the Stringhams, or other Springfield-area Mormons offer Lincoln a copy of the Book of Mormon to read, as was done with Jonathan Browning? Did they ever invite him to their worship services?

The Mormons' undaunted adherence to their un-Protestant Christian beliefs was akin to Lincoln's unwillingness to separate himself from his own biblical interpretations in spite of the personal and political challenges that it caused and would continue to cause him. Like the Mormons, Lincoln lived as a religious outsider in his community. He clung tenaciously to biblical beliefs that kept him from membership in the Protestant sects around him. He often attended worship services with various congregations, yet even if he had interest in joining any, some of them would have rejected him for his "infidel" beliefs.

Throughout Lincoln's youth, he was surrounded by a variety of Christian religions, some of them contentious toward one another in their competition for converts. Over the previous half-century, these churches grew, then divided and splintered over doctrines, personalities, and slavery.

Camp meetings held on the Illinois prairie by itinerate preachers were often frenetic. Listeners and sometimes whole congregations were sometimes driven to uncontrolled jumping and jerking referred to as "the jerks."[26] These were often acclaimed by the preachers as manifestations of divine approbation, though it was more likely a product of their often fiery sermons. It was not different in Lincoln's New Salem, where among the two hundred or so residents were Baptists, Methodists, Campbellites, and Presbyterians. These, at times, disagreed and contended with one another as well. Mrs. Robert Johnson of New Salem was noted as "particularly susceptible to the exhortation of the frontier preachers, being seized with the jerks almost every year."[27]

## MISUNDERSTOOD

While in New Salem, Lincoln, then in his early twenties, joined a group of young intellectual locals, mostly bachelors like himself, who debated and read on sundry topics including religion. Some of these young thinkers espoused American Revolution patriot Thomas Paine's assertions in *Age of Reason*, in which Paine criticized the corruption of organized religions and challenged the Bible's legitimacy on the basis of biblical contradictions and impossible stories. Some from this group of free thinkers, including, possibly, Lincoln, questioned some of the pronouncements of the various local preachers.

Most New Salem residents belonged to the Baptist group known as Hard Shells, the same sect that Lincoln's parents joined when he was fourteen in Indiana. The Hard Shell Baptists embraced the doctrine of predestination to such a degree that their church had no Sunday school and they did no proselytizing because such actions were, in their view, fruitless. God had already predestined each person from infancy to either heaven or hell, and nothing done on earth could change that course. Lincoln's friend Charles J. F. Clarke said that his Hard Shell Baptist neighbors in New Salem:

> Preach the hardest election doctring that I ever heard. They say they were created for Heaven . . . and such as die in their sins were created for Hell, or in other words, God made part of mankind for eternal happiness and the ballance for endless misery. This kind of doctering I can't stand.[28]

Young Lincoln couldn't understand it either. At an early age, he argued against the idea of a cruel and unjust God. He grew fond of the poems of Scottish poet Robert Burns—particularly those considered blasphemous by the local clergy for challenging the hardness of their predestination doctrine. But after closer examination, it is clear that Lincoln was not against the Bible or the worshiping of Christ. He was, however, against the failure of many Christians to live the virtues that Jesus demonstrated and taught.

Benjamin Thomas observes:

> While [Lincoln] eventually attained to a deep faith, emotionally the bitterness of sectarian prejudice must have been repellent to him, and was probably a cause of his lasting reluctance to affiliate with any sect.[29]

We see in Robert Burns's poem "Holy Willie's Prayer," one of Lincoln's favorites, not a challenge to Christianity as a whole (as it has been interpreted by many), but was rather an exposé on hypocrisy among some Christians. In the poem, holy Willie is a self-righteous yet admittedly sinful Scottish clergyman who offers his prayer of thanksgiving to God for having been predestined to heaven, chosen above the other poor wretches whose destiny was the brimstone of hell forever and ever. Lincoln liked to recite this poem:

> O Thou, that in the heavens does dwell,
> As it pleases best Thysel',
> Sends [one] to Heaven an' ten to Hell,
> For Thy glory,
> And no for [one's] guid or ill
> They've done afore Thee![30]

From these accounts, it has been frequently inferred by many that Lincoln scoffed at and rejected the Bible and Christianity. Evidence proves otherwise—Lincoln was somewhere in between. He did have a lifelong conviction that far too many students of the Bible failed to obey Christ's first and great commandment to love God "with all thy heart, and with all thy soul, and with all thy mind," (Matthew 22:37) and then to "love thy neighbor as thyself" (Matthew 22:39). Lincoln lived this Christian principle throughout his life, but he rarely pointed out his friends' failure to live it. Jesus's injunction to "judge not, that ye be not judged," (Matthew 7:1)—a direct biblical quote that Lincoln used in his Second Inaugural Address—likely kept him from saying much about it. He was not one to judge others; his patience and magnanimity were monumental, and it is a marvel to discern their depth and consistency throughout his life. US Representative Henry C. Deming once asked Lincoln his reason for never joining any church. In a memorial address given before Connecticut's legislature in June 1865 (just days after Lincoln's assassination), Deming shared Lincoln's response:

> [I] have never united [my]self to any church, because [I] found difficulty in giving [my] assent, without mental reservation, to the long complicated statements of Christian doctrine which characterize their Articles of Belief and Confessions of Faith. When any church . . . will inscribe over its alter as its sole qualification for membership the Savior's condensed statement of the substance of both the law and Gospel, Thou shalt love the Lord thy God with all thy heart, and with all thy soul, and with all thy mind, and thy neighbor as thyself,—that Church will I join with all my heart and soul.[31]

It is an irony that Lincoln, whose command of biblical scripture easily exceeded that of his disapproving friends and even many ministers, would be tagged with the label of infidel. As a young boy, Lincoln cherished long moments with his mother, who taught him to read until her tragic death. Nancy Lincoln taught Abraham and his sister Sarah not only the words and grammar of the Bible (the only book the family owned) but more importantly, she imprinted a deep sense of right and wrong and love for God and for all mankind into the fabric of Lincoln's character. Her skill at teaching transcended what any formal education could by creating in her son a heart of unmatched faith, kindness, humility, forgiveness, and integrity. Nancy Lincoln also instilled in her son a love for the Bible and its teachings that he continually searched. After Nancy's death, his stepmother, Sarah Bush Johnston, continued to reinforce this teaching. In fact, just three weeks before his assassination, Lincoln sat with his wife and a few others and expounded on numerous scripture references to visions and dreams as modes of divine communication to man from God, contrary to Thomas Paine's assertions decrying the notion of revelation from God.

As a boy he was known to keep "the Bible and Aesop's Fables always within reach and read them over and over again."[31] As president he carried a pocket-sized New Testament in his lapel pocket and was continually seen reading its passages when he would have moments of rest from his relentless schedule. Again, unlike Thomas Paine, Lincoln believed, "But for [the Bible] we could not know right from wrong."[33]

If Katherine Mulliner or any of the other Springfield Latter-day Saints ever entered into gospel discussions with Lincoln, he would likely have been intrigued to learn that the Mormons also espoused many of his unconventional biblical interpretations. As noted earlier, they and Lincoln both adhered to non-Protestant beliefs that all mankind may be saved and that time in hell for the unrepentant was finite. Lincoln and Mormons also believed that men are not punished for Adam's original transgression and that the proper mode of baptism was by immersion. On other Christian beliefs, Lincoln, the Mormons, and the Protestants agreed. To name a few: God hears and answers prayers, forgives repentant sinners through Christ's sacrifice on the cross, and expects obedience to His commandments.

As also noted earlier, Lincoln came to avoid religious discussions during the 1840s because his beliefs brought consternation to friends who loved him but were certain that he was on a fast track to eternal damnation. Lincoln's friend and law partner, John Todd Stuart, stated that even though they never conversed on the subject of religion, he believed "that Mr. Lincoln was in the earlier part of his life an infidel."[34] He went on to say that later Lincoln regularly attended the First Presbyterian Church with his family, rented a pew, and taught in the Sunday school but never accepted invitations to join the congregation in membership. The beliefs Lincoln held in common with Protestants seemed overcast by the biblical views he shared, perhaps unknowingly, with the Mormons.

## Chapter Five Endnotes

1. John Wesley Hill, *Abraham Lincoln: Man of God* (New York: G. P. Putnam's Sons, 1920), 51.

2. Ibid.

3. T. Walter Johnson, "Peter Akers: Methodist Circuit Rider and Educator (1790–1886)," *Journal of the Illinois State Historical Society* 32, no.4 (December 1939): 433.

4. Hill, *Abraham Lincoln*, 52.

5. Ibid.

6. Johnson, "Peter Akers," 433.

7. Hill, *Abraham Lincoln*, 53.

8. Carl Sandberg, "Abraham Lincoln: the Prairie Years and the War Years," in *Reader's Digest*, illustrated ed. (New York: Harcourt Brace Jovanovich, 1970), 64.

9. Ibid.

10. Ibid., 64–65

11. Ibid., 1, 52.

12. John Browning and Curt Gentry, *John M. Browning: American Gunmaker* (n.p.: Browning, 1994), 12–14.

13. Ibid.

14. Susan Easton Black, "James Adams of Springfield, Illinois: The Link between Abraham Lincoln and Joseph Smith," *Mormon Historical Studies* 10, no.1 (March 2009): 33, http://mormonhistoricsites.org/wp-content/uploads/2013/04/James-Adams-of-Springfield-Illinois-The-Link-between-Abraham-Lincoln-and-Joseph-Smith.pdf.

15. Ibid.

16. Ibid., 36.

17. Abraham Lincoln, "Lyceum Address" (address, the Young Men's Lyceum of Springfield, IL, January 27, 1838), http://www.abrahamlincolnonline.org/lincoln/speeches/lyceum.htm.

18. Ibid.

19. "Wilford Woodruff, 1807–1898: History of Wilford Woodruff (From His Own Pen)," entry in Wilford Woodruff's journal on September 4, 1838, Book of Abraham Project, last modified January 22, 2006, http://www.boap.org/LDS/Early-Saints/WWoodruff.html.

20. "Samuel Mulliner Research Biography," June Howe Johnson, David Hammond Allred. and Inez H. Allred, printed in *The Samuel Mulliner Book of Remembrance*, accessed January 30, 2014, https://sites.google.com/site/allredhistory/home/samuel-mulliner/samuel-mulliner-research-biography.

21. The term stake comes from a metaphor in Isaiah 54:2, where the prophet describes an ever-enlarging tent being spread wider and wider, held in place by the ever-increasing numbers of tent stakes: "Enlarge the place of thy tent, and let them stretch forth the curtains of thine habitations: spare not, lengthen thy cords, and strengthen thy stakes."

22. Julia Harmon Kesler, *Briant Stringham and His People* (n.p.: Horizon Publishers, n.d.), 25.

23. "Samuel Mulliner Research Biography," Johnson, https://sites.google.com/site/allredhistory/home/samuel-mulliner/samuel-mulliner-research-biography.

24. Walter B. Stevens, (edited by Michael Burlingame), *A Reporter's Lincoln,* 6.

25. William E. Gienapp, Abraham Lincoln and Civil War America: A Biography (New York: Oxford University Press, 2002), 14.

26. Benjamin Thomas, *Lincoln's New Salem* (Carbondale, IL: Southern Illinois University Press, 1954), 52.

27. Ibid.

28. Ibid., 53.

29. Ibid., 135.

30. Robert Burns, "Holy Willie's Prayer," stanza 1, lines 1–6.

31. William J. Wolf, *The Almost Chosen People: A Study of the Religion of Abraham Lincoln* (Garden City, NY: Doubleday, 1959), 74–75.

32. Thomas Freiling, ed., *Abraham Lincoln's Daily Treasure: Moments of Faith with America's Favorite President* (Grand Rapids, MI: Fleming H. Revell, 2002), 10.

33. William Lee Miller, *Lincoln's Virtues: An Ethical Biography* (2002; repr., New York: Vintage Books, 2003), 84.

34. Hill, *Abraham Lincoln,* 226.

*Chapter Six*

# THE MORMONS ARE NOW IN ILLINOIS!

## A New Belle in Town

In Lincoln's day, families of substance would often send their daughters of marrying age to visit friends or relatives in other communities. These visits were often made with the unspoken objective of finding suitable suitors of similar (or better) social class and affluence. Such was the case with Elizabeth Todd of Lexington, Kentucky, who made a visit to Springfield and landed the most eligible bachelor in Illinois, Ninian Edwards. He was the son of the former governor on Illinois and a lawyer. Together they built a two-story brick home said to have been large enough to contain "a dozen prairie-farmer cabins,"[1] making it one of the most stately homes in Springfield. Ninian was also a friend and fellow state assemblyman of Lincoln's. At Elizabeth's prompting, her younger sister Mary Todd, age twenty-one, made an extended visit to the Edwardses in Springfield. She left a spacious home in Lexington that had all the trappings of a wealthy southern aristocrat's plantation: a coach house, stables, servants, servants' quarters, and flower gardens. But Mary missed few of these comforts; Elizabeth's home was the commodious center of the high society in the small frontier town. The vivacious Mary Todd quickly made friends. James Conkling described her as the "very creature of excitement . . . and never enjoys herself more than when in society and surrounded by a company of merry friends."[2]

Mary Todd was establishing herself in Springfield at the same time that the Saints in Nauvoo were feverishly planting crops, building homes, and laboring to survive the approaching winter of 1839. With the eyes of America following the Mormons' plight, Mary would certainly have been apprised of the Illinoisans' view of their hardships. A few months later, she visited family in Boonville, Missouri, and surely heard the Missouri version of the Mormon dilemma. While in Boonville, Mary was courted by a young man whom she described as "an agreeable lawyer & grandson of *Patrick Henry—what an honor!* I shall never survive it—I wish you could see him, the most perfect original I ever met."[3] Nothing, however, developed further with this youthful infatuation.

Bachelorhood was becoming a concern for thirty-year-old Lincoln, and when the "glowing girl whose neat little figure dressed in the latest feminine finery"[4] moved to Springfield, his marrying instincts were piqued—as were those of the other eligible bachelors in the area. When introduced, Lincoln mustered all of his courage to say, "Miss Todd, I want to dance with you the worst way." Later that evening, Mary laughingly told a friend that he "certainly did."[5] In spite of Lincoln's awkwardness on the dance floor, he did impress her, and their relationship blossomed. Amidst the stunning saga of ten thousand exiled Mormons pouring into his state, Lincoln was building his law practice, paying off his debt, and pursuing Mary Todd.

In the course of his growing acquaintance with the vivacious and highborn Mary, Lincoln could not withhold is admiration for a woman who not only shared his esteem for Henry Clay but also knew him well, had often heard him speak, and was a frequent guest in his Lexington home. Moreover, Mary was a Whig and was much more passionately engaged in politics than most women. This impressed Lincoln. They talked of politics for hours. Mary and Lincoln shared the same birth state of Kentucky, and even though she'd grown up with slaves as her servants, she, like Lincoln was torn at the injustice of it all. They both had seen firsthand the horrors of the slave auction, Lincoln in New Orleans and Mary just down the street from her grand Lexington home, where chained men, women, and children were marched to the auction blocks.

They both loved and wrote poetry. They recited Shakespeare, and, to Lincoln's amazement, Mary admired Robert Burns as much as he did. Mary, who had often said that the man she married would be President of the United States, appreciated Abe's congeniality, humor, and sincerity. He had a promising career as her cousin's law partner and was a three-term state legislator. She had, to be sure, other suitors. One in particular, Stephen A. Douglas, would also be a candidate for President—but Lincoln won both of these campaigns. Finally, both Lincoln and Mary had lost their mothers at early ages. Mary's was taken from her at age seven. This alone brought an unspoken bond of mutual empathy for the losses they had endured through the years.

During their courtship, they would both have very likely read the following in their local Whig newspaper:

## Sangamo Journal.

Vol. VIII. No. 22 Springfield, Illinois, March 23, 1839. Whole. 386.

LOCOFOCOISM.—It will be recollected that Gov. Boggs of Missouri, in the late disturbances, ordered Gen. Clark, in the event of not being able to capture the Mormons, to "EXTERMINATE THEM." The Mormons surrendered. They were then plundered of their property—many of them sent to prison, and the remainder compelled to sign an agreement to leave the State. Even after the

Mormons were permitted to leave, they were compelled to obtain "passes," such as are given to slaves on certain occasions, to prevent them from being arrested as "runaways." The annexed is a copy of one of these "passes."

I permit John D. Lee to remove from Davis to Caldwell County, there to remain during the winter, or to pass out of the State.

R. Wilson, Brig. Gen.
By F. G. Cochral, Aid.

No wonder that the Van Buren Legislature of Missouri refused to permit an investigation into the outrages committed upon the Mormons.

With Joseph Smith in a Missouri jail awaiting trial for murder and treason, the Mormons, bereft of their prophet's leadership, were driven east to the nearest crossing of the Mississippi. They had no idea of their destination. The dilemma was solved when the generous residents in Quincy and the surrounding communities in western Illinois heroically and warmly received them. The fleeing Mormons numbered between eight and twelve thousand. Heartened by the reported compassion of the western Illinois citizens, they crossed the Mississippi. Along with the rest of the church members, Emma Smith, herself four months pregnant and her four young children ranging from eight months to seven years old, crossed the Mississippi by ferry. Upon arriving in Quincy, Emma wrote a letter to her imprisoned husband:

> No one but God knows the reflections of my mind and the feelings of my heart when I left our house and home and almost all of everything that we possessed excepting our little children and took my journey out of the state of Missouri, leaving you shut up in that lonesome prison.[6]

## POLITICAL FODDER

The town of Quincy, home to Jonathan and Orville Browning, became the unexpected safe haven for the hordes of hapless Mormons. Led by the local Democratic Association, citizens held meetings to discuss the dilemma. As would be expected, not all in the town were in favor of rescuing the Mormons. The local Whigs were wary of the Democrats' motives. When the Democratic Association asked the directors of the local Congregational Church for use of their chapel to address the Mormons' plight, they refused, not wanting to help the Mormons. In Illinois, as it was in Missouri and Ohio, much of the animosity against the Mormons would come from local Protestant ministers and their congregations. They likely feared— and rightly so—that the Mormons would win converts from their congregations. This did happen. Undaunted by the directors' refusal, the Quincy Democratic Association held their meetings in the courthouse and issued the following resolution:

> Resolved, That the strangers recently arrived here from the state of Missouri, known by the name of the "Latter-day Saints," are entitled to our sympathy and kindest regard, and that we recommend to the citizens of Quincy to extend all the kindness in their power to bestow on the persons who are in affliction.[7]

But no sooner had the cold, wet, shelterless Mormons arrived in Illinois than political battlefronts began being drawn at their expense. The local Whigs responded with the following:

Bartlett & Sullivan] Quincy, Illinois, Sat., Mar. 2, 1839. [Vol. 1 - No. 44.

We have just returned from rather a queer meeting convened at the court house. From what leaked out on the occasion, it appears that a little knot of politicians denominated the "Quincy Democratic Association," have been tampering with the Mormons now among us, for purposes which the reader can well imagine. This "Association" at their secret caucus of the Saturday night previous [Feb. 23], among other equally wise and prudent efforts to gain strength to their cause, resolved to bait a hook for this oppressed people, and approach them under the plea of sympathizing in their sufferings, and offering relief conditionally—all in the name and behalf of the "Quincy Democratic Association!!"

Thus, the Mormons must see themselves, that this move of the secret caucus, was purely and entirely selfish—immaterial how much the great body of our citizens sympathized with this people—immaterial how much money they contributed, or what efforts they might make in aid of this said people—it all must be done in the name of the miscalled "Democratic Association,". . . . How contemptible the object of this knot of third-rate politicians!

Other leading political leaders like Illinois Governor Thomas Carlin, Secretary of State Stephen A. Douglas, Judge James Adams, and General John C. Bennett of the Illinois State Militia, all Democrats, were vocal in their support of the Quincy citizens' compassion toward the distressed new arrivals. Despite the political wrangling, many western Illinois citizens from both political persuasions set about in earnest to organize relief efforts. Respected citizen Dr. Isaac Galland stepped forward and offered properties north of Quincy for the Mormons' resettlement at very reasonable terms. He also wrote the governor of Iowa, Robert Lucas, to investigate possible land acquisitions for the saints in Iowa. Lucas responded with an executive order decrying the actions of the Missouri governor and mobs, saying, "[The Mormons'] religious opinions, I consider, has nothing to do with our political transactions. They are citizens of the United States, and are entitled to the same political rights and legal protection that other citizens are entitled to."[8] He offered safe haven for the Mormons in his state as well, and many Mormons, encouraged by Governor Lucas's rectitude, settled on the Iowa side of the Mississippi.

## ALLOWED TO ESCAPE

Back in Missouri, Joseph Smith, Hyrum Smith, and three other Mormons continued to languish in the cold squalor of the jail at Liberty. They paid for legal representation but received none. Emma Smith and Hyrum's wife, Mary, managed to travel three times to Liberty in the freezing winter months to visit and comfort their husbands before they too were forced to leave Missouri at gunpoint in

February 1839. Amidst an avalanche of criticism, state authorities soon saw that a trial of Joseph Smith on scant evidence for the charges of murder and treason would only bring more uncomfortable scrutiny and negative press from a nation of disapproving observers. The atrocities in Missouri managed to turn public opinion throughout the country in favor of the Mormons, albeit for only a few months.

In February 1839, Judge Joel Turnham met with the prisoners and flatly stated that he dared not admit them bail lest it should cost him his life as well as theirs. He was certain that he and they would be hunted down and murdered if the prisoners were released. He informed them that the recent mass expulsion of the Mormons was planned months earlier and that "every officer in the State from the governor down was connected with the plot."[9] He then told them that the governor was now "heartily sick of the whole transaction and would grant them a release if he dared."[10] The prosecutors lacked the necessary evidence to convict the prisoners of the charges, but setting them free would likely set off a violent response by the Mormon-haters in the state. Governor Boggs had concluded that they could save face if the Mormon leaders were to escape. In fact, rumors that the governor would release the Mormon leaders were circulating through Quincy in early March, as evidenced in a letter to Joseph Smith from his youngest brother, Don Carlos.

After nearly five months of incarceration, the prisoners were suddenly granted a change of venue to Boone County under the charge of a sheriff and four guards. During their journey, the sheriff informed Joseph that he had secretly received orders to allow the prisoners to escape once they were safely out of harm's way. The prisoners were allowed to purchase horses and clothing, and on the third day, the guards were given whiskey by the sheriff and soon became drunk. The sheriff informed the prisoners that he was going to take a drink and go to sleep and that they could do as they pleased. One guard who remained awake helped the prisoners mount their horses and bid them farewell as they left in the night for the Quincy ferry.[11]

# Sangamo Journal.

Vol. VIII. No. 28 Springfield, Illinois, May 3, 1839. Whole. 392.

The Quincy Whig of the 27th ult. states that the celebrated Mormon leader, Joseph Smith, had arrived at that place. He, with Lyman Wright, Caleb Baldwin, Hiram Smith, and Alex'r M'Rae, escaped from the guard, who got drunk, while taking them to Boone county [sic] for trial. Considering the little justice they had reason to expect from a trial in the Boone Court, their escape was justifiable.— There are five more Mormons confined in Ray county jail.

We can only speculate whether Lincoln discussed the Mormon prophet's release with Katherine Mulliner or any of the other Springfield Latter-day Saints that he had come to know. But the topic would have been of interest to both of them, Katherine from a religious view and Lincoln from a political. How would the thousands of Mormons, with their leader now back at their head, change the political landscape in Lincoln's state? Would Lincoln and the Illinois Legislature be able to manage the so-called Mormon problem any better than the leaders and citizens of Missouri, Ohio, or New York?

These questions were likely on the minds of every Illinois legislator and official in 1839. At the time of the Mormons' arrival, Western Illinois Whigs were clinging to a small majority over the Democrats. Twenty-six-year-old Stephen A. Douglas, referred to by some as the Generalissimo of his party, was already recognized as the foremost Democrat in that part of the state. Both political parties began wooing the new residents without delay.

With the national spotlight now on them, the Illinois leaders set their hands to address the most precarious political, social, and religious issue of the day: the Mormons. Lincoln would have had an exceptional opportunity to investigate the Mormon mind and culture through Katherine Mulliner and the growing number of local

Springfield Mormons. The largest organized congregation of Latter-day Saints in Illinois prior to the Missouri expulsion was the Springfield branch, of which Katherine Mulliner and the Stringhams were a part. Few other Illinois legislators would have had the opportunity to become acquainted with a Mormon at that time. It seems illogical that Lincoln, with his astute political mind and open sociability, would not take the opportunity to acquaint himself with the Mormon predicament through conversations with his Mormon fellow residents.

On April 22, 1839, Joseph Smith was joyfully reunited with Emma and his children. They had endured, on their own, the rigors of the winter expulsion while he was being held in jail. In the early days of Joseph's incarceration, he wrote a letter to Judge John Cleveland, whose wife, Sarah, had joined the Mormon Church some three years earlier and had since then moved to Quincy. In the letter, he supplicated the Clevelands that they open their home to Emma and their children, whom, he was sure, would be forced like all the others to flee to Illinois. Judge Cleveland was not a Mormon, but he supported his wife in her worship, and they both graciously accepted the Smith family into their home in their time of distress. Emma and Sarah became close friends, and a few years later, Emma included Sarah in the presidency of the women's Relief Society of the Church of Jesus Christ of Later-day Saints. When Joseph arrived in Quincy, he lived with the Clevelands for about three weeks until he and Emma were ready to strike out on their own. The Clevelands would later move to Nauvoo when Joseph offered them property there in payment for their kindness.

## WOODRUFF AND THE SPRINGFIELD MORMONS

Through the winter months of 1838–39, the Saints in and around Springfield looked to Wilford Woodruff as their spiritual leader while Joseph remained confined in Liberty Jail. After presiding over a conference held in Springfield on March 8, 1839, Woodruff was ready to take his family to join the Saints in Quincy, some 120 miles west of Springfield. On their journey, they were fortunate to avail themselves of the ever-growing network of Mormon families

throughout Illinois who willingly opened their homes to the Woodruff family for their overnight lodging and meals. Woodruff's journal records:

> I accordingly set out . . . accompanied by my wife & child &
> also Brother & sister Stephens. We rode to Springfield & dined with
> Brother Whittle. From thence we rode to Brother John Herrets &
> spent the night. We had a pleasant interview together. Distance 32 mi.
>
> 14th Rode to Jacksonville visited some of the Saints & rode to
> Exeter & dined with Brother Phineas Young. From thence to Brother
> Samuel Fowler & spent the night.
>
> 16th MOST INTERESTING DAY I rode to Mr. Cleave-
> lands & once more had the happy privilege of greeting Sister Emma
> Smith who had taken up her abode for a season with her Children
> in the house of Sister Cleavland. . . . We next rode to Quincy four
> miles . . .[12]
>
> I then went on to the bank of the river near Quincy, and
> saw a great many of the Saints, old and young, lying in the mud
> and water, in a rainstorm, without tent or covering, which suf-
> fering was caused by the unhallowed persecution of the State of
> Missouri. The sight filled my eyes with tears, while my heart was
> made glad at the cheerfulness of the Saints in the midst of their
> affliction.[13]

Shortly thereafter, Woodruff returned to Rochester to collect the
remainder of his possessions. He stopped again in Springfield and
called a meeting of the local Mormons where, among other church
matters, he described the deplorable state of many of the homeless
Saints at the river's edge near Quincy and called for a collection for
their relief. He succeeded in gathering seventy dollars, and a messenger was immediately dispatched to Quincy with the donations.
On April 8, Woodruff passed one more time through Springfield
on his return to Quincy. Once settled, he wrote the following in his
journal:

> On the 3rd, in company with five of the Twelve [Apostles], I
> went to Judge Cleveland's, and had a happy interview with President
> Joseph Smith, who had just escaped out of the hands of his persecu-
> tors in Missouri; it was the first time I had seen him for more than
> two years, and it was a happy meeting.[14]

News of the Mormon prophet's arrival in Quincy was greeted with unmatched gratitude by his followers. Deeply moved by the kindnesses being extended, Joseph wrote a letter to the citizens of Illinois that was printed in the Quincy Argus. In it he expressed his thanks for those who had "so nobly and kindly received"[15] the members of the Church in their homeless poverty.

## NAUVOO

Within two weeks of his arrival in Quincy, "Brother Joseph," as he was affectionately called by the Latter-day Saints, consulted with the church elders to choose a location to settle the Saints. They made their primary land purchases in Dr. Galland's tiny, declining community of Commerce in Hancock County. Joseph Smith renamed the community Nauvoo, which is Hebrew for *beautiful*. The town was set on a bend of the Mississippi River forty miles north of Quincy. It had struggled because of severe and deadly outbreaks of malaria. For the Mormons, an undesirable place, uncoveted by neighbors, was just what they sought. With remarkable resolve, they set about draining the swamp.

Their selection came with a cost: an estimated eighteen hundred people stricken with malaria-like symptoms, many of whom died. The first thriving business enterprise in Nauvoo was coffin making.[16] Joseph and Emma's cherished fourteen-month-old son, Don Carlos, was one of the casualties, as was his namesake, Joseph's brother. Both were buried in the rapidly expanding Nauvoo cemetery. The Stringham clan in Springfield also gathered with the Saints in Nauvoo, but so many of them were stricken with the disease that they felt compelled to return to the safe haven of Springfield. Funerals with Joseph addressing the mourning families became so frequent that a city ordinance was passed restricting funerals to Mondays through Thursdays. The funeral procession on August 15, 1840, was almost a mile long.

Shortly after the Saints' arrival in Illinois, two events caused the Illinoisans to question the wisdom of their generosity. First, Liberty Jail prisoner Lyman Wight, a member of the Quorum of the Twelve Apostles, began a series of letters to the Quincy Whig in which he laid the blame for the Mormons' expulsion on the Missouri Democrats, indirectly implicating the Democrats who had led the magnanimous rescue effort in Illinois. Upon hearing of Wight's indiscretion, Joseph Smith quickly published his own rebuttal in the same paper, saying:

> We have not at any time thought there was any political party, as such, chargeable with the Missouri barbarities, neither any religious society, as such. They were committed by a mob, composed of all parties, regardless of difference of opinion, either political or religious.
>
> The determined stand in this State, and by the people of Quincy in particular . . . have entitled them equally to our thanks and our profoundest regards . . . We wish to say to the public, through your paper, that we disclaim any intention of making a political question of our difficulties with Missouri, believing that we are not justified in so doing. [17]

The second damaging event occurred on July 21 and 22, 1839. By this time, thousands of Mormons had congregated in and around Nauvoo in an intense effort to drain the swamps, plant crops, and build homes before winter's onset. Joseph Smith was among those stricken with malaria, and his small home was so crowded with the sick that he and Emma were obliged to sleep outside with the dozens of sick and homeless saints who congregated around his house. On July 21st, Joseph arose from his sick bed and began to administer to the sick around him by the laying on of hands as prescribed in the New Testament. Many witnesses reported that those in the house immediately recovered.

Joseph then proceeded to heal those camped around his house. He continued from family to family throughout the whole area, then crossed the Mississippi to the Mormon settlement of Montrose, Iowa, where he commanded the sick to be healed in the name of Jesus Christ, and one after another regained their strength. Mormon historian B. H. Roberts gives the following account:

> One case is mentioned by all who have written on the subject as being very remarkable. This was the case of Elijah Fordham. He was

almost unconscious and nearly dead. Bending over him, the Prophet asked the dying man if he knew him, and believed him to be a servant of God. In a whisper he replied that he did. Joseph then took him by the hand, and with an energy that would have awoke the dead, he commanded him in the name of Jesus Christ to arise from his bed and walk. Brother Fordham leaped from his bed, removed the bandages and mustard plasters from his feet, dressed himself, ate a bowl of bread and milk, and accompanied the Prophet to other houses on his mission of love.[18]

At length, Joseph returned to Nauvoo, but he charged Wilford Woodruff to continue to heal the remaining sick in the Iowa settlement, which he did with the same degree of success.

As clearly demonstrated by the funerals that followed, not all received this healing recovery, but accounts abound that many did regain their health that day. The Mormons received this manifestation as a gift from God through their Prophet. But many of the surrounding Protestant congregations and their ministers decried the two days of miracles as the work of a false prophet. The Mormons soon found that the same troubling issues that caused their expulsion from Missouri were developing in Illinois. The accounts of healings and a prophet that received revelations from God were characterized as blasphemy in many Illinois religious circles, just as in Ohio and Missouri.

Though a northern state, Illinois was made up of predominantly pro-slavery Democrats, and this huge infusion of anti-slavery Mormons stirred concerns. Moreover, the number of Mormons was greater than ever before. This had an immediate and dramatic impact on the general political landscape, which was recognized by Democrats and Whigs alike. Whoever could control the Mormon vote would essentially control the polls. The Mormons instantly became the political focus of both the Whig and Democratic parties.

The work of draining the swamp had its desired effect—incidents of malaria dramatically declined by late summer. In a matter of weeks, the population of Nauvoo, surrounding Hancock County, and eastern Iowa exploded with the immigration of some six to eight thousand Latter-day Saints. After two more years of continual growth, Nauvoo's population rivaled that of Chicago's. New converts arrived regularly from the Eastern and Southern States as well as Great Britain and Scandinavia. And to the chagrin of some Illinoisans, significant numbers of their fellow citizens, including Dr. Isaac Galland, General John C. Bennett, and Judges Daniel H. Wells and James Adams also joined the Church. On July 3, 1839, Joseph Smith recorded in his personal journal, "I baptized Dr. Isaac Galland, and confirmed him at the water's edge."[19]

## "LET THEM IMPORTUNE AT THE FEET OF THE PRESIDENT"

On December 16, 1832, Joseph Smith had received one of his numerous revelations. In it, God brought attention to the failings of the Latter-day Saints in Missouri before they were expelled from Jackson County:

> I, the Lord, have suffered the affliction to come upon [the Latter-day Saints] . . . in consequence of their transgressions . . . Therefore, they must needs be chastened and tried, even as Abraham who was commanded to offer up his only son. . . . Behold, I say unto you, there were jarrings, and contentions, and envyings, and strifes, and lustful and covetous desires among them. (D&C 101:2–6)

The revelation goes on to instruct Joseph to appeal for redress for the Saints' losses:

> Let them importune at the feet of the judge; and if he heed them not, let them importune at the feet of the governor; and if the governor heed them not, let them importune at the feet of the president; and if the president heed them not, then will the Lord arise and come forth out of his hiding place, and in his fury vex the nation. (D&C 101:86–89)

Joseph Smith had concluded that appealing to local or state authorities would not result in justice for the murders, rapes, plunderings, and massive property losses of Missouri. After the Mormons' fourth expulsion in seven years, he decided that he could no longer delay his appeal to the President of the United States. He would do it personally. So in late October 1839, he and three associates struck out for Washington, D.C., in a two-horse buggy to meet with President Martin Van Buren. Their journey took them through Springfield. On the night of November 4, Joseph's journal states that they "put up with John Snider,"[20] a local Springfield Mormon. They soon met a group of thirty Mormon coverts from Canada led by William Law on their way to Nauvoo. Joseph's journal records that these saints "tarried while we did, until the 8th. I preached several times while there."[21] This circumstance placed Joseph and Lincoln in the same town for four days.

The notorious Prophet's presence in Springfield could not have gone unnoticed by the locals. Did Lincoln and Mary have enough curiosity to listen to any of Joseph Smith's Springfield sermons? This would have been another unique opportunity for Lincoln, who was now the Whig party floor leader in the legislature, to better understand the Mormon leader from both a religious and a political standpoint. Lincoln had probably read, a few months earlier, the *Sangamo Journal*'s account of Joseph's escape from Missouri and his arrival in Illinois. A number of other newspaper articles had since chronicled his actions and those of the Nauvoo Mormons. Joseph's sermons would surely have interested both serious searchers and the curious. It is entirely possible that the political and religious issues of the Mormons were topics of conversation by the soon to be engaged Abraham and Mary. Would Katherine Mulliner or Lincoln's other Mormon acquaintances have invited him to any of the sermons? We have no record of Lincoln attending a sermon or meeting Joseph, but on other hand there is no proof that he did not attend. We are left to wonder.

Records do show that Lincoln returned to Springfield on November 2 after tending to legal matters in the towns of Clinton and Decatur. He came back to see his law partner, John Todd Stuart, off to Washington to begin his term as an Illinois congressman. As Stuart's cousin, Mary Todd would certainly have been at this send-off as well. Noting his partner's departure for Washington, Lincoln good-naturedly made the following entry in the Stuart & Lincoln fee book on November 2: "Commencement of Lincoln's Administration."[22]

Court records show that Lincoln, now running a law firm of one, was very busy in legal and political matters during Joseph

Smith's days in Springfield. Lincoln was also in his third term in the Illinois legislature, and he was certainly aware of the dramatic political implications that the Mormons brought with them. Mormon immigration was debated in the Illinois statehouse with a generally compassionate slant from both sides of the aisle. In Lincoln's later years, many political advisors commented on his uncanny ability to read political signs and predict outcomes accurately. But at this early stage of his career, the Mormon political machine proved to be a mystery. In a few short months he would feel the repercussions of their political might firsthand.

Had Joseph Smith arrived in Springfield two days earlier, Lincoln would have almost certainly met him. One of Joseph's main purposes for remaining in Springfield for those four days was to personally consult with political leaders in the State Capitol. Joseph knew of John Todd Stuart's successful election to Congress just a few weeks earlier, and almost certainly would have sought out the Stuart & Lincoln Law office to plead his case with the new Congressman had Stuart still been in town. He must have been disappointed to hear that the new Congressman had left just two days ahead of him.

Upon Joseph's arrival in Springfield, Judge James Adams sought out the Prophet and offered him lodging and meals during Joseph's remaining nights in Springfield. In light of the intense pursuit of the Mormon vote, it is likely that Adams, Douglas, and other Democrats were attempting to insulate the Mormon leader from Whig politicians, particularly Floor Leader Abraham Lincoln. And it is quite probable that Judge Adams would not have included Lincoln on any guest list after their contentious court battle two years earlier. Adding to the intrigue of this Lincoln-Adams drama, Joseph Smith's journal records, "General James Adams, judge of probate, heard of me, sought me out, and took me home with him, and treated me like a father."[23] But Adams's generosity did not stop there. He gave the Mormon prophet a liberal amount of money to fund his trip to Washington and wrote a letter of introduction to his fellow Democrat, President Martin Van Buren.

We do not know why Adams invited Joseph to his home or whether the visit was an influencing factor in Adams's 1840 conversion to Mormonism. James Adams and Joseph Smith were both from western New York, and it is possible that Adams heard stories of Joseph Smith while there in the 1820s. Three weeks prior to Joseph's visit, Brigham Young and Heber C. Kimball, members of the Quorum of the Twelve, visited with James Adams in Springfield on their way to England. They could have influenced Adams's interest in the Mormon prophet and apprised him of Joseph's upcoming journey to Washington. Adams could also have been warmed to the Mormon message from one or more of the Mormon residents of Springfield.

## PRESIDENT MARTIN VAN BUREN

Joseph slept comfortably on James Adams's couch and ate at his table in the large new home Adams had built on the courtroom-contested Sampson and Anderson properties. James Adams's offer of money for the journey proved to be a great assistance as Joseph and his Washington delegation were still suffering the financial distress caused by their Missouri losses. And the letter of introduction to President Van Buren gave them renewed hope of resolution.

Joseph Smith and Elias Higbee arrived in Washington on November 28, 1839, after an arduous, month-long journey through cold and inclement weather. They carried 491 personal claims for redress, itemized accounts of Missouri losses by members of the Church, and a petition to the US Senate and House of Representatives detailing the events that led to their expulsion from Missouri. The petition concludes, "For ourselves we see no redress, unless it is awarded by the Congress of the United States. And here we make our appeal as *American Citizens*, as *Christians*, and as *Men*."[24] The following day, Joseph recorded:

> We proceeded to the house of the President [The White House]. We found a very large and splendid palace, surrounded with a splendid enclosure, decorated with all the fineries and elegancies of this world. We went to the door and requested to see the President, when we were immediately introduced into an upper apartment, where we met the President, and were introduced into his parlor, where we presented him our letters of introduction. As soon as he read one of them, he looked upon us with a kind of half frown, and said, "What

can I do? I can do nothing for you! If I do anything, I shall come in contact with the whole state of Missouri."[25]

But we were not to be intimidated; and demanded a hearing, and constitutional rights. Before we left him he promised to reconsider what he said, and [we] observed that he felt to sympathize with us, on account of our suffering.[26]

In their discussion, President Van Buren enquired into how their religion differed from other religions of the day. "Brother Joseph said we differed in mode of baptism, and the gift of the Holy Ghost by the laying on of hands."[27]

The following days were spent in "hunting up the Representatives in order to get our case brought before the House. . . . "[28] They succeeded in holding a meeting with the Illinois delegation, which included Lincoln's law partner, John Todd Stuart. In a letter to his brother Hyrum, Joseph wrote, "The gentlemen from Illinois are worthy men, and have treated us with the greatest kindness, and are ready to do all that is in their power."[29] The Illinois delegation agreed to take their petition to the Senate for referral to a proper committee.

Throughout his stay in Washington, Joseph Smith received regular communications from the Saints in Illinois as well as from missionaries in the eastern states and Europe. On December 7, 1839, he recorded in his journal, "Elders Hiram Clark, Alexander Wright and Samuel Mulliner [Katherine's husband] arrived in Preston [England] from America."[30] On Christmas Day, he recorded, "Elders Wright and Mulliner left Preston for Scotland, and soon commenced preaching and baptizing in Paisley and vicinity."[31] While in Washington, Joseph took opportunity to preach his gospel message. One such discourse was described by a Matthew Davis in a letter to his wife, Mary:

> I went last evening to hear "Joe Smith," the celebrated Mormon, expound his doctrine. . . . Everything he says, is said in a manner to leave an impression that he is sincere.[32]
>
> Throughout his whole address, he displayed strongly a spirit of charity and forbearance. . . . *I have changed my opinion of the Mormons.* They are an injured and much-abused people.[33]

Joseph continued to importune the Illinois State legislature through letters, to which State Senator Adams [not James Adams] responded:

I had the gratification of the receipt of yours of the 16th of December . . . I also saw yours of the 19th December to Mr. Weber. We are now consulting and feeling the pulsations relative to your case being brought before the legislature, now in session, by a series of resolutions, instructing our senators, and requesting our representatives to argue relief in your case.[34]

The Mormon prophet was heartened by the support from the Illinois delegation in Washington and that of the Illinois State Legislature. It is interesting that Joseph would write Senator Adams and Mr. Weber but not Stuart's law partner and Whig Floor Leader Abraham Lincoln. It may be that James Adams recounted the harsh treatment he received from Lincoln and his friends in his trial during Joseph's four-day stay in Springfield. It could also be that Joseph was referred to the Democrat friends of James Adams and Stephen A. Douglas, who were clearly as covetous of the Mormon vote as the Whigs. As time went by and ever-increasing numbers of Mormons arrived in Illinois, the initial tide of compassion waned. Illinois State legislator John B. Weber received Joseph's appeal and responded that he had:

Called upon many of the prominent members of the Democratic party . . . all of whom expressed a willingness to aid in bringing about justice. But I regret to inform you that but few have exhibited that energy . . . which might reasonably be expected from all lovers of liberty.[35]

After several discouraging weeks in Washington, Joseph Smith was successful in gaining one final audience with President Van Buren, "who treated me very insolently, and it was with great reluctance he listened to our message, which, when he had heard, he said: 'Gentlemen your cause is just, but I can do nothing for you;' and 'If I take up for you I shall lose the vote of Missouri.'"[36] Joseph also met with the pro-slavery champion of South Carolina, John C. Calhoun, whose response towards Joseph was equally sympathetic yet empty. After these interviews, Joseph recorded, "I became satisfied there was little use for me to tarry, to press the just claims of the Saints on the consideration of the President or Congress."[37]

Joseph soon left for Illinois, leaving Elias Higbee in Washington to continue their pursuit of justice with Congress. A few sparsely attended committee hearings followed in which the Mormons' plight was heard as well as the position of the Missourians. Senator Thomas Hart Benton and the rest of the Missouri delegation prevailed, contending that their militias deserved the confiscated Mormon property as compensation for their service in expelling the Mormons from their state. On February 26, 1840, Higbee wrote to Joseph, saying:

> I am just informed . . . that the decision is against us . . . that they believe redress can only be had in Missouri, the courts and legislature. . . . We have a right now . . . of asking God for redress and redemption, as they have been refused us by man.[38]

## LINCOLN'S COURTSHIP CONTINUES

1839 was an exciting year for Lincoln. His affection for Mary Todd was growing, and he had just taken part in his law partner's successful campaign for Congress. This victory probably incited Lincoln's aspirations for his own future bid for Congress. In Stuart's absence, he was successfully managing the law practice, and he continued stumping around the state to garner support for the Whig Party's presidential nominee, William Henry Harrison.

Harrison was running against the incumbent Democrat, Martin Van Buren, who most Mormons had supported four years earlier. Lincoln set his sights on becoming an Illinois member of the Electoral College, and in the following year successfully had his name placed on the ballot for electoral delegates. This was his first involvement in a presidential campaign, and he took it seriously.

## LINCOLN COURTS THE MORMON VOTE

Lincoln's recorded references regarding the Mormons are few, but one of them was made in a letter he wrote on March 1, 1840, to John Todd Stuart in Washington—coincidentally, the same day Joseph Smith was passing through Springfield on his return from Washington. In the letter, Lincoln reported on the campaign efforts of the Whig Party, saying, "I have never seen the prospects of our party so bright in these parts as they are now,"[39] and then listed some former Van Buren supporters who had "come out for Harrison."[40] Regarding the newly arrived Mormons, Lincoln entertained the notion that their anti-slavery sentiments might lead them to support the Whig political platform as well. This conclusion was reinforced by some apparently positive comments made by Joseph Smith about Congressman Stuart in Springfield that day. Whether Lincoln heard these comments directly from Joseph or through a third party is not known. It is also uncertain whether Joseph made these comments in his November visit or upon his return in March. Knowing that Joseph met with John T. Stuart and others of the Illinois delegation various times while in Washington, it is more likely that he made the statement on March 1st. Lincoln's letter to Stuart continues: "[Joshua] Speed says he wrote you what Jo. Smith said about you as he passed here. We will procure the names of some of his people here and send them to you before long."[41] Joshua Speed was one of Lincoln's closest friends. Lincoln boarded with him in an upstairs apartment above Speed's general store, which Joseph may have entered during his visits to Springfield. The comments about Congressman Stuart might have been made directly to Speed, and it is possible that Lincoln was present at the time. We are, of course, unable to prove this for certain with the records we currently have.

Lincoln's letter to Stuart brings to mind two intriguing points regarding Abraham Lincoln and Joseph Smith. First, did these two American icons ever meet? They had ample opportunities to do so. Exhaustive research has uncovered no known record of them meeting, but Joseph Smith was in Springfield on at least two more occasions after his return from Washington. The second point arises from Lincoln's statement that "We will procure the names of some of his people here and send them to you before long."[42] This comment confirms that Lincoln was aware of the substantial Mormon community living in the Springfield area. People like Samuel and Katherine Mulliner, Wilford Woodruff, John Snider, Nicolas Groesbeck, George Stringham, Almon and Julia Ann Babbitt, and many others were probably known to Lincoln.

One other Latter-day Saint in Springfield was James Adams, but it is not known for certain when he became a Mormon. One account suggests it was as early as 1836, just before Lincoln's excoriation of him in the *Sangamo Journal*, which would mean that Adams was a Mormon during the unfortunate affair. The more plausible account indicates that he was baptized in 1840. Ebenezer Robinson, co-editor with Don Carlos Smith of Nauvoo's Mormon newspaper, the *Times and Seasons*, wrote to Brigham Young on December 27, 1840, saying, "The gospel is spreading rapidly in almost all parts of the United States . . . Judge Adams of Springfield, Ill., has been baptized."

Adams kept his membership in the much-maligned church a secret for a time, saying that he could be of more assistance to the Church if his membership remained concealed. At that time, an abundance of careers and relationships disintegrated upon affiliation with the Church of Jesus Christ of Latter-day Saints. Word of Adams's new religion would likely have created difficulties for him and his influential position in Springfield society. James Adams and Joseph Smith would later become business partners, and the two would participate together in some of the most sacred Mormon ordinances in Nauvoo. Joseph and Adams remained close and admiring friends until Adams's death three years later.

## Chapter Six Endnotes

1. Carl Sandberg, "Abraham Lincoln: the Prairie Years and the War Years," in *Reader's Digest,* illustrated ed. (New York: Harcourt Brace Jovanovich, 1970), 71.

2. Ruth Painter Randall, *Mary Lincoln: Biography of a Marriage* (Boston: Little, Brown, 1953), 3.

3. Ibid., 5.

4. Ibid., 12.

5. Ibid.

6. Carol Cornwall Madsen, "'My Dear and Beloved Companion': The letters of Joseph and Emma Smith," *Ensign,* September 2008, https://www.lds.org/ensign/2008/09/my-dear-and-beloved-companion-the-letters-of-joseph-and-emma-smith?lang=eng.

7. B. H. Roberts, *History of the Church of Jesus Christ of Latter-day Saints: An Introduction and Notes* (Salt Lake City, UT: Deseret News, 1968) vol. 3, 268.

8. B. H. Roberts, *The Rise and Fall of Nauvoo* (repr., Provo, UT: Maasai, 2001), 10.

9. B. H. Roberts, *The Missouri Persecutions* (Salt Lake City, UT: Bookcraft, 1965), 271.

10. Ibid.

11. Roberts, *History of the Church*, 321.

12. Scott G. Kenney, ed., *Wilford Woodruff's Journal: 29 December 1833 to 31 December 1840* (Midvale, UT: Signature Books, 1983), vol. 1, 320.

13. "Wilford Woodruff, 1807–1898: History of Wilford Woodruff (From His Own Pen)," entry in Wilford Woodruff's journal on March 13, 1839, Book of Abraham Project, last modified January 22, 2006, http://www.boap.org/LDS/Early-Saints/WWoodruff.html.

14. Ibid.

15. Roberts, *The Rise and Fall of Nauvoo*, 18.

16. Susan Easton Black, BYU Education Week, August 2011

17. Roberts, *The Rise and Fall of Nauvoo*, 20.

18. Ibid., 24.

19. Roberts, *History of the Church*, vol. 3, 393

20. B. H. Roberts, *History of the Church of Jesus Christ of Latter-day Saints: An Introduction and Notes* (Salt Lake City, UT: Deseret News, 1968) vol. 4, 20.

21. Ibid.

22. The Lincoln Log, November 2, 1839

23. Roberts, *History of the Church*, vol. 3, 20.

24. Roberts, *History of the Church*, vol. 4, 38.

25. Ibid., 40.

26. Ibid.

27. Ibid., 42

28. Ibid., 40.

29. Ibid.

30. Journal Histories, LDS Church History Library, December 7, 1839, image 175.

31. Ibid, image 177.

32. Roberts, *History of the Church*, vol. 4, 78.

33. Ibid., 79

34. Ibid., 53.

35. Ibid., 55.

36. Ibid., 80.

37. Ibid.

38. Ibid., 88.

39. Roy Basler, ed., *The Collected Works of Abraham Lincoln* (New Brunswick, NJ: Rutgers University Press, 1953), vol. 1, 206.

40. Ibid.

41. Ibid.

42. Ibid.

*Chapter Seven*

# "BENEVOLENT AND KIND-HEARTED CITIZENS"

In early March 1840, thousands of destitute Mormons hailed the return of their Prophet from Washington, only to lament the disheartening news that their hundreds of claims of lost homes, furnishings, livestock, and land in Missouri were not to be considered. Not one Mormon was willing to risk reentering Missouri to petition the state legislature and courts for recovery of their lost property. They had already petitioned that state's legislature, governor, and courts. With so many local civic leaders complicit in their exile, including the governor, all hope of redress from Missouri was already extinguished.

In Washington, a number of Congressmen had expressed and demonstrated sympathy for the Mormon cause, but not one of them stood up to champion it. With the nation still crippled from the financial Panic of 1837, large cash settlements would have been difficult to extricate from the strained national budget. Land grants would have been a feasible solution, but no resolution was made.

## Lincoln drubbed by the Mormons

Three years earlier, most Mormons had voted for Martin Van Buren, but the one thing that Joseph Smith did acquire in Washington was a conviction to not support the Democrat in his bid for reelection. Joseph's journal records, "On my way home I did not fail to proclaim the iniquity and insolence of Martin Van Buren, toward myself and an injured people, which will have its effect upon the public mind; and may he never be elected again to any office of trust or power, by which he may abuse the innocent and let the guilty go free."[1] Van Buren ran for office again, but he never won another election. Joseph threw his support for the Whig candidate, William Henry Harrison. Most of his Latter-day Saints, now deep in disappointment and mistrust of government at all levels, followed suit.

As noted earlier, Assemblyman Lincoln and quite certainly Mary Todd were excited for this 1840 presidential election. Lincoln embarked on his own campaign to become a presidential elector in support of William Henry Harrison.[2] He left Mary Todd in Springfield and spent the last half of August and nearly all of September 1840 in the towns of southern Illinois, stumping for Harrison. Like Joseph Smith, he had few good things to say about incumbent Martin Van Buren, but Lincoln had different reasons.

In Springfield's *Illinois Register*, local Democrats expressed their wariness of this Whig political operation: "The Junto [Whigs] have determined in secret conclave to revolutionize the southern part of the State, and have appointed A. P. Field and A. Lincoln missionaries to . . . the benighted region."[3] During Lincoln's six years in the state legislature, he was active in supporting a number of local and state officials in their election campaigns, and he was eager here to step, for his first time, into the national arena as one of the state's ten electors for the 1840 presidential race. Just days before Lincoln's Southern Illinois "mission" and less than five months after the Mormons' arrival into Hancock County, their political influence descended abruptly upon the old county residents.

# Illinois Register.

Vol. ? Springfield, Friday, August 14, 1840. No. ?

HANCOCK COUNTY.

CARTHAGE, Ill., Aug. 4, 1840.

I hasten to communicate to you the result of the elections in this county.

The whigs have carried their entire ticket by a majority of about 300 votes. The Democracy were active and vigilant, and when the polls were closed, it was generally believed that we had elected our Representatives and Sheriff; but when the news came in from Commerce [Nauvoo] Precinct, every body was surprised. The average vote against us there was about 290. Joseph Smith took an active part, and sustained the entire whig ticket.

While Lincoln and his Whigs had to be delighted with this news, Illinois Democrats were alarmed by this turn of political events. Whether by coincidence or by design, Stephen A. Douglas was at that time using his influence to gain an appointment as the circuit court judge for west-central Illinois, the district that included Nauvoo in Hancock County. He gained the appointment—becoming the youngest state supreme court judge in Illinois—then moved to Quincy and wasted little time in paying a visit to Nauvoo. There he met Joseph Smith for the first time. Their meeting was cordial and proved to be the beginning of a genuine yet guarded friendship. Shortly after Joseph Smith's meeting with Douglas—and in spite of the fact that he was throwing his vote for the Whig party candidate Harrison—Joseph and more than two hundred Nauvoo voters scratched out the last name on the ten-name presidential elector ballot and wrote in another's. The delegate list had included four Democrats and six Whigs. To make an even five Whigs and five Democrats, the last Whig candidate was removed, and Democrat

James Ralston was written in. The scratched-out name was that of Abraham Lincoln.

It appears here that Joseph and the Mormons, keenly aware of the political implications that their large numbers now played in Illinois politics, were trying to placate both Whigs and Democrats. Both parties were nervously watching the Mormons' rising power at the polls. Their numbers were significant enough in this case to make Lincoln lose his bid and put Democrat James Ralston in as an elector. Again, it's apparent that Joseph had not met Lincoln, though he would likely have heard of him as Congressman Stuart's law partner and the Whig Floor Leader in the Illinois Legislature. Joseph probably also remembered Lincoln as Judge Adams's nemesis, but there is no evidence that this was the motive for removing his name. If another Whig candidate had been the last name on the list, his probably would have been removed instead of Lincoln's. Some cite the article below as evidence that Steven A. Douglas influenced the removal of Lincoln's name.

### Illinois Register.

Vol. V Springfield, Friday, November 13, 1840. No. 37.

WHIG VERACITY.

The Missouri Republican and Quincy Whig both assert that the Hon. Richard M. Young and Stephen A. Douglass, Esq., were at Nauvoo, in Hancock county, on the day of the election, and it is insinuated by these Federal prints that they "induced two hundred Mormon voters to erase the name of A. Lincoln from the Whig electorial ticket, and substitute the name of James H. Ralston in its stead."

The Quincy Whig speaks of the erasure of Mr. Lincoln's name as a trick played upon two hundred Mormon voters." We do not view it in this light. It is very certain that Mr. Lincoln runs near 200 votes behind his ticket in Hancock county, and it is equally as certain that

Judge Ralston runs near 200 ahead of his ticket, but this the voters had a perfect right to do.

There is something connected with the vote at Nauvoo precinct, which needs explanation. Two hundred Mormon voters were induced to erase the name of A. Lincoln, from the whig electoral ticket, and substitute the name of James H. Ralston, in his stead. Rumor says that the Hon. Richard M. Young, of the U. S. Senate, and the "little giant," Stephen A. Douglass, who wants to go to Congress, were present at this election, and of course their names were freely used in connection with this little petty trick. If these rumors should prove correct, we shall have a column to spare for their benefit hereafter.

Of note here is the fact that Senator Richard M. Young proved to be the most earnest supporter of Joseph Smith's futile appeal for justice in Washington one year earlier. If nothing else, Joseph was probably sincerely pleased to see Senator Young.

A few days later, Lincoln's disappointment at losing his bid to serve as a Whig delegate at the hand of the Mormons was softened by William Henry Harrison's victory over Van Buren. Days before the presidential election, the Whigs of Springfield staged a rally and parade that embraced the Harrison campaign slogan of log cabin and hard cider. The highlight of the parade was a miniature cabin pulled by a team of four oxen. George Stringham's seventeen-year-old son, Briant, who had an excellent singing voice, had the honor of being seated on the limb of a buckeye tree on the log cabin float. It was quite certain that the Stringham family and others from the Mormon branch were present at the parade along with Lincoln and Mary. Briant and his sister wrote the following ditty that was sung at the campaign celebration:

> Oh where, tell me where, was your buckeye cabin made?
> It was made among the merry boys who wield the hoe and spade,
> Where the log cabin stands in the bonny buckeye shade.

Lincoln also won his re-election to the legislature by a large margin, despite the fact that he did very little campaigning. The Whigs in and around Springfield were very pleased with Lincoln as their representative, and it can be easily inferred that some local

Mormons cast their votes for Lincoln. E. R. Thayer, one of Spring-field's oldest merchants at the time, stated:

> When Harrison defeated Van Buren, there was great frolic in Springfield. I do not believe there has ever been such a jollification since then. The center of the celebration was a high saloon, and there champagne flowed like water. It was a favorite trick to knock off the head of the bottle by striking it on the stove. Lincoln was present and made a great deal of sport with his speeches, witty sayings, and stories. He even played leap-frog, but he did not drink a thing.[4]

It is likely that Mary Todd, with her ardent Whig sentiments, joined in this celebration with Lincoln.

There can be little doubt that Lincoln knew the Mormons had removed his name from the elector ballot, costing him the election. Lincoln was, essentially, the first state-level political casualty of the Mormon vote in Illinois. There is no recorded indication of how Lincoln felt about the Mormons dashing his hope to act as a Whig delegate, but if nothing else, he had to have been disappointed. Mary was also likely disheartened, though probably less forgiving than Lincoln.

While many politicians harbored resentment and used their influence to retaliate, history shows that in the many political set-backs Lincoln experienced, he rarely if ever resented his opponents for their victories, no matter the tactics they employed to defeat him. When Lincoln ran for the US Senate against Stephen A. Douglas in 1858, Lincoln's friend John J. Crittenden, a fellow Whig, governor of Kentucky, and former US Attorney, unexpectedly swung his support from Lincoln to Douglas, likely shifting the balance enough for Douglas to win the seat. Following his defeat, Lincoln wrote Crittenden a letter in which he expressed the following: "The emotions of defeat, at the close of a struggle in which I felt more than a merely selfish interest, and to which defeat the use of your name contributed largely, are fresh upon me; but even in this mood, I can not for a moment suspect you of anything dishonorable."[5] In another instance, upon winning his re-election for a second presidential term, he received the following telegram from H. Hoffman of Baltimore, MD: "The Maryland soldiers in the Army of the Potomac cast a total vote of fourteen hundred and twenty-eight, out of which we get eleven hundred and sixty majority. This is directly from General Meade and General Grant." Lincoln responded:

TELEGRAM TO H. W. HOFFMAN. WAR DEPARTMENT, WASHINGTON, D. C. November 10, 1864

I am thankful to God for this approval of the people; but, while deeply grateful for this mark of their confidence in me, if I know my heart, my gratitude is free from any taint of personal triumph. I do not impugn the motives of any one opposed to me. It is no pleasure to me to triumph over any one, but I give thanks to the Almighty for this evidence of the people's resolution to stand by free government and the rights of humanity.[6]

Two days later, he expressed nearly identical sentiments to a group of supporters:

I do not impugn the motives of any one opposed to me. It is no pleasure to me to triumph over any one. . . . So long as I have been here I have not willingly planted a thorn in any man's bosom. May I ask those who have not differed with me, to join with me, in this same spirit towards those who have?[7]

The courtship of Mary and Abraham was long. They first met in late 1839, but Lincoln's proposal of marriage did not come until the fall of 1840, about the time of his erasure from the ballot in Nauvoo. The disappointment of this loss was compounded by complications with his courtship.

## A MIGHTY ROUGH MAN

Mary's sister and brother-in-law, Elizabeth and Ninian Edwards, seemed to like Lincoln well enough personally, but his poverty and lack of prospects made him far from fit to marry into the highborn Todd family. They were certain that Mary could do much better, and they made this known to Mary. Lincoln came to know it as well, and it troubled him deeply. Elizabeth described Lincoln as a "mighty rough man."[8] Her son Albert later recalled, "My mother did what she could to break up the match."[9] To the Edwardses, thirty-one-year-old

Lincoln had proven himself incapable of providing the life and comforts that Mary would require to sustain her high social status. To their point, Lincoln did not own a home, was still in debt, and continued to take on legal cases out of compassion rather than financial necessity—he routinely accepted clients who were snubbed by other lawyers for their inability pay for legal services.

Mary seemed unconcerned about Lincoln's financial standing and was disturbed by her sister's discouragement of their relationship. From the beginning, Lincoln was fearful that he would not be able to provide Mary that which she would need to be happy. It was not his nature to seek social status or wealth, and knowing of her family's doubts toward him in this regard led him to doubt himself even further.

When he did propose to Mary, she at first declined out of a coquettish play to test his resolve and to show the Springfield socialites that she was not to be too easily won. She went as far as to follow up with an open flirtation with their mutual friend (and her former suitor) Stephen A. Douglas, fully expecting Lincoln to continue his pursuit for her. But her test of Lincoln's resolve only confirmed his own uncertainties, and Lincoln responded by breaking the engagement just days before their planned wedding day of January 1, 1841.[10] In so doing, he broke both of their hearts. Immediately after ending the engagement, Lincoln became ill for weeks with a flu-type virus, which, compounded by his despondency for having hurt Mary, caused him to miss some days in that year's legislative session. The town was abuzz with the news of the breakup, and the pair remained apart for more than a year.

With the broken engagement, Lincoln continued to need Katherine Mulliner's ironing services. On December 19, 1840, Samuel Mulliner returned safely to Springfield after converting some two hundred people in Scotland. It is likely that Katherine would have found occasion to introduce her husband to the forlorn lawyer friend that she had written him about. It is even more probable that Lincoln would have sought to meet the husband that he likely had heard so much about over the past two years. If, in 1839, Lincoln had met Mormon Apostles Wilford Woodruff, John Taylor, Brigham Young, or Heber C. Kimball, all of whom spent days in Springfield while journeying to Great Britain like Samuel Mulliner, he and Samuel would have been able to reminisce about their common acquaintances. The remarkable success of these missionaries was bringing thousands of new converts from Great Britain to Illinois, something of interest to Assemblyman Lincoln.

Samuel and Katherine likely thanked God many times for their decision to settle in Springfield, where Katherine and their daughters were spared the horrors of Missouri and where they encountered such an unusual degree of tolerance from the Springfield locals. Yet in spite of their good fortune in Springfield, the Mulliners were anxious to join their friends and Samuel's Scottish converts in Nauvoo. When circumstances and weather permitted, they bid farewell to their Springfield friends.

## JOHN C. BENNETT

It is unclear what brought physician John C. Bennett to Fairfield, Illinois, from the vicinity of Kirtland, Ohio, in 1839, but the authorities' discovery of his printing and selling bogus college diplomas probably contributed. Bennett's diplomas were prepared and printed by Eber D. Howe, the editor of the *Painesville Telegraph*. Howe had developed a dislike for the nearby Mormons, and in 1834 he published and distributed *Mormonism Unveiled*, a book that delineated the folly of The Church of Jesus Christ of Latter-day Saints. John C. Bennett, Howe's business colleague, likely read it.

While in Ohio, Bennett met William E. McLellin, a recent convert to Mormonism, and attended some Mormon worship services with him. McLellin introduced Bennett to Joseph Smith, and on January 13, 1832, Bennett had an extended conversation with Joseph Smith. If Joseph shared his gospel message, it had no apparent effect on Bennett, who maintained his affiliation with Alexander Campbell and his fast-growing Campbellite denomination. As noted earlier, Campbell was a frequent and ardent critic of Joseph Smith, the Book of Mormon, and the Church. He had produced a pamphlet entitled *Campbell's Delusions: An Analysis of the Book of Mormon*, which was, like Howe's, an anti-Mormon tract that Bennett likely read.

Bennett's rise to prominence in Illinois was meteoric. In 1840, Illinois Governor Thomas Carlin commissioned him to the prestigious rank of brigadier general of a three-county private militia in southern Illinois. Just weeks later, Governor Carlin commissioned him quartermaster-general of the Illinois Militia.[11] Also in 1840, Bennett displayed an apparent change of heart toward the Mormons. Through the summer he wrote three letters to Joseph Smith expressing his willingness to support him and his homeless thousands. Joseph did not respond until after receiving Bennett's third letter, which said:

> My anxiety to be with you is daily increasing, and I shall wind up my professional business immediately, and proceed to your blissful abode, if you think it best. . . . You are aware that at the time of your most bitter persecutions, I was with you in feeling, and proffered you my military knowledge and prowess.[12]

Bennett's pleas to join the Mormons in Nauvoo had every appearance of sincerity, and it is not surprising that Joseph, anxious that Nauvoo be populated with friends of other faiths, welcomed him to the new city. Especially intriguing to Joseph was the prospect of encountering an influential figure in Illinois to back the massive Mormon migration; Bennett's high position and expression of support were desperately needed and warmly welcomed. In his written response to Bennett, Joseph said, "Therefore my general invitation is, Let all that will, come, and partake of the poverty of Nauvoo freely."[13] He then alerted Bennett that with so few dwellings in Nauvoo he would need to establish his own residence. Yet when Bennett arrived in September 1840 without a place to stay, he was invited to board in Joseph and Emma's small cabin. Bennett accepted and stayed with the Smith family for several months, during which time he was baptized and gained the respect and confidence of Joseph Smith and his fellow Nauvoo citizens as he had done with the state and local officials in Springfield.

## THE NAUVOO CHARTER

Joseph Smith's foremost goal was to prevent, in Illinois, the bitter outcomes that had befallen him and his followers in New

York, Ohio, and Missouri. Fully aware that Nauvoo's population would shortly surpass that of Springfield, Joseph considered obtaining a city charter for Nauvoo like the ones enjoyed by Chicago, Quincy, and Springfield. Bennett's numerous connections to the governor and other prominent Illinois political leaders immediately proved to be valuable assets. Bennett and Joseph drafted an ambitious charter that included permission to form a militia and a university. It was expected that frontier communities organize militias for protection against Indian uprisings and maintaining civil order. The Mormons also wanted to protect themselves from government-sanctioned persecution with a government-sanctioned militia. Their sheer numbers would make it a strong one—too strong, in the view of neighboring communities. The inclusion of a university reflected Joseph's vision of a complete and thriving city, which impressed the legislature in Springfield.

With their proposed charter in hand, John C. Bennett left for Springfield to promote the cause of his newfound friends. Bennett was an accomplished lobbyist, having written and passed bills in Ohio, Virginia, Indiana, and Illinois, and his petition to end the opposition to the beleaguered Mormons was well received in Springfield. He also reminded the Mormons to demonstrate that they would be law-abiding citizens in their new state. He appealed to his fellow Democrat and Free Mason Stephen A. Douglas to assist. Douglas, who had recently opposed similar incorporations, readily took up the cause for Nauvoo, and together they lobbied friends and colleagues in the legislature before submitting the charter proposal.

With Lincoln being the Whig Floor Leader, it is probable that Bennett had conversations with him on the subject as well. While Douglas pushed the majority Democrats, State Senator Sydney Little from Hancock County, the bill's chief sponsor, rallied the Whigs' endorsement. With the new state capitol still under construction, Lincoln and his Assembly met in a nearby church to address the charter matter. They found a high degree of support, and both Democrats and Whigs overwhelmingly approved the very generous Nauvoo charter through a voice vote. Stephen A.

Douglas, as the new secretary of state, signed the seal for the charter on December 16, 1840, empowering the residents of Nauvoo to protect and defend their religious and civil liberties.

This vote would have been an opportunity for Lincoln to retaliate against the Mormons for removing his name from the ballot a few weeks earlier, but there is no evidence that he used his influence to oppose the charter. In fact, he voted in favor of the charter and made a point afterward to congratulate Bennett for its passage. Bennett heralded the passage of their charter in the new Nauvoo newspaper, the *Times and Seasons*:

> Many members in this house, likewise were warmly in our favor, with only one or two dissenting voices . . . and here I should not forget to mention that Lincoln, whose name we erased from the electoral ticket in November, (not, however, on account of any dislike to him as a man, but simply because his was the last name on the ticket, and we desired to show our friendship to the Democratic party by substituting the name of Ralston for some one of the Whigs,) had the magnanimity to vote for our act, and came forward, after the final vote, to the bar of the house, and cordially congratulated me on its passage.[14]

The passage of the generous city charter filled each Mormon with a grateful optimism in spite of their extreme poverty. Never before had they received such genuine support from state and local governments. Prominent political leaders were bold and vocal in fomenting support. This experience, so completely opposite from that in the other states in which they had assembled, left Joseph Smith with a hope for his people that he had never been able to feel before.[15]

The Mormons responded with heartfelt veneration for both Senator Sydney Little and Secretary of State Stephen A. Douglas for their influence in passing charter. This generosity on the part of the Illinois Legislature reflected the widespread sympathy for what the Mormons had suffered in Missouri. Yet despite the efforts of Senator Little, twenty-seven-year-old Stephen A. Douglas benefited the most from passing the charter. Shortly after its passage, Douglas again visited Nauvoo and praised the new community for its orderly and rapid development. The Mormons eagerly reciprocated by granting him the Freedom of the City award, at which time Joseph complemented Douglas, saying, "No man stands more deservedly high in the public estimation, as an able and profound jurist, politician, and statesman."[16] It is difficult to calculate the depth of the Mormons' gratitude for such distinguished, influential friends as Douglas.

## THE NEW GATHERING PLACE

Lincoln likely read this pro-Mormon article in the Sangamo Journal a few days after the passage of the charter:

# Sangamo Journal.

Vol. X. No. 5. Springfield, Illinois, December 18, 1840. S. Francis.

### MORMONS ARRIVED FROM ENGLAND.

The packet ship North America, which arrived at New York last week, brought in her steerage 200 passengers, the whole of whom were "Latter Day Saints" or Mormons, bound for the Mormon settlement at Quincy. The Liverpool Chroncile [sic] states that upward of 2000 are entreating to embark early next spring for the same locality. A great portion of those who sailed in the North America, are members of the abstinence society, and are from Leicestershire and Herefordshire.

We find the above in the Baltimore Patriot of the 2nd inst. The information seems to be vertain that during the ensuing summer, several thousand additional emigrants, attached to the church of the "Latter Day Saints" will be added to the population of Adams and Hancock counties. A late number of the "Times and Seasons," published at Nauvoo, contains letters from England, showing that the success of the Mormon Missionaries there is most extraordinary: we believe that their success even astonished themselves. It is not all surprising that the English converts are disposed to emigrate to the neighborhood of their leader; as, in doing so, they will find the most fertile and healthy country, and a liberal population ready to welcome them. We have understood that, generally, these emigrants are not wealthy; but they bring with them what is of far more value—sobriety, industry, and intelligence—with which qualities they will make good citizens, and add much to the prosperity of the state.

As connected with the subject, we will add, that the senate of this state have passed a bill incorporating the "City of Nauvoo," in Hancock County, which embraces the most liberal provisions. The bill will undoubtedly pass the house. The infant city now embraces a population, as we understand, of about three thousand; and is fast improving. The stagnant waters near it have been drained off and it may now be considered a decidedly [sic] healthy location.

It's a safe assumption that Lincoln shared in this welcoming sentiment. Throughout his young life, Lincoln often stood alone in his compassion for the plight of Native Americans, slaves, alcoholics and religious outcasts. Indications are that he was sympathetic to the trials of the Mormons and supportive of their rights to settle in his state and to worship as they chose. As a non-drinker, the suggestion that many of the British Saints had sworn off alcohol as he had suggested a healthy and sober addition of fellow abstainers in Nauvoo. But two thousand additional Latter-day Saints immigrating to Illinois had major economic and political implications; it turned out to be a portent of more strife to come. Given the atrocities so recently observed in Missouri, Lincoln probably wondered how resilient Illinoisans' compassion for the Mormons would be.

The British immigrants were not the only converts gathering to Nauvoo. In 1839, fifteen-year-old Jane Manning, a free black in Connecticut, had disregarded her minister's warning and listened to the recently arrived Mormon elders. By the next Sunday, she had left her Presbyterian congregation and joined the Church of Jesus Christ of Latter-day Saints. Many in her family followed her into the new religion, and eighteen months later, she led her family of nine on a pilgrimage to Nauvoo. They traveled by boat to Buffalo, but they were refused further passage because they were black. So they walked the final eight hundred miles. In her autobiography, which she dictated to Elizabeth Roundy in 1898, Jane described their journey:

168

> We walked until our shoes were worn out and our feet became
> sore and cracked open and bled until you could see the whole print of
> our feet with blood on the ground. We stopped and united in prayer
> to the Lord; we asked God the Eternal Father to heal our feet and our
> prayers were answered and our feet were healed forthwith.[17]

When Jane Manning's party arrived in Peoria, Illinois, they were
apprehended by local authorities who suspected them of being runaway slaves. They were then threatened with incarceration until they
produced their free papers. Being freeborn blacks from Connecticut,
they were unfamiliar with the required documentation and unprepared for the suspicion of pro-slavery Illinois officials of blacks who
were unattended by a white overlord. After telling their story and
destination, they were, at length, allowed to proceed with their journey. Jane continues:

> [The] next day we walked for a considerable distance and stayed
> that night in a forest out in the open air. The frost fell on us so heavy
> that it was like a light fall of snow. We rose early and started on our
> way, walking through that frost with our bare feet, until the sun
> rose and melted it away. But we went on our way rejoicing, singing
> hymns, and thanking God for his infinite goodness and mercy to us
> in blessing us as he had, protecting us from all harm, answering our
> prayers and healing our feet.[18]

Upon arriving in Nauvoo, they, like the dozens of other new
converts who arrived each month, were homeless. They asked to see
the prophet and were directed to the small Smith log home and were
kindly greeted by Emma with, "Come in. Come in!"[19] Joseph and
Emma fed all nine Mannings and listened to the account of their
journey. After this, Joseph clapped Dr. John Bernhisel, who had
joined them for the evening, on the knee and exclaimed, "What
do you think of that, doctor; isn't that faith." Then, to the Mannings, he solemnly said, "God bless you, you are among friends now
and you will be protected."[20] He then invited them to stay in their
cabin until their own housing could be secured. It is telling that the
Smiths, in an era of white superiority and with so many other new
arrivals, would welcome a black family into their home and attend to
their needs as equals. In fact, he and Emma were so taken by Jane's

courage and faith that they discussed adopting her into their family. Jane later married Isaac James, and she and her family were some of Utah's first settlers.

Joseph and Emma's willingness to receive the Manning family into their home reflected Lincoln's belief in the equality of all men. One day years later, President Lincoln was walking down a path with some companions. Coming down the path the other way was a black woman. Recognizing the President immediately, she stepped off the path in customary deference to whites. But to everyone's surprise, the President stepped off the path as well, motioning for his companions to do the same. The woman stared at him in complete bewilderment—what was she to do? The magnanimous President Lincoln smiled at her, removed his hat, and kindly motioned for her to pass by him and his party. While it was common for a white gentleman to tip his hat to a white lady, it was rare indeed for a white gentleman—and especially the president—to not only tip his hat but also step aside. And to do so for a black person was unthinkable. The woman sensed, however, his kind sincerity, and she cautiously and gratefully passed by, thanking the President. The perplexed traveling party was beyond words.

Joseph Smith never intended his new city to be for Mormons only. In January 1841, during Lincoln's despair over his broken engagement, Joseph gave a public address in which he stated:

> We claim no privileges but what we feel cheerfully disposed to share with our fellow-citizens of every denomination, and every sentiment of religion . . . let all those who desire to locate in this place (Nauvoo) . . . come, and we will hail them as citizens and friends, and shall feel it not only a duty, but a privilege, to reciprocate the kindness we have received from the benevolent and kind-hearted citizens of the State of Illinois.[21]

## FALL FROM GRACE

John C. Bennett returned to a hero's welcome in Nauvoo after his success with the charter in Springfield. Shortly thereafter, Joseph selected Bennett as his interim assistant to the President of the Church, essentially the number-two man in the Church hierarchy, while current assistant Sidney Rigdon recovered from an extended illness. Soon after that, Bennett was elected the first mayor of Nauvoo, appointed chancellor of the Nauvoo University, and then appointed major general of the newly organized Nauvoo Legion by Secretary of State Stephen A. Douglas.

# Sangamo Journal.

Vol. X. No. 5. Springfield, Illinois, February 25, 1841. S. Francis.

Gen. J. C. Bennet, has been elected Mayor of Nauvoo, under the late act incorporating that city.

Shortly following Bennett's return, Joseph received an anonymous letter warning him not to place his trust in John C. Bennett. But Bennett's invaluable assistance with the Nauvoo Charter, his eloquence in his preaching to the Mormons in their worship services, and his promotion of the Mormon plight to his powerful circle of friends in the state, left Joseph, his cadre of leaders, and the general Mormon population little reason to question his intentions. He was the clear choice for the first mayor of Nauvoo.

In the same month that Bennett won the election for mayor, Joseph sent George Miller to Ohio to inquire about Bennett's past. Miller was a prosperous Quincy farmer who had sheltered Lucy, Don Carlos, Joseph Smith Sr., and many other homeless Saints during their first difficult days in Illinois and later became converted.[22] Unlike with Bennett, Joseph encountered no reason to question Miller's integrity.

Miller returned in early March 1841 and reported that Bennett's wife had left him after a number of acquaintances had confirmed Bennett's adulterous behavior. These acquaintances also accused him of being an imposter who was not to be trusted. Joseph seriously considered the report, yet he tempered it with the fact that many men with unsavory pasts had come to God, repented, and continued on a course of integrity and righteousness. Joseph was well acquainted with some of these men. So Joseph let Mayor Bennett continue in his service to the citizens of Nauvoo with a strong admonition to conduct himself honorably. It was not long after this, however, that Bennett was again accused of adultery. When confronted by President Smith and other leading elders of the Church, Bennett tearfully confessed. He promised again to end the behavior and pled for forgiveness, which the Elders agreed to grant to him. But his conduct became known among the citizens, and their confidence and high regard for him began to deteriorate.

## FREEMASONRY

On December 29, 1841, the first meeting of the Masonic Lodge of Nauvoo was held in Hyrum Smith's office. Newly appointed Worshipful Master George Miller and his secretary, John C. Bennett, lead the organization. One year earlier, James Adams was doing the same in Springfield.

Freemasonry is the oldest fraternal organization in the world; it has existed for some six thousand years, tracing its history back to the builders of King Solomon's temple. It is based on the fatherhood of God and the brotherhood of man, and its members practice a search for truth and pledge to sustain each other in a spirit of brotherly love.

The first Masonic Lodge in Illinois was organized in March 1805 in Kaskaskia, Illinois. In 1839, James Adams founded the Springfield Lodge of Freemasonry. Most honorable men in the community were drawn to this respected organization, which often led to business and community collaborations. Following in the footsteps of Presidents George Washington, James Monroe, Andrew Jackson, and James Polk, as well as prominent Americans like Davey Crockett, Kit Carson, Henry Clay, and Paul Revere, Stephen A. Douglas became a Mason in Springfield Lodge Number Four in June 1840. Judge Adams, still an undisclosed Mormon, was the Worshipful Master at the time. One prominent Springfield resident who was conspicuously absent from the Masonic Lodge was State Assemblyman and attorney Abraham Lincoln.

It is not known why Lincoln was excluded from the Masons.

Few people in Springfield were more popular than Lincoln, who could entertain friends for hours with his stories and good nature. Could it be that Lincoln applied for membership and was declined by James Adams? Did Lincoln forbear from applying because of Adams's prominent position? Was Stephen A. Douglas's former interest in Mary Todd a deterrent, and did Mary herself encourage or discourage his involvement? The answers are unknown, but two facts are certain. First, Lincoln's political aspirations could have been significantly bolstered by membership in the nationwide network of Masonic Lodges. Second, despite being socially outgoing, Lincoln seemed to prefer to work alone.

Even after the key role he played in forming the Illinois Republican Party, Lincoln primarily operated alone. It was said of him that he followed no one. In the early 1840s, the Springfield Temperance Society was developing, and few in Springfield were more widely known to abstain from alcohol than Lincoln. It would seem logical that Lincoln would be drawn to such an organization, but he declined their invitations of membership. He seemed to sense that membership in any organization often meant lining up under political and organizational positions that he did not fully embrace. For instance, one of the primary political planks of the Republican Party in the mid-1850s was to eradicate what they called the twin relics of barbarism, slavery and polygamy.[23] And while Lincoln spoke incessantly against slavery, he did not speak against polygamy. His independence from alliances and organized societies allowed him to speak and act as he felt inclined to speak and act, free from any obligation to back positions unsavory to him.

## CHAPTER SEVEN ENDNOTES

1.  B. H. Roberts, *History of the Church of Jesus Christ of Latter-day Saints: An Introduction and Notes* (Salt Lake City, UT: Deseret News, 1968) vol. 4, 89.

2.  Ruth Painter Randall, *Mary Lincoln: A Biography of a Marriage* (Boston: Little Brown, 1953), 23–24.

3.  "The Lincoln Log: August 18, 1840," The Papers of Abraham Lincoln, last modified February 20, 2014, http://www.thelincolnlog.org/Calendar.aspx?year=1840&month=8&day=18.

4.  William Lee Miller, *Lincoln's Virtues* (New York: Vintage Books, 2002), 33.

5.  Roy Basler, ed., *The Collected Works of Abraham Lincoln* (New Brunswick, NJ: Rutgers University Press, 1953), vol. 3, 335–36.

6.  Ibid.

7.  Ibid., vol. 8, 96.

8.  Ruth Painter Randall, *Mary Lincoln: Biography of a Marriage* (Boston: Little, Brown, 1953), 41.

9.  Ibid., 40.

10. Ibid., 30.

11. B. H. Roberts, *The Rise and Fall of Nauvoo* (repr., Provo, UT: Maasai 2001), 59–60.

12. Roberts, *History of the Church*, vol. 4, 172.

13. Ibid., 178.

14. "Truth Will Prevail, January 1, 1841," in *Times and Seasons, November 1840–October 1841* (Brigham Young University, 2006) vol. 2, no. 5., http://files.restorationbranches. org/AD%201830-1844/Times%20&%20Seasons/Volume%202/Vol.%202%20No.%20 05%20pp.%20257-272.pdf.

15. Roberts, *The Rise and Fall of Nauvoo*, 68.

16. "Truth Will Prevail, May 15, 1841," *Times and Seasons*, vol.2, no.14, http://files.restora- tionbranches.org/AD%201830-1844/Times%20&%20Seasons/Volume%202/Vol.%20 2%20No.%2014%20pp.%20407-422.pdf.

17. *Jane E. Manning James: Autobiography, Holograph and Typescript* (LDS Church Archives, 1898), 1.

18. Ibid., 1–2.

19. Ibid., 2.

20. Ibid.

21. B. H. Roberts, *The Rise and Fall of Nauvoo* (Provo, Utah: Maasai Publishing, 2001), 68.

22. Lucy Smith was never shy about witnessing to the work of God through her son, and it's likely that the other appreciative Mormons shared testimony of their faith to Miller as

well. His benevolence brought him in contact with the Mormon prophet who was deeply grateful for Miller's rescue of his aging parents, brother and followers from the winter elements during his days of incarceration.

In August 1839, Wilford Woodruff and John Taylor had embarked on their journey for England and passed by George Miller's place to visit with Don Carlos Smith and his family. In the course of their visit, they along with Joseph Smith's brothers Samuel and Don Carlos, shared their gospel message to a small group there that included George Miller and to the surprise of his many friends, he too sought inclusion into the Church of Jesus Christ. He was baptized the next day, August 12, by John Taylor. Miller gave the impoverished missionaries Woodruff and Taylor, a horse to help them on their way. On August 15, the missionaries arrived in Springfield where they met with the saints there. The next day Taylor engaged a printer to make 1,500 pamphlets that described the Mormons' persecutions at the hands of the Missourians. They then continued to Rochester where Woodruff was reunited with friends and fellow Mormons.

Miller sold his farm a year later and moved to Montrose, Iowa, with his fellow Mormons. He, like Bennett, became highly regarded to the point that Miller was called to be the bishop over one of the many Mormon congregations called wards, appointed president of the Nauvoo House Association, the board of regents for the Nauvoo University and elected as worshipful master for the newly organized Nauvoo Lodge of Freemasons.

23. The Republican Platform in Philadelhphia of 1856 created and hosted by the Independence Hall Association in Philadelphia, last modified February 17, 2013, http://www.ushistory.org/gop/convention_1856republicanplatform.htm.

*Chapter Eight*

# TEETOTALLERS

The year 1841 was a long and troublesome one for Lincoln. He was unable to contain his sadness at his estrangement from Mary. In Springfield, people often inquired regarding the breakup. He spent the year avoiding social events that Mary might attend. In June, Mary Todd wrote her friend Mercy Levering that Lincoln "deems me unworthy of notice, as I have not met him in the gay world for months. I would that the case were different, that he would once more resume his station in Society."[1] Adding to Lincoln's gloom, his closest friend, Joshua Speed, had left Springfield for Louisville, Kentucky. Lincoln was left doubly empty.

He found relief as a circuit-riding attorney for the Eighth Judicial Circuit, which allowed him to be away from Springfield's painful associations twice each year. He travelled with a judge and other attorneys from town to town in nine counties of central and eastern Illinois each spring and fall. These circuit runs took him away from Springfield for eight to ten weeks at a time. They also took him farther away from the growing Mormon city of Nauvoo and news of developments there. Upon his return from the spring circuit of 1841, he formed a law partnership with Stephen T. Logan (John Todd Stuart was still in Washington). By the summer of 1841, Mary had managed to convey to her estranged fiancé that even though she had agreed to break the engagement, "she would hold the question an open one,"[2] making it clear that she still loved him. She understood that his wavering was not a result of an uncertain love for her but rather of his reticence to enter into the aristocratic life that her family would expect of him. Throughout this difficult time, "her sisters . . . showered her with objections to the marriage,"[3] reminding her that Lincoln's family was "on a different social plane"[4] than they, and that there were other eligible suitors who would make more appropriate marriage partners. She endured references to Lincoln's insufficient social graces and other ridiculing comments throughout 1841, but these did little to dissuade her feelings for him.

## OPPOSITION DEVELOPS AGAIN

By S. M. Bartlett. Quincy, Illinois, Sat., April 24, 1841. Vol. 3—No. 52.

Proceedings at Nauvoo.

The ceremony of laying the cornerstone of the Temple at Nauvoo, passed off yesterday with great parade. The number assembled is variously estimated; we should think, however, about 7000 or 8000, some say as high as 12,000. The Nauvoo Legion consisting of 659 men, was in attendance, and considering the short time they have had to prepare, made a very respectable appearance. On the whole the exercises passed off with the utmost order, without accident or the slightest disturbance. Gen. Bennet commanded the Legion, under the direction of the Prophet, and acquitted himself in a truly officer-like manner.—We have no time for further comment this week.—Warsaw World, April 7.

In a goodwill gesture, people from the neighboring communities were invited to attend the ceremonial laying of the cornerstone of the new Mormon temple, and many attended. As related above, it was a cordial day of community support and collaboration. There was, however, at least one of the attendees who came away troubled at the intimidating size and strength of the Nauvoo Legion, the vast and continually increasing number of Latter-day Saints, and the unprecedented city charter granted to them by the legislature. His name was Thomas Sharp.

Sharp was the twenty-two-year-old editor of the *Warsaw Signal*, and he used his newly acquired newspaper to express his consternations. His denunciations of Joseph Smith and his followers began as respectful questions and observations but soon escalated to sharp and relentless attacks against the Mormons. His voice represented many in Warsaw who saw their chances of building a thriving river-trade port dashed by the success of nearby Nauvoo. By mid-1841, Sharp organized a new political party blatantly called the Anti-Mormon Party. This new organization gained significant traction in Hancock County, especially in Warsaw and the county seat of Carthage. Sharp successfully fomented a growing resentment of the Mormons, their optimism, and their political clout.

Appointing Masters in Chancery of two Counties was one of Stephen A. Douglas's first orders of business as the new State Supreme Court Judge in western Illinois. His provocative selection for the vacancy in Hancock County was his friend and fellow Democrat John C. Bennett. With this appointment, what had been unthinkable to many was suddenly a reality: Mormons were becoming public officials.

By S. M. Bartlett. Quincy, Illinois, Sat., May 15, 1841. Vol. 4—No. 3.

The New Judiciary System—Rewards.
At the late sitting of the Circuit Court in this place, Judge Douglass appointed Calvin A. Warren, Esq. of this city—a zealous

and somewhat ambitious member of the locofoco party—Master in Chancery, for this county.

At the sitting of the court in Hancock county, Gen. John C. Bennett, of Nauvoo, was appointed by the same Judge, Master in Chancery, for Hancock. Gen. Bennett, is a prominent member of the Church of Latter Day Saints or Mormons, and a friend of the fallen Van Buren dynasty.

## THE EYES OF THE NATION ON NAUVOO

By 1841, the success of Nauvoo was becoming a marvel to many outside of Illinois and a growing consternation to an increasing number within it. Two years had passed since the Mormons' expulsion from Missouri, but their status and conditions remained newsworthy in many parts of the country. Stories of the Mormons' resilience and growing prosperity in a nation still crippled by the Financial Panic of 1837 were printed in many newspapers throughout America. The rise of Nauvoo was of such interest around the country that it became a travel destination for people who wanted to see this American phenomenon for themselves. Most of these visitors were favorably impressed and returned to their home and friends. Descriptions of a growing city, a sizeable and well-drilled militia, a temple under construction, and industrious, sober citizens drew additional tourists. These curious visitors were often invited to make their homes in Nauvoo to participate in its development, and some did. An inn called the Mansion House was built for the purpose of lodging and entertaining these guests. Joseph and Emma made their home at the inn and hosted the travellers.

One such visitor to Nauvoo was a Mr. Jonas, the Grand Master Mason in Ohio. He wrote of his visit to the editor of the *Advocate*, a newspaper printed in Columbus, Ohio:

> MR. EDITOR.—Having recently had occasion to visit the city of Nauvoo, I cannot permit the opportunity to pass without expressing the agreeable disappointment that awaited me there. I had supposed, from what I had previously heard, that I should witness an impoverished, ignorant and bigotted population, completely priest-ridden, and tyrannized over by Joseph Smith, the great prophet of these people.

On the contrary, to my surprise, I saw a people apparently happy, prosperous and intelligent. Every man appeared to be employed in some business or occupation. I saw no idleness, no intemperance, no noise, no riot . . . With the religion of these people I have nothing to do . . . But I protest against the slanders and persecutions that are continually heaped upon these people. . . .

While at Nauvoo I had a fine opportunity of seeing the people in a body. There was a Masonic celebration, and the Grand Master of the state was present [and likely James Adams] for the purpose of publicly installing the officers of a new lodge. An immense number of persons assembled on the occasion, variously estimated from five to ten thousand persons, and never in my life did I wittness a better-dressed or a more orderly and well-behaved assemblage: not a drunken or disorderly person to be seen, and the display of taste and beauty among the females could not well be surpassed anywhere.

During my stay of three days, I became well acquainted with their principal men, and more particularly with their Prophet, the celebrated "Old Joe Smith." I found them hospitable, polite, well-informed and liberal. With Joseph Smith, the hospitality of whose house I kindly received, I was well pleased; of course on the subject of religion, we widely differed, but he appeared to be quite as willing to permit me to enjoy my right of opinion, as I think we all ought to be to let the Mormons enjoy theirs; but instead of the ignorant and tyrannical upstart, judge my surprise at finding him a sensible, intelligent, companionable and gentlemanly man. In frequent conversations with him he gave me every information that I desired, and appeared to be only pleased at being able to do so. He appears to be much respected by all the people about him, and has their entire confidence. He is a fine looking man about thirty-six years of age, and has an interesting family. . . .

From all I saw and heard, I am led to believe that, before many years, the city of Nauvoo will be the largest and most beautiful city of the west, provided the Mormons are unmolested in the peaceable enjoyment of their rights and privileges, and why they should be troubled while acting as good citizens, I cannot imagine; and I hope and trust that the people of Illinois have no disposition to disturb unoffending people who have no disposition but to live peaceably under the laws of the country, and to worship God under their own vine and fig tree."[5]

## Political Turbulence

When John Todd Stuart returned from his Congressional term in Washington, Lincoln was weighing his chances for a future run for Congress. He was likely eager to sit with his friend and hear details of Stuart's experience in Washington. Among many topics of mutual interest would have been Lincoln's breakup with Mary, Stuart's cousin. Stuart would likely have heard Mary's version of the unfortunate affair upon his return. The two politicians probably also discussed the Mormon phenomenon that had so abruptly developed in their state during Stuart's absence. Stuart would likely have shared with Lincoln his impressions of Joseph Smith from their interactions in Washington, and Lincoln would probably have described the remarkable and unintentional political upheaval that the amassing Mormons had brought to Illinois' political landscape.

Stuart returned to find that the local Whig Senator for Hancock County, Sidney Little, had lost his bid for re-election in Hancock County, and this was blamed primarily on his support of the Mormons. Little had been targeted by local Democratic newspapers for showing interest in helping the new Mormon constituency (this despite the fact that Democrat Stephen A. Douglas exceeded him in his support for the Mormons). Pinning a friendship between the Mormons and Stuart might garner the Democrats a similar victory, and Stuart was the Democrats' next target.

Lincoln would very likely have read the following articles about John Todd Stuart with great interest:

# Sangamo Journal.

Vol. V Springfield, Friday, June 11, 1841. No. 15

MR. STUART AND THE MORMONS.

The Missouri Republican a few days since contained some absurd remarks, pretended to be founded upon the report of a steamboat Captain, to the effect that the Mormons were erecting a fort at Warsaw [Illinois] under the pretence of erecting a temple, and that Gov. Carlin had united with them, not only in their creed, but also in some embryo schemes . . . The design of the Republican was to make political capital out of the slander it originated. Here the whigs have another game to play. It is their great object to palter with the Mormons. They need their votes to elect John T. Stuart. Therefore he and they are coquetting with this sect, and have made great efforts, if not pledges, to secure their votes, by making them believe that their particular views will be promoted, by the instrumentality of Mr. Stuart.

We have not any prejudices against the Mormons, believing that every man has a right under his own vine and fig tree to worship God as to him shall seem right. But we think it portends some danger, when a candidate for Congress, bargains in advance with any particular sect . . . [Let] Mr. Stuart beware that he does not dig a pit for himself to fall into; he may meet the fate of Mr. Little of Hancock, who after having paid his addresses with great assiduity to the Mormons, while he was toying with others, has been jilted, and he now finds himself the discarded of all. A word to the wise is said to be sufficient, but to John T. Stuart, many words may be necessary.

Lincoln's friend Simeon Francis, editor of the *Sangamo Journal*, responded to the rival Springfield newspaper *Illinois Register*'s censure of Stuart with the following:

# Sangamo Journal.

Vol. X. No. 43. Springfield, Illinois, June 18, 1841. Whole 511.

The Mormons have been driven from Missouri and under such circumstances that constituents of Mr. Stuart who was bound as their representative to prefer their claims before Congress. Yet for doing this plain act of duty, the register reads him a lecture. That paper says, 'Let Mr. Stuart beware that he does not dig a pit for himself to fall into." Is Mr. Stuart to dig a pit for himself by doing a simple act of justice to a portion of his own constituents?

# 𝕿𝖍𝖊 𝖖𝖚𝖎𝖓𝖈𝖞 𝕬𝖗𝖌𝖚𝖘.

Vol. 6. Quincy, Illinois, Sat., June 5, 1841. No. 39.

THE MORMONS.

An officer of one of the steamboats that lately arrived at our warf [sic] from above, informs us that the Governor of Illinois has, bona-fide, become a Mormon.

There had been several hundred Mormons in New York and England, who lately made a "descent" upon Nauvoo,—and the circumjacent regions by way of making settlement there. This colony was beheld with alarm by many of the dispassionate inhabitants in that part of the State.

So far as the above relates to Gov. Carlin, the editor of the Republican has been wholly misinformed. We did not even hear the report here, that his excellency had become a convert to Mormonism, until we saw the paper containing the [aforesaid] article.

## RELENTLESS MISSOURI

In early June 1841, the Mormon prophet accompanied his brother Hyrum and William Law as far as Quincy as they left to embark on a mission to the eastern states. While there, he visited Church members who were able to settle in Quincy and surrounding Adams County. Two and a half years had passed since Governor Boggs's extermination order had successfully evicted the Mormons from his state, and Missouri continued to receive censure for it. Many in Missouri felt that a conviction of Joseph Smith would be a step toward their exoneration, and when word came that Joseph was just across the Mississippi in Quincy, away from Nauvoo and his masses of followers, Missouri officials quickly pressed Governor Carlin for permission to arrest Joseph as a fugitive from justice. Governor Carlin complied.[6]

Just hours after authorizing the arrest warrant, Governor

Carlin found, to his surprise, that Joseph Smith was at the door of his residence in Quincy, asking for an audience. The Mormon prophet was unaware of the warrant, and Governor apparently felt no need to mention it during their lengthy and cordial conversation. Shortly after the visit, Carlin dispatched a posse led by Sheriff Thomas King and a Missouri marshal to apprehend Joseph. They caught up with him at Bear Creek, some twenty-eight miles south of Nauvoo, where he was arrested.

George Q. Cannon recorded, "as the officer from Missouri did not conceal the vindictive hate with which he viewed his prisoner nor smother his threats, many of the party [posse] left in disgust and returned to their homes, declaring that they would have nothing to do with such outrageous proceedings."[7] Sheriff King and the Missouri marshal escorted their prisoner toward Monmouth, in northern Illinois, where a hearing would be conducted on the matter. On the way, Sheriff King became very ill. When they arrived at Nauvoo, Joseph brought King to his home, where he and Emma attended to the sick officer "like a brother, and continued this assiduous care for his captor."[8]

Joseph was stunned to have spent such an amiable meeting with a governor who had authorized his arrest just hours earlier. There are indications that Governor Carlin had been pressured for some time by Missouri officials to issue an arrest warrant for Joseph Smith.[9] Why he finally complied at this time is unknown, but the false rumor of his conversion to Mormonism—a potentially career-killing hazard for any politician—may have influenced his decision. Governor Carlin had to be aware of the political repercussions being endured by Little, Douglas, and Stuart for simply helping the Mormons. Signing the warrant might have doubled as a measure to quickly extinguish the rumor. At the same time, it would have contributed to bettering relations with Missouri.

Missouri was charging Joseph with the same crimes for which they had lacked evidence to convict him in 1838: treason, fraud, and murder. So when the posse and their prisoner returned to Quincy, Joseph appealed for a writ of *habeas corpus*, which required the arresting officials to provide evidence of cause for the arrest. Newly appointed Master of Chancery Calvin A. Warren obtained the writ. Procedure then required that writ of habeas corpus be viewed by an Illinois judge. Taking the matter to the sitting judge in the Western Illinois District would settle two important matters: the strength of Missouri's case against Joseph Smith and the resolve of Judge Stephen A. Douglas, who, fortuitously for Joseph, had just arrived in Quincy.

## On Trial

Having sat before starkly dishonest judges in Missouri, Joseph hoped that his professed friend, Judge Douglas, would provide a fair hearing. Judge Douglas consented to give the matter a hearing in the following week. Douglas was well aware of the mounting opposition to Joseph Smith and ordered that the hearing be held at the next scheduled circuit court opening, which would be in Monmouth, some fifty-seven miles northeast of Nauvoo. Douglas had already received abundant criticism for his friendship with the Mormons and knew that voters would be watching him and his handling of this highly volatile court case. Now it was Douglas's turn to address the same political dilemma that Governor Carlin faced just days earlier: what would the political consequences be for him if he ruled in favor of the notorious Mormon prophet?

A warning from citizens opposed to Joseph was quickly circulated among local lawyers, promising serious repercussions for anyone foolish enough to represent Joseph Smith. Lincoln's friend Orville Browning, who was living in Quincy at the time, dismissed the warning and stepped forward to defend Joseph in Monmouth. His legal team included former Senator Sidney Little and James Ralston, whom the Mormons had written in over Lincoln on the election delegate ballot. In his case, Browning drew from his personal observations of the Mormons that sought refuge in his community in 1839.

The prosecution was led by a young lawyer from Missouri. He also had a team to assist him, and records indicate that Abraham Lincoln, in Springfield at the time, was assigned by the state to assist in the prosecution of Joseph Smith. This could have been a documented meeting of these two iconic Americans (albeit in adversarial roles), but it was not to be. There is no evidence that Lincoln contributed anything to the case, and there is evidence as to why he did not participate in the hearing. The only facts available are those regarding the timing of the case. Lincoln would have had little time to participate. Joseph Smith was arrested on June 5, and the hearing commenced on June 9 and concluded on the 10. It could have taken up to two days for Lincoln to receive word from Quincy of his assignment to the case, and assuming he immediately responded and struck out for Monmouth, he would likely have arrived on June 12—two days too late. The fact is that Lincoln did not even go to Monmouth; he was occupied in the courts at Taylorville and Springfield on the days of Joseph Smith's hearing. Once again, the two presidential prophets failed to meet.

Word of the trial rushed through western Illinois like a flood. By the day before the trial, spectators were pouring into Monmouth. Joseph Smith arrived on June 8 with an entourage of some twenty supporters, including George Miller, who was well known and highly regarded in the Monmouth area. A large crowd was assembled when they entered the village. Many of them had traveled some distance to get a glimpse of Joseph Smith, who was arguably the most notorious man in America at the time. Some hoped to see some miracle performed, while others had violence on their minds. This latter group tried to apprehend Joseph, but Sheriff King, whose health had improved, would have none of it. Upon arrival, Joseph Smith dutifully submitted to orders that he be held in the jail, which was likely one of the safest places for him to spend the night under the circumstances. He likely saw the hastily erected gallows from which some in the crowd hoped to see him hang.[10] Joseph Smith recorded the following:

> In the evening, great excitement prevailed, and the citizens employed several attorneys to plead against me. I was requested to preach to the citizens of Monmouth; but as I was a prisoner, I kept closeted in my room, for I could not even come down stairs to my meal, but the people would be crowding the windows to get a peep at me, and there fore I appointed Amasa Lyman to preach in the Court House Wednesday evening.[11]

The trial was the most electrifying event to occur in the village; it is still recounted by Monmouth historians to this day.

Early in the proceedings, the Missouri prosecutor became ill and vomited in front of Judge Douglas. He was quickly replaced. Spectators in the overflowing courtroom grew disorderly, prompted by the unruly crowd outside the building. Judge Douglas called upon the court bailiff to maintain order. The bailiff, fearful of the crowd or perhaps complicit with them, made only a cursory effort to quiet them, which worked for a few moments. Shortly thereafter, Judge Douglas again ordered the bailiff to control the boisterous courtroom. Judge Douglas became so dissatisfied with the bailiff's halfhearted effort to maintaining order that he fined the man ten dollars, which stunned the audience to silence—but again, only for a few moments. When the spectators continued their disruptions, Judge Douglas fined the bailiff another ten dollars. The sheriff then turned his indignation on the crowd, and the force of his anger at being fined twice finally quieted them enough to continue the proceedings.

The defense argued that the arrest warrant was illegally filed because it was an unserved and expired warrant from two years earlier. But Orville Browning did not stop there. He delivered a stirring defense of the Mormon prophet and his beleaguered followers, reminding the court of the illegal and unpunished atrocities against the Saints in Missouri and their cold winter exile in Quincy. With deep emotion, he exclaimed:

> Great God! have I not seen it? Yes, mine eyes have beheld the blood-stained traces of innocent women and children, in the drear winter, who had traveled hundreds of miles barefoot through frost and snow, to seek a refuge from their savage pursuers. It was a scene of horror, sufficient to enlist sympathy from an adamantine heart.[12]

Then, turning to the Joseph Smith, he continued:

> And shall this unfortunate man, whom their fury has seen proper to select for sacrifice, be driven into such a savage land, and none dare to enlist in the cause of justice? If there was no other voice under heaven ever to be heard in this cause, gladly would I stand alone, and proudly spend my latest breath, in defense of an oppressed American citizen.[13]

Joseph Smith's journal confirms the strength of this defense:

> Afterwards Mr. Browning resumed his pleadings which were powerful; and when he gave a recitation of what he himself had seen at Quincy, and on the banks of the Mississippi river . . . where he tracked the persecuted women and children by their bloody foot-marks in the snow, they were so affecting that the spectators were often dissolved in tears. Judge Douglas himself and most of the officers also wept.[14]

Browning's impassioned defense markedly subdued of the violent segment of the crowd. After the deliberations, Judge Douglas adjourned the case until the next morning. That evening, Amasa Lyman addressed a large audience that was surprisingly passive and attentive following Browning's moving defense. The next day, Judge Douglas dismissed the case on procedural grounds, and the pacified crowd seemed content with the verdict.

Douglas's decision, centered on the legality of using an old and expired arrest warrant, was an easy ruling for any judge. It is hard to imagine that Governor Carlin was surprised with the verdict. It is even possible that he anticipated that his warrant would not hold up in court and expected Douglas would exonerate Joseph Smith in a fair hearing. While issuing the expired warrant weakened the trust that the Mormons might have had in him, Carlin was able to placate, at least momentarily, the perplexing Missourians and the growing anti-Mormon element in Illinois. Issuing the warrant may also have extinguished the inaccurate rumor of his conversion. In hindsight, Governor Carlin's actions could be considered politically astute.

Stephen A. Douglas won the gratitude of the Mormons with his decision, but it aroused even more suspicion among some in western Illinois that he had a political agenda with them. Some Whig newspapers, including Sharp's *Warsaw Signal*, accused him of openly courting the Mormon vote by dismissing the case. From this point on, Whigs began to back away from wooing the Latter-day Saint vote and stepped up their criticism toward them as the gubernatorial election of 1842 approached. Douglas's appointment of John C. Bennett as master of chancery infuriated some in nearby Warsaw and Carthage who felt that no Mormon should hold public office.

Within days of Joseph Smith's trial in Monmouth, former State Senator Sidney Little, one of Joseph's defense lawyers, was tragically killed when he leaped from a careening carriage drawn by a runaway horse. Saddened by the news of their friend's passing, the Mormons held a day of fasting and prayer for their fallen benefactor from Hancock County. This gesture of gratitude pacified many neighbors who could not conceal their alarm at the Mormons' stunning growth and success. It is unclear whether Lincoln knew of this expression of faith and friendship, but if he did, he would likely have been impressed with the Mormons' reverent expression of goodwill. As President of the United States, Lincoln called on the nation to observe nine different days of fasting and prayer in almost prophet-like fashion. He was convinced that the outcome of the Civil War rested in the hands of Almighty God and in the repentance of the "almost chosen"[15] American people, not in himself, his government, or his military.

In August of that year, Lincoln again escaped Springfield by boarding a steamboat to visit Joshua Speed in Kentucky. Speed, unlike Lincoln, was successfully courting the woman he would marry in the coming months. Lincoln stayed for three weeks in the spacious home on the Speed plantation, which was powered by more than sixty slaves. It was Lincoln's first look at the life and conditions of slaves on a plantation. The tedious boat trip home to Springfield was broken by one scene that tormented Lincoln after he returned home. He described it in a letter to Joshua Speed:

> By the way, a fine example was presented on board the boat for contemplating the effect of *condition* upon human happiness. A gentleman had purchased twelve negroes in different parts of Kentucky and was taking them to a farm in the South. They were chained six and six together. A small iron clevis was around the left wrist of each, and this fastened to the main chain by a shorter one at a convenient distance from the others; so that the negroes were strung together precisely like so many fish upon a trot-line. In this condition they were being separated forever from the scenes of their childhood, their friends, their fathers and mothers, and brothers and sisters, and

many of them, from their wives and children, and going into perpetual slavery where the lash of the master is proverbially more ruthless and unrelenting than any other where; and yet amid all these distressing circumstances, as we would think them, they were the most cheerful and apparently happy creatures on board. One, whose offence for which he had been sold was an over-fondness for his wife, played the fiddle almost continually; and the others danced, sung, cracked jokes, and played various games with cards from day to day. How true it is that "God tempers the wind to the shorn lamb," or in other words, that He renders the worst of human conditions tolerable, while He permits the best, to be nothing better than tolerable.[16]

Within a few days of his arrival, Lincoln was off again for another two-month round of the Eighth Judicial Circuit, relieved once again to be away from Springfield.

## THE MORMONS' REMARKABLE RESILIENCE

It is safe to assume that Lincoln heard Orville Browning's first-hand account of successfully defending Joseph Smith. It does not appear that the Springfield newspapers carried news of the trial in Monmouth, but many other Illinois papers did. With Lincoln being assigned to the prosecution of the case, he would likely have been interested in Browning's observations regarding the trial.

Vol. II. Ottawa, Ill., July 30, 1841. No. 10.

MORMONS.

Within the last ten days between three and four hundred Mormons passed through this place on their way to the Mormon settlement in Hancock county, in this State. On Tuesday last we counted seventeen wagons, occupied with men, women and children, all wending their way towards the settlement of the "Latter Day Saints." We understand they were from Western New York, and their appearance was quite respectable, apparently being chiefly composed of farmers.

We notice that a large number from Europe have recently arrived at the same settlement, and that others from different portions of the old and new world are on their way. The settlement is now said to contain between ten and fifteen thousand inhabitants, and the town of Nauvoo is represented as being in a flourishing condition. A large Temple is being created, which is to contain a Baptismal Font, supported by twelve oxen, overlaid with gold, all the most costly and magnificent structure.

We notice by the Warsaw Signal, published in the vicinity of Nauvoo, that considerable prejudice exists in that section against this class of people. The editor battles Prophet Smith with much spirit, and denounces him as a hypocrite and impostor, and comments severely on their military parades and warlike preparations.

It is truly a marvel that the Mormons in their deep poverty could and would build an impressive temple. The effort was inspired by their prophet, who informed them that God had commanded them to build a house to his name wherein sacred ordinances could be performed and the Saints could be instructed from on high.[17] Each man and woman was counseled to donate one day in ten—a tithe of their time—to the construction of the impressive edifice. And they did.

In patterning the Church's organization after the original church established by Jesus Christ, Joseph Smith chose twelve faithful followers as Apostles. Citing Acts chapter one, where Peter and the remaining apostles chose Matthias to replace Judas Iscariot, Joseph called new apostles whenever an old one died or was excommunicated.

In the midst of their impoverished resettlement in Illinois, Joseph Smith announced that the Lord had called nine of the Apostles to preach the gospel in England, including Brigham Young and Wilford Woodruff. They relied on the generosity of Mormons still residing in the eastern states for food, shelter, and other necessities as they made their arduous trek to England. On October 5, 1839, Brigham Young and Heber C. Kimball were received by the Saints in Springfield, "where they were kindly treated and nursed, for they were yet very feeble."[18] And they tarried there until October 11. It is possible that Judge James Adams met with them while there, which might explain why Adams would approach Joseph Smith just days later as Joseph passed through Springfield on his way to Washington. It is also entirely possible that Katherine Mulliner, the Stringhams, or other Mormons in Springfield might have introduced Lincoln to the traveling Apostles, but yet again, no record has been found confirming that possibility.

## TEETOTALERS

After six months of travel, the Apostles arrived at Liverpool, England on April 6, 1840. From there they traveled to Preston, England, where it was decided they would conduct their ministry. It would be in Preston that the Apostles, along with the handful of earlier European missionaries, like Samuel Mulliner, would experience the remarkable success mentioned in the December 18, 1840 Springfield's *Sangamo Journal* article referenced earlier.

In 1832, Preston, England, became the first British city to organize a temperance movement calling for total abstinence from liquor. The number of these Preston "teetotalers," as they came to be called, swelled. The next year a temperance hotel was opened, a temperance magazine published and the British Association for the Promotion of Temperance was organized in 1835. By 1838, nearby Liverpool alone boasted some 27,000 pledged teetotalers. Whether by chance or divine design, the Mormon Apostles came to Preston with a Gospel message that included Joseph Smith's 1832 revelation on abstaining from alcohol.

Mormon Apostle Willard Richards expressed that this common view of full abstinence from spirits opened the doors and hearts of the English people. Just three weeks after their arrival in Preston, the Apostles held their first conference in Preston's spacious Temperance Hall, which was attended by more than sixteen hundred new converts and investigators. Three months later, a second conference was held in Manchester, which 2,513 members and investigators attended. On September 8, 1840, the ship *North America* sailed for New York with the 200 British converts aboard as referenced by the December 18 *Sangamo Journal* article. The next month, the quarterly general conference convened in Manchester had 3,626 faithful attending. After a year of preaching, the Apostles left England in April 1841 for Nauvoo, leaving an estimated seven to eight thousand new Latter-day Saints in Great Britain, many of whom were intent upon joining the Saints in Illinois. This signaled dramatic implications for Lincoln and his fellow legislators.

On February 3, 1841, three days after the Nauvoo charter was officially in force, Mayor Bennett called for restriction on tippling houses. The following week, the city council passed a temperance ordinance against the sale of whiskey in small amounts, essentially outlawing saloons in Nauvoo.

Since the advent of high-quality rum in the Americas, drinking rates on both sides of the Atlantic had skyrocketed. Abstinence, or at least moderation, was the message of the concerned citizenry of the European and American temperance societies. Springfield, like most American cities, had its own temperance society. The Springfield organization was made up primarily of reformed alcoholics (or drunkards, as they were referred to then), clergy, and concerned citizens. They called themselves the Washington Society after George Washington. One would think that Lincoln, who was never known to drink, would be an enthusiastic participant in the temperance movement, but he remained aloof from the organization.

In early 1842, the Washington Society was looking for a speaker to commemorate Washington's Birthday. Famously sober Abraham Lincoln was their choice. At this time in Lincoln's career, he was a respected lawyer, legislator, and public speaker, and hundreds came to Springfield's Second Presbyterian Church to hear the colorful orator. But many left the meeting disappointed. Others were offended by his temperance speech. While Lincoln was in full agreement with his audience on the destructive nature of liquor, he varied with them on the means to address the problem. To many temperance advocates, abusers of alcohol were considered the dregs of society, and many a clergyman and other temperance spokesmen lectured vigorously and often on the repulsive nature of these drunkards. It was on this condescending abhorrence for the victims of alcohol addiction that Lincoln spoke, and some in the audience perceived his message as an affront.

Unlike the Mormons, who viewed abstinence from alcohol and tobacco as a religious observance, Lincoln's abstinence appeared to be motivated by a promise he made at the age of nine to his dying mother. Years after the tragic passing of Nancy Lincoln, while traveling in a stagecoach, Lincoln reportedly had the following conversation with a gentleman from Kentucky:

> "Mr. Lincoln, won't you take a drink with me?"
>
> Lincoln replied, "No, Colonel, thank you, I never drink whiskey."
>
> They rode along together for a number of miles more, visiting very pleasantly, when the gentleman from Kentucky reached into his pocket and brought out some cigars saying, "Now Mr. Lincoln, if you won't take a drink with me, won't you take a smoke with me? . . ."
>
> And Mr. Lincoln said, "'Now Colonel, you are such a fine, agreeable man to travel with, maybe I ought to take a smoke with you. But before I do so, let me tell you a little story—an experience I had when a small boy. . . . My mother called me to her bed one day when I was about nine years old. She was sick, very sick, and she said to me, 'Abey, the doctor tells me I am not going to get well. I want you to promise me before I go that you will never use whiskey or tobacco as long as you live.' And I promised my mother I never would. And up to this hour, Colonel, I have kept that promise. Now would you advise me to break that promise to my dear mother, and take a smoke with you? . . . "
>
> "No, Mr. Lincoln, I wouldn't have you do it for the world. It was one of the best promises you ever made. And I would give a thousand dollars today if I had made my mother a promise like that, and kept it as you have done."[19]

Lincoln knew well the damage that uncontrolled drinking could do. A number of New Salem and Springfield residents operated backyard stills. In his early adult days, two prominent men of New Salem lost their lives to whiskey. George Warburton, one of the first merchants in New Salem, was found face down in the shallows of the river after a drunken debauch, and Peter Lukins died from a drinking binge. Lincoln's New Salem business partner, William Berry, died at the age of twenty-four from the effects of excessive alcohol, leaving Lincoln with a debt that would take him seventeen years to repay. In Lincoln's early days in New Salem, he worked the latter part of one winter "in a little still-house, up at the head of a hollow,"[20] but he was never known to drink the product.

In Lincoln's early adult years, religions revivals, funerals, weddings, and house-raisings were rarely complete without a barrel of whiskey for all to enjoy. R. B. Rutledge of New Salem, in reference to Lincoln's sheer strength, exclaimed that he had seen Lincoln take a very heavy barrel of whiskey "by the chimes . . . and lift it up to his face as if to drink from the bung hole."[21] On another occasion, Bill Green made a bet for a fur hat that Lincoln could do the same. Upon lifting the barrel, Green claimed that Lincoln filled his mouth with whiskey, then rolled the barrel to his knees and spat out the whiskey to the ground, thus winning Green the fur hat. After Lincoln's assassination, another old acquaintance offered $50.00 to anyone who had seen Lincoln take a drink. He got no takers. Friends marveled that Lincoln could remain so popular with his drinking associates and not incur their disdain for not joining them. Yet throughout his life, Lincoln was associated with men and women who participated in the consumption of liquor while he abstained, and through it all endeared himself to a wide and loyal circle of friends.

Just days after his remarkable and unlikely election as America's sixteenth President, he and Mary had an argument. A delegation was on their way to the Lincoln home in Springfield to officially present the results of the election and to formally extend him the Presidency. Mary plead with Lincoln to make an exception to his long-held prohibition on alcohol in his home for these guests. Friends even stepped forward, supporting Mary's assertion that a proper alcoholic beverage needed to be offered to the most distinguished group of gentlemen to ever come to Springfield. He considered the request, but in the end he would not relent, and with deep embarrassment, Mary served them each a glass of water. Lincoln apologized to the illustrious delegation and briefly explained that liquor had never been imbibed in the Lincoln home, so in its place he was offering them a drink of Adam's ale.

Lincoln's temperance speech was delivered with an abundance of biblical references, once again adding to the quandary of his religion. By this time in his life, he had begun avoiding religious discussions because no matter how hard his acquaintances tried to point out the error of his Biblical views, they failed. And although he would frequently attend Sunday religious services, he remained outside of any organized denomination.

In his address, Lincoln exhorted his fellow abstainers with Sermon-on-the-Mount-like expressions such as to be merciful, to love thy neighbor as thyself, and to refrain from judging and condemning others:

> The warfare heretofore waged against the demon of Intemperance, has, some how or other, been erroneous. . . . Too much denunciation against dram sellers and dram drinkers was indulged in. . . . When the dram-seller and drinker, were incessantly told, not in accents of entreaty and persuasion, . . . but in the thundering tones of anathema and denunciation, . . . that *they* were the authors of all the vice and misery and crime in the land; . . . that *their houses* were the workshops of the devil; and that *their persons* should be shunned by all the good and virtuous, as moral pestilences—I say, when they were told all this, and in this way, it is not wonderful that they were slow, *very slow*, to acknowledge the truth of such denunciations, and to join the ranks of their denouncers, in a hue and cry against themselves.
>
> To have expected them to do otherwise than as they did—to have expected them not to meet denunciation with denunciation, crimination with crimination, and anathema with anathema, was to expect a reversal of human nature, which is God's decree, and never can be reversed.[22]

As unwelcomed as young Lincoln's message was, he was extraordinarily accurate and astute. He seemed to recognize, at an early age, the fine line between judging others by decrying their errors (which had the by-product of aggrandizing the judger) and respectful and kindly persuasion. Joseph Smith taught similar principles in D&C 121:41–44. Lincoln's paradigm was remarkably parallel to Jesus's Sermon on the Mount messages of love our enemies, bless them that curse us, do good to them that hate us, pray for them that despitefully use us, and forgive our debtors. He was essentially entreating his listeners to heed Jesus Christ's teaching of not focusing on the mote in another's eye when our own may contain a beam. Lincoln was remarkably consistent in living these principles in his daily interactions with others. In his temperance message, he seemed to be attempting to explain his personal understanding of pure religion. He continued:

> When the conduct of men is designed to be influenced, *persuasion*, kind, unassuming persuasion, should ever be adopted. . . . So with men. If you would win a man to your cause, *first* convince him that you are his sincere friend. . . . On the contrary, assume to dictate to his judgment, or to command his action, or to mark him as one to be shunned and despised, and he will retreat within himself, close all the avenues to his head and his heart . . .
>
> Such is man, and so *must* he be understood by those who would lead him, even to his own best interest.[23]

For those who have questioned Lincoln's regard for Jesus Christ as the grantor of an infinite sacrifice for the redemption of all, here is a glimpse of his true, yet rarely expressed inclinations:

> Another error, as it seems to me, into which the old reformers fell, was, the position that all habitual drunkards were utterly incorrigible, and therefore, must be turned adrift, and damned without remedy.[24]
>
> If they believe, as they profess, that Omnipotence condescended to take on himself the form of sinful man, and, as such, to die an ignominious death for their sakes, surely they will not refuse submission to the infinitely lesser condescension, for the temporal, and perhaps eternal salvation, of a large, erring, and unfortunate class of their own fellow creatures. . . . Indeed, I believe, if we take habitual drunkards as a class, their heads and their hearts will bear an advantageous comparison with those of any other class.[25]

Lincoln's abstinence from alcohol was not likely known by the Mormon prophet, but the Mormon doctrine of abstinence from tobacco and alcohol was probably known to Lincoln. Again, he would have found an intriguing commonality with his Springfield Mormon friends who observed this religious and healthful practice.

# CHAPTER EIGHT ENDNOTES

1. "The Lincoln Log: June 17, 1841," The Papers of Abraham Lincoln, last modified February 20, 2014, http://www.thelincolnlog.org/Calendar.aspx?year=1841&month=6&day=17.

2. Ruth Painter Randall, *Mary Lincoln: Biography of a Marriage* (Boston: Little, Brown, 1953), 49

3. Ibid., 50.

4. Ibid.

5. B. H. Roberts, *History of the Church of Jesus Christ of Latter-day Saints: An Introduction and Notes* (Salt Lake City, UT: Deseret News, 1968) vol. 4, 565–66.

6. B. H. Roberts, *The Rise and Fall of Nauvoo* (repr., Provo, UT: Maasai, 2001), pp, 84–85.

7. George Q. Cannon, *Life of Joseph Smith the Prophet* (Salt Lake City, UT: Deseret Book, 1972), 372.

8. Ibid., 373.

9. Roberts, *The Rise and Fall of Nauvoo*, pp, 84–85.

10. Hogan, Terry, *In a Monmouth Courtroom*, In Backtracking, The Zephyr, last modified January 14, 2006, www.thezephyr.com.

11. B. H. Roberts, *History of the Church of Jesus Christ of Latter-day Saints: An Introduction and Notes* (Salt Lake City, UT: Bookcraft, 1975), 366.

12. Cannon, *Life of Joseph Smith the Prophet*, 376.

13. Ibid.

14. Roberts, *History of the Church*, 368–69.

15. Roy Basler, The Collected Works of Abraham Lincoln (New Brunswick, N.J.: Rutgers University Press, 1953), vol. 3, page?

16. Mark E. Neely Jr., "Lincoln, Slavery, and the Nation," *Journal of American History* 96 (September 2009): 456–58.

17. Joseph Smith, et al., *Doctrine and Covenants of the Church of Jesus Christ of Latter-day Saints Containing Revelations Given to Joseph Smith, the Prophet with Some Additions by His Successors in the Presidency of the Church*, Section 124:26–31.

18. Roberts, *History of the Church*, 11.

19. The Church of Jesus Christ of Latter-day Saints, "Lesson 42: Honor thy Father and thy Mother," in *Preparing for Exaltation: Teacher's Manual* (n.p.: 1998) 249, http://www.lds.org/manual/preparing-for-exaltation-teachers-manual/lesson-42-honor-thy-father-and-thy-mother?lang=eng.

20. Benjamin J. Thomas, *Lincoln's New Salem*, rev. ed. (1954; repr.,Carbondale, IL: Southern Illinois University Press, 1987), 48.

21. Ibid., 144.

22. Roy Basler, ed., *The Collected Works of Abraham Lincoln* (New Brunswick, NJ: Rutgers University Press, 1953), vol. 1, 271–73.

23. Ibid., 273.

24. Ibid., 275.

25. Ibid., 277–78.

*Chapter Nine*

# "WE CARE NOT A FIG FOR WHIG OR DEMOCRAT"

In 1842, the editor of Nauvoo's *Times and Seasons* and future Church president John Taylor described the precarious political dilemma faced by the Mormons in Illinois:

> There were always two parties, the Whigs and Democrats, and we could not vote for one without offending the other; and it not unfrequently happened that candidates for office would place the issue of their election upon opposition to the Mormons, in order to gain political influence from the religious prejudice, in which case the Mormons were compelled, in self-defense, to vote against them, which resulted almost invariably against our opponents. This made them angry . . . yet they raged on account of their discomfiture, and sought to wreak their fury on the Mormons.[1]

Regarding this growing political quandary, Joseph Smith addressed the citizens of Nauvoo with a message that gained coverage in a number of additional newspapers throughout Illinois.

# PEORIA REGISTER AND NORTH-WESTERN GAZETTEER.

Vol. V. Peoria, Illinois, January 21, 1842. No. 43.

THE MORMONS RELIGION AND POLITICS.

The last number of the "Times and Seasons," the Mormon paper published under the direction of this sect at Nauvoo, contains the following extraordinary document:

STATE GUBERNATORIAL CONVENTION.

City of Nauvoo, Illinois,

December 20th, A. D. 1841.

To my friends in Illinois:—
The Gubernatorial Convention of the State of Illinois, have nominated Colonel Adam W. Snyder for GOVERNOR, and Colonel John Moore for LIEUTENANT-GOVERNOR of the State of Illinois—election to take place in August next . . . They are sterling men, and friends of equal rights—opposed to the oppressor's grasp, and the tyrant's rod. With such men at the head of our State Government we have nothing to fear.

In the next canvass we shall be influenced by no party consideration . . . we care not a fig for Whig or Democrat: they are both alike to us; but we shall go for our friends, our TRIED FRIENDS, and the cause of human liberty which is the cause of God. DOUGLASS is a Master Spirit, and his friends are our friends—we are willing to cast our banners on the air, and fight by his side in the cause of humanity, and equal rights . . . Snyder, and Moore, are his friends—they are ours. These men are free from the prejudices and superstitions of the age, . . . and such men will ever receive our support . . . We will never be justly charged with the sin of ingratitude—they have served us, and we will serve them.

JOSEPH SMITH.
Lieutenant-General of the Nauvoo Legion.

# PEORIA DEMOCRATIC PRESS

Vol. II. Peoria, Wednesday, Jan. 26, 1842. No. 50.

The last Sangamo Journal devotes a column and a half of its editorial matter to the address of Joseph Smith to his friends in Illinois, in which Smith states that he and his friends will vote for Snyder and Moore at the next August election. He tells the story of the Farmer and Asp; that when the farmer had warmed the poisonous reptile in hos bosom, so that returning life appeared, the asp began hissing and curling itself up preparatory to a deadly attack upon the farmer, who seeing its intent and aim, destroyed it. The Journal then adds, "the moral is perceptible, and needs no words of explanation." We must confess we read these remarks of the Journal with amazement and alarm. That paper was mute so long as the Mormons, or "latter day saints," voted for Harrison and sleepy John [Stuart]; but when there is an indication that they, like thousands of other citizens, are becoming disgusted with Whig rule, or rather misrule, then they are treated with scorn and ignominy, and there is a giving out in no unmeaning terms, that if they act the part of freemen and vote as they think right, a terrible vengeance awaits them: "The moral is perceptible, and needs no words of explanation." Truly the meaning of the Journal is plain and cannot be misunderstood—it means this: The whigs have been courting and fawning about the Mormons, but now "seeing their intent and aim," to vote for Snyder and Moore, they must be destroyed; yes, "DESTROYED!" Indeed, this is the moral the Journal inculcates. Does the editor of the Journal want another Missouri war? Does he wish our state disgraced? It is from such a course as that paper pursues that mobs are excited to acts of violence and encouraged to trample all laws, human and divine, all rights of individuals and the community under foot. We sincerely hope that the Journal will find no sympathy or support from other whig presses for the blood-thirsty sentiments it has uttered.

## TOGETHER AGAIN

The editor the *Peoria Democratic Press* referred to was Simeon Francis, who by this time had developed a friendship with Lincoln.

It was well known in Springfield that Lincoln seemed to spend nearly as much time at the *Sangamo Journal* office as at his own law office.[2] Francis admired Lincoln's wit and noble qualities and occasionally allowed him to write articles for the *Journal*; Lincoln wrote editorials under pseudonyms like Johnny Blubberhead, Sampson's Ghost, Old Settler, and Rebecca. Simeon Francis and his wife, Eliza, took such a liking to Lincoln that they treated him much like a member of their family.[3]

The Francises were saddened at the breakup of Abraham Lincoln and Mary Todd and more particularly the reasons for the separation. By this time, Lincoln's friends and Lincoln himself were all wondering if he, now thirty-three, would ever make it to the altar of matrimony. The affable yet unkempt lawyer had few possessions and still lived in boarding houses and with friends (due largely to his dogged determination to pay the debt from his New Salem store failure). These facts must have made eligible bachelorettes doubt his ability to adequately provide for a family.

Abraham and Mary entered 1842 just as they had the previous year, neither seeing nor speaking to one another. That Lincoln still pined for Mary is reflected in a letter to his closest friend, Joshua Speed, written on March 27, 1842:

> I am not going beyond the truth, when I tell you, that the short space it took me to read your last letter, gave me more pleasure, than the total sum of all I have enjoyed since that fatal first of Jany. '41. Since then, it seems to me, I should have been entirely happy, but for the never-absent idea, that there is *one* still unhappy [Mary] whom I have contributed to make so. That still kills my soul. I can not but reproach myself, for even wishing to be happy while she is otherwise. She accompanied a large party on the Rail Road cars, to Jacksonville last monday; and on her return, spoke, so that I heard of it, of having enjoyed the trip exceedingly. God be praised for that.[4]

Their separation rolled into mid-1842 until Eliza Francis determined that something had to be done about it. Unbeknownst to Mary or Abraham, Eliza invited both of them over for a visit at the same time. The two unwittingly complied, and when Mrs. Francis marched Lincoln into the parlor where Mary was sitting, the two stunned lovers gazed at each other, speechless and bewildered, for the first time in a year and a half. Mrs. Francis placed their hands together, flatly told them to be friends again, and walked out. This unexpected reunion kindled the embers of their mutual affection. The reunited couple determined to meet again. But where? Mary's sisters would certainly rise up in protest at reviving the relationship they thought they had successfully extinguished, and Lincoln had no place to offer. Mrs. Francis was quick to assure them that her home would be a more than adequate meeting place, and thus the two continued their undisclosed courtship at the Francis home throughout 1842, saying nothing to others about their renewed relationship.

On July 4, 1842, either shortly before or shortly after this unexpected reunion, Lincoln wrote another letter to Joshua Speed. Lincoln thanked Speed for some relationship advice that Speed had apparently given Lincoln regarding Mary. The letter seems to express some guarded optimism: "I believe God made me one of the instruments of bringing your Fanny and you together, which union, I have no doubt He had fore-ordained. Whatever he designs, he will do for me yet."[5]

## ANOTHER TURBULENT ELECTION

Gubernatorial candidate Adam Snyder, a Democrat, was a vocal proponent for the Nauvoo Charter in the State Senate, a fact remembered by the Mormons in Nauvoo. He had successfully become an elector representing incumbent Martin Van Buren when Lincoln had unsuccessfully tried to become one for William Henry Harrison. In the days after Adam Snyder's nomination to the governorship and endorsement by Joseph Smith, his health deteriorated. He died before the 1842 election could even take place. At Snyder's untimely death, the Democrats nominated Thomas Ford, a relatively unknown candidate who appeared ambivalent toward the Mormons.

The Whig's nominee for governor was Joseph Duncan, who saw the strength of Nauvoo and its Mormon residents as a growing menace to the state. Redrawing the Nauvoo Charter was one of the planks in his campaign platform. When the charter was being debated in the legislature two years earlier, both Whigs and

Democrats saw the political ramifications of a large body of Saints residing in their state, and each tried to demonstrate friendship to the new residents. While genuinely motivated by compassion for the Mormons' plight, they gave Nauvoo a charter with political powers that far exceeded those of other Illinois cities. Nauvoo was essentially a sovereignty above the laws of the state.

Nauvoo's power to form a militia also exceeded that of other cities. Nauvoo was allowed to appoint a lieutenant general over its militia, and Joseph Smith held the post. Up to that time, only one other American in the history of the United States had ever held the rank of lieutenant general: George Washington. Joseph Smith was the only living Lieutenant General in the nation, which theoretically placed him above all other military commanders. Many Illinoisans shared Duncan's fear that the thousands of foreign converts migrating to the state had more allegiance to their Prophet than to the Republic. Some even accused Joseph Smith of intending to build an independent Mormon empire in Illinois.

Duncan called for a reduction in these exceptional powers and for placing Nauvoo on equal terms with other Illinois cities. Other Illinoisans, led by Thomas Sharp, wanted to entirely revoke Nauvoo's charter and the Mormons' right to exist in Illinois; they too sided with Duncan. Duncan stood to capitalize on Thomas Sharp's growing Anti-Mormon political party, which was garnering supporters from both Whigs and Democrats, especially in Hancock County. But many Illinois Whigs were repulsed by the extreme rhetoric of driving the Mormons from the state in spite of their unease with Nauvoo's success.

Few Mormons had any fondness for Thomas Ford, but they cast their votes against Duncan as a matter of survival. As a result of their formidable voting bloc, Ford was elected governor of Illinois, leaving many Whigs like Simeon Francis more troubled than ever by the Mormon problem.

And what of Lincoln? No record is found of Lincoln expressing his position on this dilemma. He appears to have remained silent on the issue. Lincoln's selective interest was seen again when the Republican Party was being organized in the mid-1850s. The new party's foundation was built upon the eradication of the "twin relics of barbarism": slavery and polygamy. While Lincoln spoke incessantly against the expansion of slavery, there is no record of him speaking against the Mormon practice of polygamy—and no explanation for why this was done. While the nation was divided on the issue of slavery, it was united in its opposition to polygamy. It is a mystery why Lincoln did not capitalize on this issue to garner votes and support for his political aspirations. This pattern of supporting some of his party's issues and remaining silent on others was common throughout Lincoln's political career.

## ILLINOIS ELECTION OF 1842

Thomas Sharp ran in the 1842 election as a Whig candidate for Hancock County's State Assembly seat. He intended to add his strident anti-Mormon voice to Duncan's campaign against the Nauvoo charter, but Sharp also lost his bid for office at the hands of the Mormons. Adding insult to injury, the winner of the race was William Smith, the Prophet's brother and a member of the Quorum of the Twelve Apostles. William Smith, who ran on the Democratic ticket, was the fiery editor of the *Nauvoo Wasp*, a new secular newspaper established just months earlier to counter Sharp's unrelenting criticism in the *Warsaw Signal*. Smith and Sharp traded points and counterpoints, barbs and insults, through most of 1842 up to the election. But in the end, Smith defeated Sharp by a large margin because of the number of Mormon voters. By losing his election, Thomas Sharp unintentionally contributed to his worst nightmare becoming a reality—a Mormon being voted into the state legislature. Sharp's fury against the Mormons was fanned even hotter at this humiliating setback. His defeat intensified his antagonism, and he broadened his attack over a ten-county area, becoming the standard bearer for the extermination or expulsion of the Mormons from Illinois.

Lincoln declined to run for a fifth term in 1842 even though he could have easily won. Probably influenced by Mary Todd, he set his sights on building a base for a run at the US Congress the next year. In doing so, Lincoln missed another opportunity to develop an acquaintance with a prominent Mormon leader, this time newly elected legislator William Smith. It is possible they chanced to meet when William was in town for legislative sessions, but history provides no evidence that they did. Lincoln was also beginning to feel disheartened that Stephen A. Douglas and other ambitious politicians were receiving important state appointments and judgeships, yet Lincoln was persistently overlooked for such distinctions. His talents seemed to go unnoticed by friends and colleagues in Illinois.

The Illinois election of 1842 poses some intriguing questions: Did Lincoln vote for Joseph Duncan for Governor? (Lincoln was not a Hancock County resident to vote for or against Sharp.) Did he campaign for Duncan like he had for so many other Whig candidates in the past? Was he for or against Joseph Duncan's plan to equalize the Nauvoo Charter? While no record exists of Lincoln's position on the matter, due in part to his reticence to speak about the Mormon question, it is likely that Lincoln would have seen some wisdom in moderating the Nauvoo Charter.

Voting against Duncan would have been inconsistent with Lincoln's continual efforts to support fellow Whig candidates. In light of all of these factors, Lincoln did cast his vote in a losing cause for his Whig colleague Joseph Duncan, doing again what he had been doing for years to strengthen his party's position in Illinois politics.[6]

By this time in Lincoln's political career, he was developing a reputation for accuracy in perceiving the minds of the people and thereby predicting election outcomes. One observer, Helen Hay, noted:

> "His crowning gift of political diagnosis was due to his sympathy . . . which gave him power to forecast with uncanny accuracy what his opponents were likely to do." . . . After listening to his colleagues talk at a Whig Party caucus, Lincoln would cast off his shawl, rise from his chair, and say: "From your talk, I gather the Democrats will do so and so . . . I should do so and so to checkmate them." He proceeded to outline all "the moves for the days ahead; making them all so plain that his listeners wondered why they had not seen it that way themselves."[7]

Lincoln was probably far from surprised at Thomas Sharp's defeat in Hancock County, in spite of the Mormons' support for fellow Whig John Todd Stuart in the previous election. But with the untimely death of Democrat Adam Snyder, Lincoln probably saw the 1842 election as a window of opportunity for his minority Whig party to gain a Whig governor. Mormon voters' fear of Joseph Duncan's rhetoric frustrated this hope. Springfield's Democratic newspaper mockingly reported that "the tears fairly came into Lincoln's eyes when the news arrived" of Duncan's defeat.[8]

## LINCOLN'S SILENCE

Lincoln, like all astute Illinois politicians, was very aware of the strong Mormon voting block and the crushing defeats they had just handed his Whig party. Yet indications of Lincoln's feelings on the Mormons in his state are few and essentially neutral, as explained by his future law partner, William Herndon. Herndon remembered that Lincoln maintained a measured silence regarding the Mormons, just as he did with his own religious beliefs during the 1840s.[9] This silence might be interpolated as a position of neutrality, especially in light of an 1846 political handbill that stated that he had never spoken ill of religion in general or toward any religious denomination in particular. This had to include the Mormons. In that same handbill, Lincoln revealed that he had chosen to remain silent on the topic of religion in general from 1841 to 1846—the very same five years as the Mormon presence in Illinois.[10]

The fact that Lincoln could maintain a measured neutrality toward a religious group that had dealt him some personal political blows is notable, and it could not have been an easy task. From mid-May to December 1842, the *Sangamo Journal* printed articles on the Mormons—mostly lengthy diatribes against them—in every weekly issue save two. For Lincoln, the issue was likely tempered by his friendship with Springfield Latter-day Saints like the Mulliners and Stringhams, or the Brownings in Quincy. Despite ample opportunities to join in the clamor, Lincoln held his peace. As he said years later, "I am rather inclined to silence, and whether that be wise or not, it is at least more unusual now-a-days to find a man who can hold his tongue than to find one who cannot."[11] Indications are strong that Lincoln's silence on religious matters extended well beyond his 1846 declaration. It must be understood that his statement was made in a political handbill for all to read. Had it not been true, opponents would have come forward to discredit Lincoln's claim. But that did not happen. Instead, his political opponents used it as evidence that Lincoln had turned his back on worshiping God. In reality, it merely meant that his deep faith and love for God were kept private to prevent contentious challenges to his personal interpretations of the scriptures.

## LINCOLN'S BAPTISM

The date is uncertain, but around this time Lincoln became quietly preoccupied with the doctrine of baptism. His continual searching in the Holy Bible might have focused on teachings such as Christ's injunction to "go ye therefore, and teach all nations, baptizing them in the name of the Father, and of the Son, and of the Holy Ghost," (Matthew 28:19) and Peter's directive to "repent, and be baptized every one of you in the name of Jesus Christ for the remission of sins" (Acts 2:38). Whatever the reason, he approached Reverend John O'Kane and asked him to baptize him—secretly. Two letters have surfaced regarding the matter, both by G. M. Weimer. They are discounted by some Lincoln scholars, but the record does exist, leaving open the possibility that it may be true.

One of Weimer's letters reads as follows:

> The statement I have about the incident of John O'Kane baptizing Abe Lincoln is not something copied from a paper or book.
>
> When I lived in Eureka, Illinois, so my 2 boys could be in College, John O'Kane stayed with me and my family during a State convention. I asked him since he knew Lincoln very well, if he knew whether Abe Lincoln ever became a Christian. Then he said, "I am now going to tell you folks (I and wife and her father) all about the matter. I have kept it in my own memory because when he first had me to arrange to baptize him, his wife assumed a bitter resentment— that it would ruin their social status. So it was postponed for a while (10 days) till the 'storm' was over. Then he and I took a buggy ride one day with a change of clothing under the seat. I then baptized him in a small river near Springfield, Ill. Of course, he became a

member of the Church of Christ. But I have kept it a secret as far as humans are concerned on account of his home condition. Now the possible people who might be hurt in their feelings are all or near dead. So, Bro. Weimer, I'll tell you three folks, but keep it a secret for some years so no storm can be suffered."

We promised. Wife and her father lie in their grave in Eureka Cemetery. I, as far as I know, am the only living messenger of the noted incident.[12]

## BANKRUPTCY

While 1842 brought new optimism to Lincoln, particularly through his rekindled relationship with Mary Todd, it brought more misfortune to the life and family of Joseph Smith. In February 1842, the nation's first bankruptcy law was passed to alleviate the widespread devastation of the Financial Panic of 1837, and the US government officially discouraged attorneys from opposing bankruptcy applications. Many of Joseph Smith's debtors filed for and were granted bankruptcy, adding to the financial strain on him and the growing church. Fraudulent claims by unscrupulous debtors forced the law's repeal just twelve months later.

## MISFORTUNE

The residents of Nauvoo recognized the opportunity for river commerce. Joseph Smith incurred a large and growing debt to acquire new land for his immigrating converts, and when he saw an opportunity to help ease the financial burdens the new European converts coming to Nauvoo by steamboat from New Orleans, he took it. In September 1840, Nauvoo Mormon Peter Haws approached Joseph Smith, Hyrum Smith, and James Adams about joining him in buying a Mississippi riverboat.[13] The craft was currently owned by the government and operated by a certain Lieutenant Robert E. Lee, who had been using it to dredge out the hazardous Des Moines Rapids nearby.[14] The project's federal funding had been cut, however, and the two steamboats used in the dredging operation were being sold at auction in Quincy. Peter Haws, as the principal in the partnership, purchased one of them on credit for $4,866. The partnership had no cash, but Illinois Governor Thomas Carlin and Senator Richard Young each signed letters encouraging the sale, inadvertently adding to the resentment of Thomas Sharp and the Warsaw residents. Lieutenant Lee, representing the US government, accepted Haws's promissory note and returned to Virginia.

The new steamboat owners had eight months to pay the debt to the government. They renamed the craft the *Nauvoo* and quickly sold 5/6 of the interest in the steamboat to three non-Mormon investors, making repayment more probable. One of the investors, Robert F. Smith (no relation to Joseph), would become an ardent Mormon-hater who in 1843 replaced Thomas Sharp as Chairman of the Anti-Mormon Party and was, in 1844, the captain of the Carthage Greys militia who were charged with protecting Joseph Smith the day he was murdered.

They then hired experienced riverboat pilots William and Benjamin Holladay to captain the steamboat. The *Nauvoo* was deployed immediately, transporting cargo and passengers along the river with promising success. But in November 1840, after just two months of operation, the pilots somehow ran the *Nauvoo* aground on the mostly cleared Des Moines Rapids, damaging it so severely that it could not be repaired. It appeared to many that the Holladays had deliberately steered the boat out of the widened channel and into the limestone outcroppings, but they denied that it was intentional.[15]

With the note for the disabled steamship *Nauvoo* now past due, Robert E. Lee was back in Washington, pressing the government to block the bankruptcy application for the steamship debt. The principle owner, Peter Haws, and his partners had, of course, been depending on the revenue from the functioning *Nauvoo* to pay for the craft. Contrary to the government's own expressed policy, Treasury Solicitor Charles B. Penrose and Secretary of War John Bell issued an order to sue the Mormon partners for collection. "Penrose and Robert E. Lee were determined that the steamboat debt must be paid."[16] For some unknown reason, the non-Mormon partners such as Robert Smith were not named in the suit. Montgomery Blair (whom Lincoln later chose as a member of his cabinet) assigned the case to local US attorney Justin Butterfield, with orders to "take the necessary steps"[17] to oppose the plea.

Butterfield was known as one of the most competent lawyers in Illinois. He was a Whig and a friend of Lincoln's. Butterfield filed the suit in May 1842. Nathaniel Pope, the most prominent and respected Federal Judge in Illinois, ordered the defendants to appear on three different occasions, but in the weeks after the *Nauvoo's* suspicious wreck, Peter Haws had left town and could not be found. Even though Mormon owners George Miller and Henry Miller and some of the non-Mormon partners had resources and property that could have been claimed in the suit, the only two targeted for repayment of the debt were Joseph and Hyrum Smith. They didn't appear at any of the three dates, so on June 11, Judge Pope entered a default judgment of $5,212 for the original note plus interest and court costs.

While Lincoln made no effort to ease the debt that he had been paying down for years, he assisted many in the courtroom with the new opportunity. Records indicate that in March of 1842, Lincoln paid two dollars for a certificate allowing him to practice law in the US Circuit Court where bankruptcy cases were heard. During the year that the bankruptcy law was in effect, Lincoln and his partner, Stephen A. Logan, handled about fifty bankruptcy cases. These cases were presented before US Circuit Court Judge Nathaniel Pope in Springfield's newly completed capitol building. In Illinois, 1,433 bankruptcy applications that were filed, and only eight were opposed by the state of Illinois. One of those eight belonged to Joseph Smith, and another to his brother Hyrum. Why these brothers were singled out for opposition is unclear, but they were pursued primarily through the efforts of John C. Bennett and Robert E. Lee.

## THE FALL OF JOHN C. BENNETT

In January 1842, Lt. General Joseph Smith had ordered Major General Bennett to began drilling the Nauvoo Legion in preparation for a much-anticipated military parade and mock battle scheduled for May. The Nauvoo residents made a point to ensure that their militia would be a city militia, not a religious one. Joseph Smith wrote in the *Times and Seasons*:

It is supposed by many abroad that all of our officers are *Mormons*—this, however, is not the case. A large number of the officers of the *Nauvoo Legion*; several members of the *City Council*, both *Aldermen* and *Councillors* [Councilors]; and a large portion of the *Regents of the University*; are not members of any church—many of them are old citizens who resided here long before we were driven from Missouri.[18]

On May 7, 1842, the day of the long anticipated military parade and demonstration arrived. Many people from surrounding towns flocked to Nauvoo, including Judge Stephen A. Douglas, who adjourned court in the nearby county seat of Carthage so that he and other curious colleagues might observe the exhibition. Upon hearing of Judge Douglas's arrival in Nauvoo, Joseph Smith rushed an invitation to him and his friends to attend the officers' banquet as honored guests at Joseph's home prior to the military parade. Douglas was reunited with John C. Bennett, whom he had appointed master of chancery in Hancock County and with whom he collaborated in the passing of the city charter eighteen months earlier in Springfield.

The military display was most impressive to the Mormons but somewhat ominous to some non-Mormons, in spite of the fact that Joseph Smith had gone to great lengths to include as many non-Mormon neighbors he could in the Legion. Now the largest militia in the nation, the Nauvoo Legion paraded its two thousand drilled and smartly uniformed militiamen with their marching band through the streets of Nauvoo to the great delight of the spectators. They then displayed their military skill in a mock battle. It was a splendid spectacle for the thousands who had gathered to watch the proceedings, but it included the intrigue of Bennett's strange orders. In his journal, Joseph Smith recorded that he sensed "mischief concealed in that sham battle."[19] He went on to write:

> I was solicited by General Bennett to take command of the first cohort during the sham battle; this I declined. General Bennett next requested me to take my station in the rear of the cavalry, without my staff, during the engagement; but this was counteracted by Captain A. P. Rockwell, Commander of my Life Guards, who kept close to my side, and I chose my own position. . . . Let John C. Bennett answer at the day of judgment, "Why did you request me to command one of

the Cohorts, and also to take my position without my Staff, during the sham battle, on the 7th of May 1842, where my life might have been the forfeit, and no man have known who did the deed?"[20]

Shortly after John C. Bennett's first censure for his indiscretions, reports of their continuance and escalation surfaced. It appears that the Nauvoo leaders demonstrated a generous forbearance toward Bennett's unfortunate behavior for some time. They finally took action when the rumors and questioning of the citizenry demanded that appropriate steps be taken against him. By 1842, far too many Nauvoo citizens knew of their mayor's ongoing improprieties for him to continue to govern with the respect of his constituency. Just days after the military display, Bennett's reputation was so tarnished by repeated allegations of adultery, homosexuality, and performing abortions that he was impeached as mayor, stripped of his leadership of the Nauvoo Legion and the Masonic Lodge, and excommunicated from the Church. John C. Bennett's illustrious career in Nauvoo was over.

Upon hearing of John C. Bennett's fall from grace, Simeon Francis reported the following:

# Sangamo Journal.

Vol. X. Springfield Illinois, June 24, 1842. No. 44.

It will be seen by the following that the Major General of the Nauvoo Legion, Chancellor of the University at Nauvoo, Judge Douglass' Master in Chancery, and author of Lieutenant General Joe Smith's Proclamation, directing the Mormons to vote the loco foco [Democratic] ticket for Governor and Lieutenant Governor . . . is excommunicated from the Mormon Church. It is now an undoubted fact, that the reports which have been in circulation in relation to Dr. Bennett, are true.

Bennett left Nauvoo in disgrace and headed straight for Springfield to *Sangamo Journal* editor Simeon Francis to begin a new and unsuccessful career as an expositor of the evils of Joseph Smith and the

Mormons. He compiled these articles into a book whose first forty-plus pages extolled his illustrious career and impeccable character. This self-aggrandizement alone left many questioning the veracity of the book's contents. The book and his speaking campaign met with minimal success except among citizens of Illinois and Missouri who were already unhappy with the Mormons. One of the first and foremost claims that Bennett made in his exposé was that he had joined the Mormons in Nauvoo two years earlier, not to help defend and support them as he'd claimed at the time, but to expose Joseph Smith and the Mormons as frauds. This claim was believed by some but not all.

By May 1842, Lincoln had returned from his spring judicial circuit ride and was in Springfield when Bennett arrived. It would be improbable to suppose that Lincoln would not have met again with Bennett, who now spent most of his days at the *Sangamo Journal* office, or at least have had frequent discussions with Simeon Francis on the matter. If Lincoln did not hear some of Bennett's accusations against Joseph Smith and the Mormons firsthand, at the very least he would have read them in the *Journal*, as Francis seemed eager to print them. One thing that Bennett's exposé did was elicit one of the few documented comments that Lincoln made about the Mormons:

> To Samuel D. Marshall
> Friend Sam: Springfield, July 14. 1842-
>
> Yours of the 15th. June, relative to the suit of Grable vs Margrave was duly received, and I have delayed answering it till now, when I can announce the result of the case.[13]
> ... As to the fee, if you are agreed, let it be as follows. Give me credit for two years subscription to your paper, and send me five dollars in good money or the equivalent of it in our Illinois paper.
> There is nothing new here. Bennett's Mormon disclosiers [sic] are making some little stir here, but not very great. Ever your friend
>
> A. LINCOLN[21]

Of interest here is that in spite of the gusto and detail with which Francis published Bennett's disclosures, Lincoln seemed unimpressed by them. Outside of Illinois and Missouri, most appeared to take Lincoln's view on the matter, as reflected in a letter written by Mormon Apostle Lyman Wight a few months later:

> Since I wrote you from Springfield, Ill. I have journeyed through all the small branches [congregations] . . . As to enemies I have found none, and as regards persecution I have never seen less; and regard to Bennett I am hardly question, and if I mention his name the people say he is too contemptible to be noticed; a Methodist preacher by the name of Waterman, in Dayton, told his congregation that he was personally acquainted with Bennett, and although Joseph Smith might be a bad man, yet he could say to them it would be an injury to their society to believe anything that Bennett said; and I can say to your that in traveling a distance of five hundred miles I have not heard a single man say but what Joseph Smith had done himself an honor in purging the church of so filthy a rascal as John C. Bennett.[22]

Bennett's betrayal appeared to be hurtful to Joseph Smith and other Church leaders and members who had truly relied on and confided in John C. Bennett during the past two years. The depth and breadth of Bennett's duplicity speaks to his true character. The following documents shared in the *Times and Seasons* seem to reflect a sadness on the part of the Nauvoo leaders at the loss their friend and colleague. Despite his careless behavior, there can be little doubt that Bennett was a strong contributor to the success of the Mormons' resettlement in Illinois.

# TIMES AND SEASONS.

### "Truth will prevail."

May 17, 1842.

"Bro. JAMES SLOAN,—You will be so good as to permit Gen. Bennett to withdraw his name from the Church Record, if he desires to do so, and this with the best of feelings towards you and General Bennett.

JOSEPH SMITH."

"In accordance with the above I have permitted General Bennett to withdraw his membership from the Church of Jesus Christ of Latter Day Saints, this 17th day of May, 1842,—the best of feelings subsisting between all parties,

JAMES SLOAN,
General Church Clerk and Recorder."

**THE WASP.**

TRUTH CRUSHED TO EARTH WILL RISE AGAIN—BRYANT

Vol. I.—No. 6. Nauvoo, Hancock Co., Sat., May 21, 1842. Whole No. 6.

New election of Mayor, and Vice Mayor, of the City of Nauvoo, on the resignation of General Bennett.

On the 17th instant, General John C. Bennett, resigned the office of Mayor of the city of Nauvoo, and on the 19th, General Joseph Smith, the former Vice Mayor was duly elected to fill the vacancy; and on the same day General Hyrum Smith was elected Vice Mayor, in place of General Joseph Smith, elected Mayor.

The following vote of thanks was then unanimously voted to the Ex-Mayor, General Bennett, by the city Council, to wit:

Resolved, by the City Council of the City of Nauvoo,

That this Council tender a vote of thanks for General John C. Bennett, for his great zeal in having good and wholesome laws adopted for the government of the city, and for the faithful discharge of his duty while Mayor of the same.

Passed May 19th, 1842.
JOSEPH SMITH, Mayor.
JAMES SLOAN, Recorder.

Even after these demonstrations of disappointed friendship, Bennett turned on his former friends with an uncanny vengeance. As noted earlier, his first declaration was designed to elevate himself above his recent humiliation by saying that his experience in Nauvoo was done, from the beginning, with the sole intent to expose them as frauds and criminals. The degree to which he had gained the trust of Joseph Smith, the other elders of the church, and the citizens of Nauvoo, as well as the degree to which he had embraced and preached their religion, leads one to believe that either his stated intrigue was not fully true or that he was, in fact, one of the most sinister imposters in America.

Bennett collected his serialized disclosures from the *Sangamo Journal* and published them as a book entitled, *The History of the Saints; or, an Expose of Joe Smith and Mormonism.* But Simeon Francis's zeal for printing Bennett's salacious accounts was not shared by most other newspapermen around the country.

# Boston Courier.

September 8, 1842. Semi-Weekly. Vol. XVI.—No. 1918.

Mormonism. We notice that the individual alluded to in the following paragraph from the New-York Journal of Commerce, has advertised a course of lectures in this city. Other New-York papers represent his lectures as improper and disgusting recitals.

Gen. Bennett. We heard this expositor of Mormonism for a short time on Friday night. The General is not fitted to make a very deep impression, either by the intellectual or moral qualities which he exhibits. A considerable portion of what he stated was written on detached sheets of paper, and read rather poorly.[23]

## THE REMARKABLE CITY OF NAUVOO

By 1842, just eleven years since its origin, membership in the Church of Jesus Christ of Latter-day Saints was estimated to be a robust eighteen thousand.[24] While their congregations still thrived in dozens of eastern towns, cities like Philadelphia and Boston, and in Europe, the majority lived in western Illinois and eastern Iowa. Nauvoo was experiencing a dramatic buildup developed by the mostly penniless immigrants who had either been driven from Missouri or were new arrivals from eastern states and Europe, many of whom sold all to make the pilgrimage. They proved to be the industrious people described months earlier by Simeon Francis in the *Sangamo Journal*, but another winter would soon be upon them, and they anxiously engaged themselves in planting crops and building homes and shops to see them through the harsh winter months. By this time, the rise of Nauvoo and the construction of the temple had become known throughout much of the country, and people were curious to see the spectacle for themselves. In fact, some historians note that during the 1840s no religion, city, or individual was mentioned in local newspapers more often than Mormonism, Nauvoo, and Joseph Smith. One curious visitor wrote:

> I have been at Nauvoo . . . and have seen the manner in which things are conducted among the Mormons. In the first place, I cannot help noticing the plain hospitality of the Prophet, Smith, to all strangers visiting the town . . . The people of the town appear to be honest and industrious . . . On Sunday I attended one of their meetings, in front of the Temple now building, and one of the largest buildings in the state. There could not have been less than 2,500 people present, and as well appearing as any number that could be found in this or any state. . . . It has been a matter of astonishment to me, after seeing the Prophet, as he is called, . . . why it is, that so many professing Christianity, and so many professing to reverence the sacred principles of our Constitution (which gives free religious toleration to all), have slandered, and persecuted this sect of Christians.[25]

## THE SHOOTING OF GOVERNOR BOGGS

The third calamity to fall upon the Mormon prophet was, oddly enough, the attempted murder of former Missouri Governor Lilburn W. Boggs in Independence, Missouri. On "Sunday, May 22 Joseph the prophet spent the day mostly at home. In looking at the papers he discovered the following in the *Quincy Whig*:"[26]

By S. M. Bartlett. Quincy, Illinois, Sun., May 22, 1842.

Lilburn W. Boggs, late Governor of Missouri, was assassinated at his residence in Independence, Missouri, by an unknown hand, on the 6th instant. He was sitting in a room by himself, when some person discharged a pistol loaded with buckshot, through an adjoining window, three of the shot took effect in his head, one of which penetrated his brain. . . . The Governor was alive on the 7th, but no hopes are entertained of his recovery. . . . There are several rumors in circulation in regard to the horrid affair; one of which throws the crime upon the Mormons . . . Smith too, the Mormon prophet, as we understand, prophesied, a years or so ago, his death by violent means. Hence there is plenty of foundation for rumor.[27]

Upon reading the article, Jospeh went immediately to his brother William and had him insert the following article in the *Wasp*:

Nauvoo, Ill. May 22, 1842. Mr. Bartlett, Dear Sir:—

In your paper (the Quincy Whig) of the 21st inst., you have done me manifest injustice in ascribing me to a prediction of the demise of Lilburn W. Boggs, Esq., Ex-Governor of Missouri, by violent hands. Boggs was a candidate for the State senate, and, I presume, fell by the hand of a political opponent, . . . but he died not through my instrumentality. My hands are clean, and my heart pure, from the blood of all men. I am tired of the misrepresentation, calumny and detraction, heaped upon me by wicked men; and desire and claim, only those principles guaranteed to all men by the Constitution and Laws of the United States and of Illinois. Will you do me the justice to publish this communication, and oblige, yours respectfully,

JOSEPH SMITH[28]

Lilburn Boggs made a surprising recovery and was not killed by the assassin's gun as was reported in the *Quincy Whig* and numerous other newspapers. Joseph was troubled at the accusation that he had predicted the violent death of Lilburn Boggs, which he declared to be false. He was deeply frustrated at yet another unsubstantiated charge against him. The date of the assassination attempt was May 6, the day prior to the military parade in Nauvoo. Joseph Smith was seen by hundreds in Nauvoo on that day. He could not have been two hundred and fifty miles away in Independence. John C. Bennett, who new full well the whereabouts of Joseph Smith on May 6 because he was with him, still chose to seize upon the situation by rushing to Missouri and spreading the rumor that Joseph Smith had ordered Orrin Porter Rockwell, one of his bodyguards, to conduct the assassination. Bennett's scheme had its desired effect, and the State of Missouri focused its investigation of the crime on Joseph and Rockwell.

Rockwell confronted Bennett at Carthage and angrily accused him of lying, but Bennett was undeterred. He contacted Boggs and persuaded him to swear to an affidavit that Porter Rockwell, acting on orders of Joseph Smith, had been the assailant. In July, Boggs appeared before a justice of the peace in Independence, Missouri, and charged Orrin Porter Rockwell with attempted murder and Joseph Smith as accessory to crime. Missouri Governor Thomas Reynolds then entered the fray by entreating the lame duck Governor Thomas Carlin, just days before handing the governorship to Thomas Ford, to send officers to arrest Joseph Smith and Porter Rockwell on these new charges. Carlin received a barrage of letters from Emma Smith, the Nauvoo Female Relief Society, and prominent Nauvoo citizens imploring him to see the impropriety of the extradition order, but Carlin nonetheless offered a reward for the arrest of the Prophet and Porter Rockwell.

Once again, Joseph Smith was headlining newspapers across the country. Joseph and Rockwell appealed to the power of *habeas corpus*, which, ironically, John C. Bennett had successfully lobbied to include in the Nauvoo Charter, and the local judge temporarily freed them based on the fact that they were not in Missouri and could not have carried out the crime.[29] Joseph Smith believed that even with the *habeas corpus* in hand, both Missouri and Illinois authorities would ignore it. He was right. He also knew that a fair trial in Missouri was extremely unlikely. If he returned to Missouri, he would probably be imprisoned again for another crime that he did not commit. Worse, he would be among dozens of Missourians intent on his murder. Knowing firsthand the Missouri authorities' blatant disregard for the rule of law and their hunger for his blood, Joseph reluctantly submitted to his friends' urgings to seek at least a partial seclusion. For his own protection, Joseph began living randomly in the homes of friends in and around the area. Rockwell fled to Pennsylvania using a fictitious name.

While in seclusion at the home of Edward Hunter, Joseph Smith penned the following message to his followers on September 1, 1842:

> Forasmuch as the Lord has revealed unto me that my enemies, both in Missouri and this State, were again in the pursuit of me; and inasmuch as they pursue me without a cause . . . I have thought it expedient and wisdom in me to leave the place for a short season, for my own safety and the safety of this people. (D&C 127:1)

In probable reference to the bankruptcy case pursued by the US government through Justin Butterfield, he continued:

> I would say to all those with whom I have business, that I have left my affairs with agents and clerks who will transact all business in a prompt and proper manner, and will see that all my debts are cancelled in due time, by turning out property, or otherwise, as the case may require. . . . When I learn that the storm is fully blown over, then I will return to you again.
>
> And as for the perils which I am called to pass through, they seem but a small thing to me, as envy and wrath of man have been my common lot all the days of my life; and for what cause it seems mysterious, unless I was ordained from before the foundation of the world for some good end, or bad, as you may choose to call it. Judge ye for yourselves. . . . But nevertheless, deep water is what I am wont to swim in. It all has become a second nature to me; and I feel, like

Paul, to glory in tribulation. . . . Let all the saints rejoice, therefore, and be exceedingly glad; for Israel's God is their God, and he will mete out a just recompense of reward upon the heads of all their oppressors. (D&C 127:1–3)

Sensing the ominous danger that their revered Prophet now faced, not just from Missouri but from lawless vigilantes in Illinois, Church leaders prepared documents answering John C. Bennett's accusations and sent three hundred and eighty elders to distribute the documents to public officials and Church members in various states. It is likely that Springfield would have been the recipient of such emissaries because of its Mormon congregation and the many important government officials living there. It is also likely that Lincoln either heard the refutations directly or read the pamphlet defending their Prophet.

When the 380 volunteers emerged to refute Bennett's poison, Senior Apostle Brigham Young, along with three other members of the Twelve, Heber C. Kimball, George A. Smith, and Amasa Lyman, set out with their clarifying message as well. These emissaries were assigned to the central Illinois communities of Quincy, Pittsfield, Jacksonville, and others. They ended their two-month mission with a two-day conference in Springfield in the latter part of October. This last meeting provided yet another opportunity for Lincoln to interact with Mormon leaders in Springfield.

## Finally a Wedding

While Joseph Smith was weathering this latest threat, Lincoln was advancing his relationship with Mary Todd. Sometime in late October or early November 1842, he had a wedding ring made for Mary on which he had engraved, "Love is eternal."[30] During their secret courtship in the Francis home, he and Mary had formulated an unusual set of wedding plans. They were set in motion early on the morning of November 4, when Lincoln knocked on the door of Reverend Charles Dresser, the Episcopal minister in Springfield, and interrupted the family breakfast by announcing, "I want to get hitched tonight,"[31] and asking Dr. Dresser to do the honors. Then, perhaps to the chagrin of Mrs. Dresser, Lincoln asked that the ceremony be quietly held in their home. At the same time, Mary shocked her sisters with the news of her upcoming wedding, setting off a firestorm of protests. Mary was fully prepared to withstand them, however, and her family saw in short order that this time they would not prevail. Nothing they could say or do would change the course set by Mary and Abraham for a marriage scheduled just hours away. Shortly after Lincoln's request of the Dressers, which they willing accepted, Lincoln happened to run into Ninian Edwards and inform him of the startling plan.

This sent Edwards racing home to confirm this upsetting report with his family. The announcement presented an unpleasant and somewhat embarrassing dilemma for the Edwards family and their high-society friends. Where they thought they had succeeded in maintaining their family honor they had now failed. And with Mary Todd living under their roof, how would they face their aristocratic circle when they were as oblivious to the revived relationship as everyone else? How could they not know of these plans? But now, even more importantly, how could Mary's sister Elizabeth Edwards allow the marriage to be held anywhere but in their spacious home? Elizabeth insisted that at the very least Mary hold the wedding in the Edwards mansion.

This request was probably not unanticipated; Mary agreed, and Lincoln acquiesced as well. It was going to be hard for him to enter a home where he had been rejected for being far too common, much less hold this sacred ceremony in a place where he would only reluctantly, possibly resentfully, be accepted from then on. He likely consented to the change for Mary's sake, as she was probably pleased to have a semblance of the wedding for which she'd dreamed, even though it was thrown together by her sisters in less than a day. Interestingly, had the original Dresser location not been replaced, the Lincolns would have been married in the very home on Eighth and Jackson Streets which they later purchased from the Dressers and lived in for seventeen years.

As the hour approached, Lincoln's best man, James Matheny, remembered that "Lincoln looked and acted as if he were going to the slaughter."[32] Yet Mary's other sister observed that he "was cheerful as he ever had been, for all we could see. He acted just as he always had in company."[33]

The couple stood before a crackling fireplace while rain descended outside, and Dr. Dresser married Abraham and Mary Lincoln. They pledged to cherish one another "for better for worse, for richer for poorer, in sickness and in health."[34] After exchanging pleasantries and enjoying the refreshments, Lincoln led Mary out to a waiting carriage that took then down the muddy street to their first home, an eight-by-fourteen-foot rented room in the nearby Globe Tavern. It was the first real residence that the thirty-three-year-old Lincoln had ever claimed and the humblest home that Mary had ever occupied.

That Mary loved "Mr. Lincoln," as she would call him for the rest of their days together, is exemplified by the fact that Mary accepted this austere and humble lifestyle without complaint. Mary faced unspoken scorn from her family as she walked away from her life of opulence. Lincoln's love for Mary, or "Molly,"[35] as he affectionately called her, is reflected in his willingness to marry into an aristocratic family, which he had never coveted and that would be a political liability in future elections. Lincoln had always been a candidate for the common people, and marrying into status and privilege opened him to accusations of turning on the common citizen in favor of position and status.

One week after the wedding, Lincoln penned a business letter to his law colleague Samuel D. Marshall. In it, he stated: "I have looked into the Dorman & Lane case, till I believe I understand the facts of it; and I also believe we can reverse it. Nothing new here, except my marrying, which to me, is matter of profound wonder."[36]

## CHAPTER NINE ENDNOTES

1. B. H. Roberts, *The Rise and Fall of Nauvoo* (repr., Provo, UT: Maasai, 2001), 416.

2. "The Journalists: Simeon Francis, (1796–1872)," on Mr. Lincoln & Friends, last modified April 1, 2014, http://mrlincolnandfriends.org/inside.asp?pageID=52&subjectID=4, 1.

3. Ibid.

4. Roy Basler, ed., *Collected Works of Abraham Lincoln* (New Brunswick, NJ: Rutgers University Press, 1953), vol.1, 282.

5. "Abraham Lincoln to Joshua Speed, July 4, 1842," *House Divided*, last modified February 27, 2014, http://hd.housedivided.dickinson.edu/print/40458.

6. "The Lincoln Log: August 1, 1842," The Papers of Abraham Lincoln, last modified February 20, 2014, http://www.thelincolnlog.org/Calendar.aspx?year=1842&month=8&day=1.

7. Doris Kearns Goodwin, *Team of Rivals* (New York: Simon & Schuster, 2005), 104–5.

8. "The Lincoln Log: August 12, 1842," The Papers of Abraham Lincoln, last modified February 20, 2014, http://www.thelincolnlog.org/Calendar.aspx?year=1842&month=8&day=12.

9. Aryeh Maidenbaum, "Sounds of Silence: An Aspect of Lincoln's Whig Years," *Illinois Historical Journal*, LXXXII, no. 3 (Autumn 1989): 173.

10. Ron L Andersen, *Abraham Lincoln: God's Humble Instrument* (Salt Lake City, UT: Millennial Mind Publishing, 2009), 73.

11. Roy Basler, ed., *Collected Works of Abraham Lincoln* (New Brunswick, NJ: Rutgers University Press, 1953), vol.4, 209.

12. Jim R. Martin, "The Secret Baptism of Abraham Lincoln," *Restoration Quarterly* 38, no. 2 (n.d.), http://www.acu.edu/sponsored/restoration_quarterly/archives/1990s/vol_38_no_2_contents/martin.html.

13. Joseph I. Bentley, "In the Wake of the Steamboat 'Nauvoo': Prelude to Joseph Smith's Financial Disasters," *Journal of Mormon History* 35, no.1 (Winter 2009): 26–28.

14. Ibid., 25.

15. Ibid., 29.

16. Ibid., 36.

17. Ibid.

18. "City of Nauvoo, Saturday, January 1, 1842: Officers," in *Times and Seasons* (Provo, UT: Brigham Young University: 2006–09), vol. 3, http://contentdm.lib.byu.edu/cdm/ref/collection/NCMP1820-1846/id/9200.

19. Joseph Smith, Journal Histories, LDS Church History Library, May 7, 1842

20. Ibid.

21. Roy Basler, ed., *The Collected Works of Abraham Lincoln* (New Brunswick, NJ: Rutgers

University Press, 1953), vol.1, 290.

22. Journal Histories, Church History Library, Salt Lake City, Utah, October 9, 1842.

23. Although John C. Bennett was giving tempestuous public lectures on "Joe Smith and the Mormons" in Boston at the very time the Courier ran the above news item, the editors of the paper took no further notice of the man and his "disgusting recitals."B. H. Roberts, History of the Church of Jesus Christ of Latter-day Saints: An Introduction and Notes, 2nd ed.; Revised Edition (Salt Lake City, UT: Deseret Book, 1966), vol. 4, 381.

24. Susan Easton Black "How Large Was the Population of Nauvoo?" BYU Studies Quarterly 35, no. 2, https://byustudies.byu.edu/showtitle.aspx?title=6985.

25. Extract from a letter written in Monmouth, Illinois for the Juliet Courier, June 1841, History of the Church, vol. IV, 381.

26. Journal Histories, Church History Library, Salt Lake City, Utah, May 22, 1842.

27. Ibid.

28. Ibid.

29. George Q. Cannon, Life of Joseph Smith the Prophet, (Salt Lake City, UT: Deseret Book, 1972), p 405.

30. Ruth Painter Randall, Mary Lincoln: Biography of a Marriage (Boston: Little, Brown, 1953), 61.

31. Ibid., 62.

32. Ibid., 64.

33. Ibid.

34. Ibid., 65.

35. Ruth Painter Randall, Mary Lincoln: Biography of a Marriage (Boston: Little, Brown, 1953), 13, 66.

36. Basler, Collected Works of Abraham Lincoln, vol.1, 305.

# "THEY SEEM BUT A SMALL THING TO ME"

While Lincoln was rekindling his romance with Mary Todd, Joseph Smith was facing myriad challenges. Missouri Governor Thomas Reynolds supported former Governor Boggs's accusation that, as an accessory to attempted murder, Joseph Smith was a fugitive from Missouri justice. The Missouri press agitated for his extradition. Even though Joseph had been cleared by the local court because of the hundreds of witnesses who saw him in Nauvoo on the day of Boggs's shooting, Governor Carlin's reward for Joseph's arrest remained open, and Joseph therefore remained in a state of semi-seclusion. In fairness to Carlin, the issue was fomenting anarchy in his state. It demanded a highly visible solution, and Carlin wanted the matter decided in the Federal Court in Springfield. The fact that Joseph could not be found fueled accusations from Thomas Sharp and his supporters that Joseph Smith considered himself above the law.

This dilemma, added to Justin Butterfield's pursuit of payment for the steamship Nauvoo, often kept Joseph from his Mayoral task of receiving the continual flow of new, mostly poor converts. To mitigate the massive responsibilities of leading the Church, he delegated many important responsibilities to his bishops, stake presidents, and Quorums of the Twelve, Seventy, and Fifty, all of whom operated without compensation in a remarkably unified manner.[1]

Also in August 1842, Joseph Smith made a disquieting prophecy, declaring to a group of his followers:

> That the Saints would continue to suffer much affliction and would be driven to the Rocky Mountains, many would apostatize, others would be put to death by our persecutors or lose their lives in consequence of exposure or disease, and some of you will live to go and assist in making settlements and build cities and see the Saints become a mighty people in the midst of the Rocky Mountains.[2]

This prophecy was disconcerting to many of the saints; it predicted yet another deadly expulsion. They had been yearning, working, and praying for a successful and peaceful settlement in Nauvoo and for an end to persecutions. But their prophet informed them that not only would persecutions mount again but that the saints would be driven to an ominous and unknown place—the Rocky Mountains. And if this troubling prophecy was not enough, Joseph punctuated his ominous message a month later by saying:

> My bosom swells, with unutterable anguish . . . when I contemplate the scenes of horror that we have pass'd through in the State of Missouri and then look, and behold, and see the storm, and cloud, gathering ten times blacker—ready to burst upon the heads of this innocent people. . . . Shall we bow down and be slaves? . . . The [Nauvoo] Legion, would willingly die in the defence of their rights; but what would that accomplish? . . . I have kept down their indignation, and kept a quiet submission on all hands, and am determined to do so, at all hazards. . . . Our enemies shall not have it to say, that we rebel against government, or commit treason; however much they may lift their hands in oppression, and tyranny.[3]

Glowing and sometimes exaggerated reports from California and Oregon inspired a westward movement to those locations during the 1840s, but the Rocky Mountains were a mystery to nearly everyone in the United States. Fur trapper and explorer Jim Bridger had been to the valley of the Great Salt Lake and was so disenchanted with the area that he offered to pay one thousand dollars for the first bushel of corn produced there.

It was soon clear to the Latter-day Saints that if they were expelled from Illinois there would be no safe place to the east. Despite the Constitution's guarantee of religious freedom, Americans had proven in New York, Ohio, Missouri, and now in Illinois that they would not tolerate the Mormon religion. If expelled from Nauvoo, they would have to go west, avoiding the established settlements in Oregon and California.[4] They would have to choose an uninhabited area, essentially undesirable to other Americans, where they could once again establish their homes, build their communities and temples, and worship God according to the dictates of their hearts.

## UNENDING LEGAL CHALLENGES

Of the more than fourteen hundred bankruptcy cases in the state of Illinois during 1842, the one involving Joseph and Hyrum Smith and the misfortune with the steamship Nauvoo received the most publicity. The Mormons' enemies, fueled by John C. Bennett's accusations of fraud by the Smith brothers to avoid paying the debt, hailed the case as further evidence of the duplicitous lives of Mormon leaders. It is likely that Bennett sought out Butterfield while in Springfield, but whether they met or not, Justin Butterfield seemed to be inspired by Bennett's allegations to press hard in opposing the Smiths' bankruptcy cases. In particular, Bennett charged that Joseph Smith had fraudulently backdated some property deeds to avoid the debt. In court, however, neither Bennett nor Butterfield entered any evidence of the backdating charge—probably because signed and witnessed county records affirmed that Bennett's allegation was false. But Bennett's intensity fomented suspicion, its desired effect, on Butterfield and many others. Federal Judge Nathaniel Pope ordered the Smiths' case to be set over for further hearings in Springfield on December 15. Given Butterfield's friendship with Lincoln and their common Whig political persuasion, Lincoln had ample opportunities to discuss the high profile case with his friend while Butterfield was in town. Such a conversation, however, remains unverified.

On December 9, 1842, Joseph Smith journalized:

> I chopped wood all day. My Brother Hyrum started for Springfield to attend to his case of bankruptcy with Benjamin Covey as witness. Willard Richards, William Clayton, Henry G. Sherwood, Peter Haws, Heber C. Kimball, Alpheus Cutler, and Reynolds Cahoon accompanied them to attend to my case; present testimony to the governor that I was in Illinois at the time Boggs was shot, consequently could not have been a fugitive from the justice of Missouri, and thus procure a discharge from Governor Ford, on Governor Carlin's writ for my arrest. The weather was very cold, and the traveling tedious, yet my messengers traveled 34 miles and staid [sic] with my brother Samuel Smith, who kept a public house at Plymouth.[5]

During December 1842, not only was the Mormon problem the most pressing matter for the outgoing Governor Carlin and incoming Governor Ford, but this Mormon delegation would find that it was the topic of debate in the Legislature, which was in session for the first time in eight years without the presence and influence of Abraham Lincoln. Joseph Smith's December 9 journal entry continues:

> Mr. Davis, of Bond County, introduced a resolution to the House of Representatives at Springfield concerning the charter of Nauvoo, and urged its repeal.
> Mr. Hicks was in favor of having the State arms taken from the Mormons.
> Mr. Owen thought that they had no more than their quota.[6]

The arms referred to consisted of three six-pound cannons, with a few score of muskets, swords, and pistols furnished by the United States to Illinois as militia supplies. In reality, the Nauvoo Legion had received but a small portion of the arms to which it was entitled.

Assemblyman William Smith, Joseph's brother, was then given the floor to defend the rights of the citizens of Nauvoo to retain their charter, their militia, and the few arms assigned to them by the state. He plead with his fellow legislators to bear in mind that:

> In the estimation of genuine democracy the rights of the people of Nauvoo were just as sacred as those of any other people. The people that live there should have just the same privileges extended to them as are awarded to Springfield, Chicago, Quincy or any other city in the State.

Nauvoo is not as some may erroneously suppose—a city composed entirely of Mormons. I can inform [you] gentlemen that Methodists, Presbyterians, Baptists, Unitarians, in short many of different
kinds of religion, and even infidels may be found there, and all these
are tolerated there, just as in any other community.

Those people consider themselves bound by the laws and
endeavor to obey them. Have they not, I would ask, contributed their
portion towards replenishing your county and state revenues? Have
they ever refused to pay their taxes? . . . Where then is the necessity
that this honorable body should enact a law taking away from them
their chartered privileges?[7]

Willard Richards records in his journal that upon their arrival
in Springfield on the morning of December 13, he rented a room in
the Globe Tavern. This made him and probably some of the others
in his entourage fellow guests with the Lincolns, who were now in
their sixth week of marriage. It is unknown how many of Willard's
companions took their lodging at the Globe (some may have stayed
with James Adams), but in those days it was common for numerous
people to crowd into a rented room. Lincoln did this regularly on his
judicial circuit runs. Included in the Lincolns' room rental of $4.00
a week, the Globe Tavern, like many others, provided meals for all
guests at the common dining table. Willard Richards and his friends
remained in Springfield until December 17, giving them five days to
have joint meals and other chance meetings with the Lincolns.

The atmosphere in Springfield was electric with the topic of
Joseph Smith and his legal challenges. Globe Tavern tenants, along
with nearly everyone else in the town, were probably curious for conversation with these Mormon visitors. Like most other Springfield
residents, Lincoln would have heard of the widely known bankruptcy case of Hyrum and Joseph Smith, and Lincoln had a well-
known propensity to approach newcomers to the town with a warm
welcome and a congenial conversation.

It is interesting that Peter Haws, who was obviously the principal owner of the Nauvoo, was in Springfield. Yet neither he nor the
other owners were pursued in the debt case, and apparently Joseph and
Hyrum did little or nothing to hold them responsible for their portion
of the debt. The Smiths appeared willing to assume full responsibility.

In the days leading up to the December 15 court date, Bennett's influence on Butterfield seemed to have waned, leading to two unexpected shifts in Joseph's favor. After his deliberations with the Mormon delegation on the Smiths' behalf, Butterfield went to Judge Pope and recommended to the court that:

> Hyrum [was] to be discharged in bankruptcy and [Butterfield] recommended approval of a proposal made by Joseph's representatives in Springfield to settle the entire debt to the United States on the following terms: The note would be paid off in four equal annual installments, secured by a mortgage on real property worth double the amount of the debt.[8]

Judge Pope accepted their terms and closed the case.

With the bankruptcy case resolved, Justin Butterfield made the surprising change from Joseph Smith's prosecutor to his defender. Butterfield would now represent Joseph against the Missouri charge of accessory to the attempted murder of former Governor Boggs. On December 20, Joseph Smith recorded the receipt of three heartening letters in his journal:

> Chopping and drawing wood, with my own hands and team, as I had done mostly since the 9th. President Young continued very sick. This afternoon the brethren arrived from Springfield, and presented me with Messrs. Ford's, Butterfield's and Adams' letters, and general history of their proceedings, which was highly satisfactory.[9]

The letter from Governor Ford, whose term had begun on December 15, revealed his determination to settle the mounting turbulence surrounding the Mormons in his opening days in office:

> Dear Sir:
>
> Your Petition requesting me to rescind Gov. Carlin's proclamation and recall the writ considered against you, has been received and duly considered. I submitted your case and all the papers relating thereto, to the Judges of the Supreme Court, or at least to six of them, who happened to be present. They were unanimous in the opinion that the requisition from Missouri was illegal and insufficient to cause your arrest. . . . If it should become necessary, for this purpose to repair to Springfield, I do not believe that there will be any disposition to use illegal violence towards you; and I would feel it

my duty in your case, as in the case of any other person to protect you with any necessary amount of force from mob violence . . .

I am most respectfully yours,
THOMAS FORD[10]

Justin Butterfield's letter read as follows:

Springfield, December 17th, 1842, Joseph Smith, Esqr.—Dear Sir:—I have heard the letter read which Gov. Ford has written to you, and his statements are correct in relation to the opinion of the Judges of the Supreme Court.—The Judges were unanimously of the opinion that you would be entitled to your discharge under a habeas corpus to be issued by the Supreme Court. . . . My advice is, that you come here without delay, and you do not run the least risk of being protected while here, and of being discharged by the Supreme Court by habeas corpus. I have also the right to bring the case before the U. S. Court, now in session here, and there you are certain of obtaining your discharge. I will stand by you, and see you safely delivered from your arrest.

Yours truly,
J. BUTTERFIELD[11]

James Adams penned this short but reassuring note:

City of Springfield, 17th Dec. 1842: Gen. J. Smith—My son— It is useless for me to detail facts that the bearer can tell. But I will say that it appears in my judgment, that you had best make no delay in coming before the court at this place for a discharge under habeas corpus.

I am, &c.
J. ADAMS[12]

Of the hundreds of friendships that Joseph Smith developed during his lifetime, one of the most intriguing was the one with James Adams. As noted earlier, their acquaintance was made in 1839, when Joseph Smith passed through Springfield on his way to Washington. Adams sought him out and invited Joseph to stay in his new home. Joseph Smith made such an impression that Adams gave him a generous amount of money to fund his journey to the nation's Capital. Adams so impressed Joseph that he would later refer to Adams as a father figure (as reflected in Adams's salutation "My son" in his December 17 letter). Joseph's father passed away in 1840, and Joseph appears to have allowed Adams to step into that void.[13]

## SACRED DOCTRINES

Adams secretly embraced the Mormon religion at first, but by the end of December 1842, he had made a number of visits to Nauvoo and was serving as the congregational leader of the LDS branch in Springfield. His friends, acquaintances, and even Lincoln would have known of his involvement with his newfound religion by then. A year previously, he helped Hyrum and Joseph organize a Masonic Lodge in Montrose, Iowa. In May 1842, the Smith brothers invited him to participate in the most sacred religious rite of the Church of Jesus Christ of Latter-day Saints. On May 4, 1842, Joseph wrote:

> I spent the day in the upper part of the Store i.e. in my private office . . . in council with General James Adams of Springfield, Patriarch Hyrum Smith, Bishops Newell K. Whitney and George Miller, and Presidents Brigham Young, Heber C. Kimball, and Willard Richards, instructing them in the principles and order of the priesthood. . . . In this Council was instituted the ancient order of things for the first time in these last days.[14]

A year would pass before these temple ordinances would be extended to other Latter-day Saints. Joseph claimed that these temple rites were the same that were practiced in Solomon's Temple and that of the ancient Israelites in their traveling tabernacle under the Prophet Moses' authority. As previously noted, Mormon theology embraces the doctrine that God extends the gift of salvation to all men and women through obedience to God's laws and ordinances. This Mormon doctrine stems from the New Testament reference to Jesus preaching to the spirits of the dead following his crucifixion:

> For Christ also hath once suffered for sins, the just for the unjust, that he might bring us to God, being put to death in the flesh, but quickened by the Spirit: By which also he went and preached unto the spirits in prison. (1 Peter 3:18–19)

In Mormon Church doctrine, the New Testament reference to baptisms for the dead, or for those who have passed to the spiritual world, requires the physical body and is therefore an earthly ordinance. So believers living on the earth go to the Holy Temples to perform this ordinance of baptism for their ancestors in the hope that they will have accepted Jesus Christ's gospel. If that ancestor embraces the Lord's gospel, then the ordinance of baptism has been performed for them vicariously, making them worthy of God's salvation and exaltation. "Else what shall they do which are baptized for the dead, if the dead rise not at all? Why are they then baptized for the dead?" (1 Corinthians 15:29).

James Adams made more visits to Nauvoo in 1842; Joseph Smith appears to have wanted Adams close to him. Earlier in 1840 he had been appointed trustee of the University of the City of Nauvoo, and that same year, while in Nauvoo, he performed vicarious baptisms in the Mississippi River for his deceased daughter Charlotte, his father, an uncle, and a grandmother. In August, Joseph Smith accompanied Adams to the Mormon settlement of Montrose, Iowa, where Adams organized the Masonic Lodge of the Rising Sun while Joseph waited for him. It is interesting that James Adams would be held in such high esteem by the Mormon prophet, while Lincoln believed him to be a swindler who was guilty of fraudulently taking adjoining properties from the widows of Andrew Sampson and Joseph Anderson.

In 1841, the matter of Anderson and Sampson strangely surfaced again. Adams received a blessing from Patriarch Hyrum Smith and then participated in more baptisms for the dead. This time he was baptized for eighty-one of his deceased ancestors, one of whom was former President John Adams. Inexplicably, however, Adams was baptized for two additional and unrelated individuals: Andrew Sampson and Joseph Anderson. Just why these two individuals would be included is an intriguing enigma.

Why Sampson and Anderson, why not any number of Adams's other deceased acquaintances? Did a repentant James Adams confess his fraud to Joseph Smith, and did Joseph recommend the ordinance as a means of repentance? Were the baptisms for these two gentlemen a solemn act of remorse and recompense on the part of Adams, done to atone for the transgression of stealing their property? Was Abraham Lincoln right all along about his nemesis, and was Joseph

Smith also correct about the converted and repentant soul of James Adams? Did Lincoln see a change in Adams after Adams's conversion to Mormonism? Did Lincoln and Adams ever make amends as they continued to live in Springfield?

## On Trial again—This Time in Springfield

Encouraged by the assurances of his trusted friend James Adams, his newfound friend Justin Butterfield, and Governor Thomas Ford, whose election had been secured largely by the vote of Nauvoo, Joseph Smith decided to follow their advice and trust in the judicial system that, with the exception of Judge Stephen A. Douglas the previous year, had been less than reliable for him. On the morning of December 26, Joseph allowed himself to be arrested by General Wilson Law of the Nauvoo Legion on Governor Carlin's warrant. That same morning, Elders Henry G. Sherwood and William Clayton rushed to the county seat in Carthage to obtain a writ of habeas corpus, which was then taken to Justin Butterfield in Springfield.

Upon returning home that day, Joseph found Emma, who had been enduring a very difficult pregnancy, in the throes of delivery of yet another son who did not survive. Having to leave Emma in the care of his mother and the other sisters of the Relief Society, Joseph was compelled to leave for Springfield the next morning in Wilson Law's custody. Because Governor Carlin's two-hundred-dollar reward for his arrest was still in force, fifteen loyal supporters accompanied him to discourage any mischief during the three-day journey.

There was much excitement as word of the Mormon prophet's impending arrival and trial spread throughout Springfield and the surrounding communities. Early in the afternoon of December 30, Joseph arrived at the home of Judge James Adams, where he and some of his friends stayed for the next six days. Justin Butterfield met him at the Adams residence, and they discussed the upcoming hearing. Butterfield expressed his approval of Joseph accepting arrest and for having obtained the writ of habeas corpus from the county court in Carthage. Butterfield was assisted with the hearing by another Springfield attorney, Benjamin F. Edwards, who was

Mary's and now Lincoln's brother-in-law. That evening, Joseph met with his brother William, and they discussed the recent proceedings in the legislature regarding the Nauvoo Charter. Joseph's journal states that:

> At 11 o'clock I was arrested thereupon by a deputy, Mr. Maxey, in presence of Mr. Butterfield, my attorney, who immediately wrote a petition to Judge Pope for a writ of habeas corpus, which I signed, and at 11½ in the morning went before Judge Pope.[15]

Butterfield presented his evidence that Governor Reynolds of Missouri had made a false statement in charging Joseph as a fugitive from Missouri. There was nothing that appeared in the affidavits to evidence that Joseph had committed a crime or that he had fled the state afterward. Then he presented compelling evidence that Joseph Smith was in Nauvoo at the time of the commission of the crime. Joseph recorded in his journal:

> The writ was granted, returned, and served in one minute, and I walked up to the bar. Mr. Butterfield read the habeas corpus and moved the court to take bail 'till I could I have a hearing, which was granted; and although it was only a case of misdemeanor, Generals James Adams and Wilson Law were bailed for me for the sum of $2000 each, and Monday was set for trial.[16]

If ever Abraham Lincoln met or saw Joseph Smith, it would have been on this Saturday morning of December 31, 1842, while Joseph was waiting in Judge Pope's courtroom for Butterfield to present his petition. Joseph's journal records that while waiting, Joseph heard a number of bankruptcy cases being deliberated by Judge Pope. It is probable that some of those deliberations were cases handled by Abraham Lincoln and his partner Stephen Logan. In the course of their normal practice, Lincoln or Logan or both would have been present in the courtroom noting Judge Pope's decisions for their clients. But given the notoriety of Joseph Smith's case, doubtless both Logan and Lincoln would have at least tried to make arrangements to be in the courtroom. If he was, he would have seen his former nemesis, James Adams, step forward to post the two-thousand-dollar bond for Joseph Smith. He would likely have seen his probably new acquaintance Willard Richards in the courtroom as well. Would Richards have introduced Lincoln to Joseph, Hyrum, and the Nauvoo associates with them?

That evening, a New Year's Eve Ball was held in honor of newly elected US Senator Sidney Breeze. Joseph Smith was invited to attend, and he did. Remarkably, instead of being met with the revulsion that he commonly received from outsiders, Joseph was the sensation of the evening. He charmed the crowd with his infectious smile and affability. By the end of the evening, he came away with an even larger group of sympathizers. One described Joseph as the lion of the evening, referring to the great attention that was afforded him and the distinguished manner in which he engaged with the guests.

This party would have been yet another opportunity for Lincoln to meet Joseph, but Breeze was a Democrat, and Lincoln may not have even been invited. He would have certainly known of the event, but we have no record of Lincoln's whereabouts that evening. Was he attending another celebration elsewhere in the town with his Whig friends, or did he spend a quiet evening with Mary in their one-room apartment at the Globe Tavern? At any rate, James Adams and Stephen A. Douglas were at the party and quite likely at the Prophet's side throughout the evening, making it even less likely that Lincoln would have attended.

# 𝕾𝖆𝖓𝖌𝖆𝖒𝖔 𝕵𝖔𝖚𝖗𝖓𝖆𝖑.

Vol. XII. Springfield, Illinois, January 5, 1843. No. 20.

Joseph Smith, the Mormon prophet, was brought before Judge Pope, of the U. S. District Court, on Tuesday, on a writ of habeas corpus, in the Bogg's case. The examination was postponed till Wednesday. Mr. Lamborn appears on the part of the State, and Mr. Butterfield on the part of the prisoner.

Major General John C. Bennett, of the Nauvoo Legion, is now lecturing on Mormonism in Chicago.

The Express says he proposes to lift the curtain a little higher
than usual in his lectures

When the court reconvened after the New Year, Joseph described
the courtroom as crowded. It was certainly filled with curious
onlookers, both Mormon and non-Mormon. Was Lincoln present
in that courtroom, standing a head taller than most others? It would
have been very easy for Lincoln to walk the one block from his law
office to the Tinsley Building and observe the legal proceedings of
Judge Pope and his friend Justin Butterfield in behalf of the Mormon
prophet. Did Lincoln listen in quiet approbation at the civil manner
in which Butterfield and Pope executed the judicial gifts of a free
Republic in behalf of a beleaguered Church founder? At the end
of this brief preliminary hearing, they proceeded to descend the
staircase to the street. Joseph recorded: "As General Law came to
the top of the stairs, one of the crowd observed, 'There goes Smith
the Prophet, and a good-looking man he is. And (said another) as
damn'd a rascal as ever lived.'" General Law and Hyrum Smith took
exception to the last comment, and by the time they had descended
to the bottom of the stairs, the man:

> Began to strip off his clothes and ran out in the street, cursing
> and swearing and raising a tumult, when Mr. Prentice, the marshal,
> interfered, and with great exertions quelled the mob. Much credit is
> due Mr. Prentice for his zeal to keep the peace.[17]

The fracas in the street immediately drew a crowd, and it is possible that Lincoln observed it. He may also have watched as Joseph
and Butterfield proceeded across the street to the America House, a
new modern hotel in which Governor Ford was lodging and recovering from an illness.

In yet another demonstration of good will owing to the recent
influx of Mormons to Springfield, some state legislators approached
Joseph Smith and offered the House of Representatives Hall for
the Mormons' Sunday worship service the next day. Joseph gratefully accepted, then prudently asked Apostles Orson Hyde and John
Taylor to provide the sermons, eliminating an opportunity for his
enemies to stir up trouble on the day before the trial. Word of the

Mormon worship service spread quickly, and, as was expected, many non-Mormons attended the service, including many members of the legislature.

With Springfield all abuzz at the arrival of Joseph Smith, one of the most infamous people in America in that day, how did Mary and Abraham Lincoln respond? There is strong evidence that Mary was very interested in the Joseph Smith trial, and it is very likely that she deliberated with her husband on a strategy to attend it. After having dined at the Globe Tavern with Willard Richards and others of the Mormons in his group two weeks earlier, would they not have been even more curious to witness these historic proceedings? Nothing is known about the Lincoln's shared evenings with the Mormons at the Globe, but it is almost certain that they shared a few, if not many, hours together in conversation. Often talk around the dining tables in taverns would go on long into the evening, and news, politics, commerce, religion, weather, gossip, and frivolity would alternately take center stage.

During these evening meals with the Mormons, Lincoln must have been cheered to note that he wasn't the only one choosing not to take a dram of whiskey. And imagine the Mormons' surprise to see Lincoln's abstinence. The Lincolns potentially had hours to hear the Mormon side of all of the issues that followed them. During these evening conversations, did the ever-enthusiastic Mormons bear their witness to the Lincolns of their faith? Was the Book of Mormon passed to the newlyweds with a challenge to read it and pray over the veracity of its contents? Was the Mormon contingent treated to Lincoln's captivating humor? The Lincolns might have discussed the Springfield Mormons that they knew. Did these Mormons find in Lincoln an unusually neutral and conciliatory listener to their plight?

In Lincoln's early days he was a tireless campaigner, ever ready to ask how he might gain a citizen's vote. Did Lincoln take advantage of the Mormon leaders' presence to promote his new campaign as a candidate for Congress? To carry part or most of the Mormon bloc vote would have been a dramatic boost to his campaign. When the Mormon prophet arrived in town two weeks later, did the Lincolns reach out to these new Mormon friends who had returned with him for the trial? Lincoln had written a note to himself regarding the Mormon religious service in the Representatives' Hall,[18] which demonstrates an interest in attending. But he apparently changed his mind or became ill, because evidence shows that they were probably not in attendance at the service.[19]

## STEPHEN A. DOUGLAS

Stephen A. Douglas was one of the six State Supreme Court Judges in Springfield. Days earlier, he had offered his opinion in favor of Joseph Smith's case. Upon Smith's arrival, Judge Douglas sought him out and renewed his acquaintance with Joseph, Hyrum, and his other Nauvoo friends. By this time Douglas was paying a political price for his friendship with the Mormons and for his handling of Joseph's first extradition case in Montrose the previous year. While many could see the propriety of his acquittal of Joseph Smith in Montrose, the Prophet's enemies targeted Douglas for doing so. Six months earlier, on July 2, 1842, in the midst of Simeon Francis's reporting of John C. Bennett's diatribes, Francis posted the following in his *Sangamo Journal*:

## 𝕾angamo 𝕵ournal.

Springfield, Illinois, July 2, 1842.

On the 29th day of June 1841, we happened to be in company with Judge Douglass and several other gentlemen, in Jacksonville, when the Mormon question, then a general topic of conversation, was introduced. After telling of the persecution which had been visited upon them, and the many hair breadth escapes of Joe Smith, whilst in Missouri, as related by him to Douglass a short time before, the Judge stated in substance that he believed there was as much true religion among them as in any other church;—that they were misrepresented—that he thought they were more upright and correct in their conduct than other denominations, because every one was watching them—he used the simile that "a new broom sweeps clean"—they were new, but when they grew old and wealthy they might become corrupt.[20]

In the months following this article, Douglas was derided for having been present at the Nauvoo Legion military review in June 1841 and was accused of believing in the Mormon faith, which he denied. It is clear that in spite of this criticism (which came mainly from Whigs), Douglas appeared to show no hesitation in befriending and defending Joseph Smith in his Springfield trial. Nor did James Adams, who was now openly Mormon. Their loyalty to the Mormon prophet quite likely influenced the mostly civil response to Joseph Smith among the local residents. In spite of the criticism, Douglas would remain the Mormons' friend for their final three turbulent years in Nauvoo. This sympathy for the Mormon plight would hound him politically for years to come.

Following lunch at the America House, Joseph and Butterfield returned to the ailing Governor's room for some informal and congenial conversation. As the topic turned to religion, Governor Ford said that he was not affiliated with religion and then shared that:

> From reports we had reason to think the Mormons were a peculiar people, different from other people, having horns or something of the kind; but I find they look like other people, indeed, I think Mr. Smith is a very good looking man.[21]

Governor Ford also revealed that Governor Reynolds of Missouri had recently presented him with the old warrant for Joseph's arrest for treason, arson, and so on. If Joseph was acquitted on the current charge, Reynolds wanted Ford to re-arrest Joseph on this former charge. Ford then assured them that this desperate gesture was ludicrous in light of the trial presided over by Stephen A. Douglas in June 1841, in which the warrant was proven defective.

Later that afternoon, a runaway team of horses charged through the streets of Springfield and past the State House, causing someone to exclaim, "Joe Smith is running away."[22] This prompted a sudden adjournment of the session in progress in the House of Representatives. The ruckus also interrupted Lincoln's court session at the State House.

On Monday morning, the courtroom was filled to standing room only with spectators described as people of a very respectable class, including the current and former Governors of Illinois, Missouri Governor Reynolds, former Governor Boggs, a self-proclaimed prophet, and his apostles. It was a sensational news story in all parts of the country. Simeon Francis was present with pencil in hand to cover the riveting story of a former governor accusing the nationally known Mormon prophet as an accessory to his attempted murder. Many other newspaper outlets throughout the country would undoubtedly seek out Francis's coverage of the trial.

Just prior to the beginning of the trial, a commotion of a different sort occurred at the top of the courtroom stairs. The crowd began to shuffle and part, creating a pathway for six young women, dressed to the nines, who were determined to make a public statement that ladies should also observe these highly-charged proceedings. It was unusual for women to attend such trials, but in this case, no man in the courtroom ventured a complaint at their attendance. Rather, they all immediately set about to find proper seating for the damsels, but none could be found.

Judge Pope was probably expecting their appearance; he was ready with a solution. They sat with him at the judge's bench in the front of the courtroom, three on one side and three on the other. This seating arrangement did not surprise the spectators much; one of the women was his daughter. And, interestingly enough, one of the others was Mary Todd Lincoln. She was not going to be denied being a part of this riveting event, and while at it, she was determined to make a splash. The former Miss Todd was back in her social saddle; her marriage to Mr. Lincoln had brought her out of the gloomy doldrums of their separation.

Mary Lincoln's education and Kentucky upbringing in the social graces placed her at an uncommon level of sophistication and confidence among the women of Springfield. She was unabashed and keenly astute in her interest in and grasp of the political landscape, a trait highly admired and valued by her husband. Politics was a vocation not generally indulged in by women of that day, and she was undoubtedly emboldened by Miss Pope's influence with her father.

Clearly Mary wanted to be at the trial, and it is quite possible that she was the women's impetuous ringleader. Without a doubt, she would have discussed her scheme with her husband, who apparently did nothing to oppose her plan. And where was Mr. Lincoln during the trial? Court records show that he was across the street at the State House, trying a case in the State Supreme Court. It is safe to say that Lincoln did not attend Joseph's trial.

Attorneys Butterfield and Edwards presented their case in a masterful manner, and Illinois Attorney General Josiah Lamborn argued for the state of Missouri. Judge Pope was exceptionally deliberate in the case, and, in the end, on January 5, 1843, he gave the ruling that nearly everyone had expected—that the affidavit from Boggs was defective and therefore Joseph Smith must be discharged. Instead of a riot over the verdict, for which the marshals and the Mormons were braced, a spirit of decorum and approbation of Judge Pope's ruling prevailed in Springfield. At the conclusion of the trial, Pope and Butterfield invited Joseph to meet with him. A most congenial conversation took place as they asked, among other topics, if Joseph really believed himself to be a Prophet of God.

Joseph Smith's six days in Springfield proved to be very productive for him and his people. The common courtesy extended to him was a rare experience in his turbulent life. He had been in the company of the leading men in Springfield—governors, judges, and legislators from around the state, all of whom extended an unusual deference and decorum toward Joseph and his representatives. Quite unexpectedly, he had become a celebrity in the city. Many Mormons and non-Mormons, including Stephen A. Douglas, sought him out. At the conclusion of the trial, the marshal who held the famous prisoner in his custody invited Joseph to a family dinner.

A New York reporter who had rushed to Springfield to cover the trial noted that the Mormon prophet seemed to have a continual smile on his countenance. Through the experience, the people of Springfield were able to see that there was little of substance to the wild accusations that John C. Bennett continued to spread throughout the country. Once again, the community of Springfield distinguished itself from so many others in their fair and tolerant treatment of the peculiar citizens known as Latter-day Saints. The winner in this historical trial was, of course, Joseph Smith, as his days of being pursued by his enemies were ended for the time being. He could finally, after more than six months, return to his family in relative peace and safety. The other winner was the criminal who shot Lilburn Boggs. Boggs and Missouri had placed all their efforts in the conviction of Joseph Smith, allowing the guilty party to remain uncaptured and unpunished. The losers were the State of Missouri, Lilburn Boggs, and John C. Bennett, whose credibility declined with the passing of each new day.

The determined entrance of Mary Lincoln and her feminine friends at the trial caused at least one anonymous citizen to censure them for their unladylike display. This prompted a number of newspapers, including Simeon Frances's, to refute his criticism, and we see that Francis himself had also softened on the topic of Joseph Smith:

# Sangamo Journal.

Vol. XII. Springfield, Illinois, January 26, 1843. No. 23.

CASE OF JOE SMITH.

Mr. Butterfield requires no defence.—There he presented the case on the part of his client in such a manner, that no one, whether versed in the legal subtleties of the law or not, who heard him, doubted for a moment that Smith was illegally under arrest, and should be duscharged.

The attack of the letter writer upon those ladies who attended court for the purpose of hearing the argument of Mr. Butterfield, and the Opinion of the Judge, is worthy of a low-bred fellow. If he will make himself known to the husbands, brothers or fathers of those ladies he has thus grossly insulted, he may receive the notice he so richly deserves at their hands.

It is not surprising that Francis would come to Mary's defense—it was in his home that the romance between her and Lincoln was allowed to blossom. Mary and Mr. Lincoln must surely have enjoyed a laugh at the reaction to her most civil of demonstrations.

There was no greater opportunity for Joseph Smith and Abraham Lincoln to meet than during the month of December 1842. Joseph's days in Springfield boasted a multitude of circumstances in which they could have met. Scholars have searched long and deep into recorded history to find evidence confirming an acquaintance between the President and the Prophet, but to date, none has been found. But it must also be remembered that no record exists claiming that they did not meet. Why, during those six days, would it have been worth mentioning their acquaintance? Lincoln's timeless and world-renowned greatness remained concealed from his friends, neighbors, and even the Mormon prophet in 1842.

On the other hand, dozens of Lincoln's friends and associates did meet Joseph Smith during the five years that these world-renowned Americans both claimed Illinois as their home. Records indicate that politicians James Adams, Stephen A. Douglas, Thomas Ford, Thomas Carlin, John C. Bennett, John T. Stuart, Richard M. Young, Orville Browning, Justin Butterfield, Nathaniel Pope, Benjamin F. Edwards, Adam Snyder, Charles A. Warren, James Ralston, Sidney Breeze, Cyrus Walker and Sidney Little all interacted with Joseph, to name just a few.

Then there were the Springfield Mormons: Katherine and Samuel Mulliner; Mary Groesbeck, her son Nicolas, and his wife, Ruth Thompson Groesbeck; George and Polly Stringham and their children Briant, Jeremiah, and Sabra; as well as Jonathan Browning in Quincy, Willard Richards in the tavern, and possibly many others. Mormon leaders who may have met Abraham Lincoln include William Smith, Wilford Woodruff, Brigham Young, Heber C. Kimball, Almon Babbitt, John Snider, Hyrum Smith, William Clayton, Wilson Law, Henry Sherwood, Peter Haws, Alpheus Cutler, Reynolds Cahoon, and Benjamin Covey.

Dozens of Lincoln's acquaintances were present in the courtroom or at the New Year's Eve celebration for Sydney Breeze. And last but certainly not least, Mary Todd Lincoln attended Joseph's trial. It is extremely improbable that so many of Lincoln's friends would meet the Prophet and that Lincoln himself would remain aloof from at least an introduction to one of the most famous persons in America. Once again, there is no record stating that they did not meet, just an absence of one confirming that they did.

The return journey to Nauvoo for Joseph and his loyal followers was a joyous yet bitterly cold one. Some fifteen thousand anxious Saints, ever mindful of their past experiences with capricious courts, politicians, and judges, had been fasting and praying for the deliverance of their Prophet, and this time those prayers were answered. The traveling party warmed their spirits by composing a song, which they sang over and over:

> And are you sure the news is true?
> And are you sure he's free?
> Then let us join with one accord,
> And have a jubilee
>
> We'll have a jubilee, My friends
> We'll have a jubilee
> With heart and voice we'll all rejoice
> In that our Prophet's free.[23]

# CHAPTER TEN ENDNOTES

1. This unity can be seen in a small drama that unfolded among the Springfield Latter-day Saints. Almon Babbitt, a one-time resident of Springfield, was the leader of the saints still residing in and around Kirtland, Ohio. He had traveled to Nauvoo on church business. While there, he observed the tumult that was mounting against the saints in Illinois and Iowa. On his return trip to Kirtland, he stopped in Springfield and began admonishing some of the saints there to either avoid Nauvoo for their own safety or consider removing to Kirtland, where it would be safer for them and their families.

   The president of the Springfield stake, Edwin T. Miriam, was troubled by Babbitt's behavior. He gathered statements from some of his members, which he forwarded to Joseph Smith for guidance. President Smith and the Quorum of the Twelve did not approve of Babbitt's unauthorized counsel, and they sent emissaries to Springfield to address the matter. Many of these Springfield Latter-day Saints and the emissaries may have been acquainted with Abraham Lincoln.

   George Stringham wrote, "I asked Brother Babbitt if I had better move to Nauvoo. He said he thought there was a scourge for that place, and I had better stay here." David Elliot wrote, "Brother Almon W. Babbitt told me I had better stay in Springfield for the scourge would fall on Nauvoo before long." Springfield Mormons David Dickson, John Pryor, John Priest, and Abram Palmer all wrote similar testimonies. President Miriam then reported that:

   "These sayings seem to have discouraged many who had a desire to gather with the saints at Nauvoo and turn their minds to Kirtland. In this situation Brother [Lyman] Wight and Brother [Brigham] Young found us, who, when they became acquainted with our situation labored diligently to restore us to a proper understanding, and I think the brethren are all restored with one exception; Reuben Daniels, we fear, is past help, and we hope there will be a stop to such teaching. Ours in the bonds of the New and Everlasting Covenant, Edwin T. Merian, President." (Quotes from Journal Histories, Church History Library, Salt lake City, Utah, August 10, 1842.)

2. B. H. Roberts, *History of the Church of Jesus Christ of Latter-day Saints: An Introduction and Notes*, 2nd ed.; Revised Edition (Salt Lake City, UT: Deseret Book, 1966), vol. 5, 85.

3. Richard Lyman Bushman, *Rough Stone Rolling*, with the assistance of Jed Woodworth (New York: Alfred A. Knopf, 2005), 475–76.

4. The *Sangamo Journal* of June 11, 1846, (vol. xv, No. 38) printed the following letter from surveyor John C. Fremont, dated January 24, 1846. His description of the Great Basin would have been of particular interest to the Mormons then leaving Nauvoo:

   "I crossed the Rocky Mountains on the main Arkansas, passing out at its very head-waters; explored the southern shore of the great Salt Lake, and visited one of its islands. You know that on every recent map, manuscript or printed, the whole of the great basin is represented as a sandy plain, barren, without water, and without grass. Instead of a plain, I found it, throughout the whole extent, traversed by parallel ranges of lofty mountains, their summits white with snow, (October) while below, the valleys had none. Instead of a barren country, the mountains were covered with grasses of the best quality, wooded with several varieties of trees, and containing more deer and mountains [sic] sheep that we had seen in any previous part of our voyage. So utterly at variance with every description, from authentic sources, or from rumor or report, it is fair to consider this country as hitherto wholly unexplored, and never before visited by a white man."

5. Journal Histories, Church History Library, Salt Lake City, Utah, December 9, 1842.

6. Ibid.

7. Ibid.

8. Joseph I. Bentley, "In the Wake of the Steamboat 'Nauvoo': Prelude to Joseph Smith's Financial Disasters," Journal of Mormon History 35, no. 1 (Winter 2009): 38, http://www.jstor.org/discover/10.2307/23290686?uid=3739928&uid=2&uid=4&uid=3739256&sid=21103603652863.

9. Journal Histories, Church History Library, Salt lake City, Utah, December 20, 1842.

10. Journal Histories, Church History Library, Salt lake City, Utah, December 17, 1842.

11. Ibid.

12. Ibid.

13. B. H. Roberts, *History of the Church of Jesus Christ of Latter-day Saints: An Introduction and Notes* (Salt Lake City, UT: Deseret Book, 1968), vol. 4, 20.

14. Journal Histories, Church History Library, Salt lake City, Utah, May 4, 1842.

15. Journal Histories, Church History Library, Salt lake City, Utah, December 31, 1842.

16. Ibid.

17. Ibid.

18. The Lincoln Law Office Museum, Springfield, IL.

19. Ibid.

20. "The Mormons" in *Sangamo Journal*, July 2, 1842.

21. Journal Histories, December 31, 1842.

22. Ibid.

23. Richard Lyman Bushman, *Rough Stone Rolling*, with the assistance of Jed Woodworth (repr., New York: Vintage Books, 2007), 481.

# Chapter Eleven

# PRESIDENTIAL PROPHETS

In August 1842, the same month that Joseph Smith uttered his prophesy on the Mormon exodus to the Rocky Mountains, Lincoln was building support for his run for a seat in the US Congress the following year. His campaign strategy included tapping into the strength of nationally known Henry Clay, Lincoln's political hero. Quite likely through the encouragement of his secret fiancé Mary Todd, who was well acquainted with the powerful Henry Clay of Kentucky, Lincoln gathered with other ambitious Henry Clay admirers to form the Clay Club of Springfield. He then invited the illustrious Senator for a visit to "the prairie-land."[1]

Lincoln and the executive committee of the Clay Club assured Clay that "should you now yield to our request, we promise you such a reception as shall be worthy of the man on whom are now turned the fondest hopes of a great and suffering nation."[2] To Lincoln's disappointment, Clay was unable to make the visit, possibly dealing a disabling blow to Lincoln's campaign.

In 1843, Joseph Smith would also pen a letter to Henry Clay, then a prominent candidate in the 1844 presidential election, but his letter did not reflect the glowing admiration that Lincoln's did.

## MR. AND MRS. LINCOLN

Mary Lincoln's love for Mr. Lincoln is reflected in her gracious acceptance of the small room at the Globe Tavern as her home after living in the spacious and well-appointed homes of the Edwards and the Todds. She stepped from a life of plenty to one of austerity with an uncommon dignity. She even endured the frequent ringing of the large and loud bell above their second-floor room, which rang at all times of the day and night to alert the stable boys that a stagecoach or carriage's team of horses needed to be stabled. As annoying as the bell was, it did elicit a certain excitement for the Lincolns with its signal of new arrivals with whom Mary and Mr. Lincoln could share their local news and hear theirs.

In writing to his friend Joshua Speed about his marriage to Fanny, Lincoln avowed that "You owe obligations to her, ten thousand times more sacred than you can owe others."[3] This sentiment, along with the inscription "Love is Eternal" on Mary's wedding ring, reflects Lincoln's own deep affection for her.

Prior to Lincoln's marriage to Mary, he had at times been portrayed as uncouth and unrefined. Mary knew that if her man was to become President of the United States, he would need some coaching in the refined decorum of the etiquette-minded leaders of the state and country. Through their years as a family, she did succeed in ensuring that he was dressed and groomed more appropriately before leaving the house each day, but she never fully succeeded in replacing all of his backwoods ways, his Hoosier drawl, or his awkward mannerisms, many of which he took with him to the White House. His common-folk ways were frequently scrutinized by the more refined eastern men and women in and around Washington—a fact that did not elude him but one to which he paid little mind.

Within a few weeks of Joseph Smith's January trial in Springfield, the Lincolns were certain that Mary was carrying their first child. Unlike today, graveyards were filled with the remains of young women who perished in the perilous process of childbirth. Both Mary and Mr. Lincoln knew this well. Both Lincoln's sister and Mary's mother had died giving birth. When spring arrived, Lincoln kissed his young and pregnant wife good-bye and left to ride

the judicial circuit once more. This he did in spite of the widely publicized Millerite (later called the Seventh-day Adventists) prophecy
of the Savior's second coming, which had all in the country looking
to April 23 as the end of the world as they knew it.[4] True believers
were busy disposing of property and buying up muslin cloth to use
as ascension robes. Joseph Smith was asked about the veracity of the
prophecy, and he responded by saying that Millerite founder William Miller would be disappointed at the results of his prediction.
Lincoln returned in early May with the world still intact and his wife
more than grateful to have her husband near during the wonders and
travail of pregnancy. The twice yearly judicial circuit runs would be a
part of their lives for years to come, and as time went on, Mary grew
to dislike them more and more.

In August, the time came for Mary's dreaded delivery, which
took place in their hot, stuffy, thin-walled boarding-house room.
Mary safely gave birth to a son. They named him Robert Todd
Lincoln, granting to Mary's father the honor of a namesake. There
was probably little disagreement from Mr. Lincoln with the name;
Lincoln's relationship with his father, Thomas Lincoln, had become
strained during his adult years for unknown reasons. One wonders
why Mary did not go to either of the comfortable homes of her sisters
for her "confinement," raising the question of whether resentment
over Mary's marriage against their advice may have still simmered. A
kind Mrs. Bledsoe and her young daughter Sophie, fellow tenants at
the Globe, would come daily to tend to needs of the baby and Mary.
Years later, Sophie would recall that Mary had no nurse to care for
her during that difficult time, leading one to conclude that her sisters
may not have come to the second-rate tavern to comfort their sister
in her time of need.[5]

Lincoln was giddy at the arrival of his healthy son, and he liked
to quip to his friends his relief that the child had not arrived with one
of Mary's short legs and one of his long ones. The cries of the infant
were heard throughout the small tavern, eliciting complaints that
prompted the Lincolns to move shortly thereafter to a small rented
home nearby.

## LINCOLN AIMS FOR CONGRESS

As trying as his judicial circuit runs were, they served Lincoln in a way that extended beyond livelihood. Men did not gain election to Congress by remaining unknown, and his circle of friends expanded each year as he traveled from town to village. His natural outgoing nature served him well, particularly among the common people, for whom he held deep affections. His drive for Sangamon County Whig nominee for Congress pitted him against one of his best friends, Edward Baker. Lincoln admired Baker so much that he named his second son Edward Baker Lincoln after his longtime friend. In 1861, US Senator Baker was President Elect Lincoln's choice to introduce him at his presidential inauguration in Washington. Shortly thereafter, Baker gallantly heeded Lincoln's call for volunteers in the Union army and was appointed a Colonel in the Civil War. Baker became a very early war casualty in a relatively small skirmish at Balls Bluff, becoming the only sitting US Senator to be killed in the Civil War and bringing the anguish of the war directly to President Lincoln's heart.

Lincoln's poverty compounded the challenge of running for office. The added expenditures and campaigning days away from the courtroom further reduced his earnings. But it is quite certain that Mary was in full support of the endeavor.[6]

Adding to their financial burden, Lincoln continued his payments on the New Salem store debt and had begun sending money regularly to his aging parents. It is quite certain that Lincoln could have increased his income had he cared enough to do it. Although frugal with his money, he regularly placed other matters in life ahead of pursuing wealth, unlike many of his successful lawyer friends. He had always felt quite content to be a mere boarder with a friend's family, and they always seemed glad to have him in their homes. In the White House, Lincoln was quoted to say, "Money, I don't know anything about '*money*.' I never had enough of my own to fret me, and I have no opinion about it any way."[7]

There was at least one member of the Todd family who did appear to admire Mary's choice of a husband, and that was her father, Robert Todd. Being aware of his daughter's humble circumstances, he began sending money to the Lincolns to help with expenses. But he apparently did not mind, having been heard to say, "I only hope that Mary will make as good a wife as she has a husband."[8]

Edward Baker defeated his friend Lincoln for the County nomination, and Lincoln enumerated two of the factors that he felt contributed to his friend's victory. One was his marriage to Mary. Mary herself was not a political liability, but her highborn heritage was. After Lincoln married into the aristocratic Todd and Edwards families, his political opponents sometimes accused Lincoln of selling out his more common friends for money and position. He and Mary marveled at this, considering their modest circumstances. But the factor that troubled him most was that in this, his first foray into national politics, his religious convictions were held against him by some voters. After his defeat, Lincoln penned these sentiments:

> There was too the strangest combination of church influence against me. Baker is a Campbellite, and therefore as I suppose, with few [ex]ceptions got [the votes of] all that church. . . . It was every where contended that no ch[r]istian ought to go for me, because I belonged to no church.[9]

He then expressed his confidence that his friend did nothing to introduce the issue of religion into the campaign; it stemmed, again, from Lincoln's reputation as an infidel. In the early years of their marriage, it was noted that Lincoln would stay home with the children while Mary faithfully attended her Presbyterian Sunday service, so it was easily deduced that Lincoln the candidate was an unfit Christian because of his apparent disinterest in religion.

## POLYGAMY

Upon Joseph Smith's return from Springfield, he was met with an enormous crowd of thankful saints who rejoiced in his vindication. They saw Missouri's pursuit of their prophet as a threat to themselves, and they felt to celebrate their own relief at Joseph's freedom. On January 17, Joseph Smith held an expansive banquet at his home to celebrate both his acquittal and his and Emma's sixteenth wedding anniversary. The significance of the anniversary celebration went much deeper for Emma and Joseph. He wanted to publicly affirm to Emma, their friends, and his followers that his love for her was undying, even at this extremely difficult time for them as husband and wife. Whispers of the doctrine of celestial marriage, or polygamy, were circling the Mormon community. Emma had known of the principle for a number of years. She knew the day would come when Joseph could no longer delay its practice, and by 1842, the time had arrived to obey what Joseph considered to be God's command.[10]

Earlier, Joseph confided with Emma that he had received a divine revelation regarding God's law of plural marriage as seen in the lives of Abraham, Moses, David and Solomon. Jehovah had commanded them to accept the additional wives that He gave to them. Joseph knew full well that this doctrine would unnerve many of his faithful saints, incense most of his enemies, bring a firestorm of indignant persecutions to him and his followers, and damage his relationship with Emma. As early as 1841, he confided the doctrine privately to some of his closest associates. They were all appalled by it, as he knew they would be. He himself had been when he'd received the commandment. Joseph asked each of them to take the matter to God in prayer, and by so doing, a number of them received compelling spiritual confirmations that God was re-introducing a sacred, eternal order again on the earth. These stood soundly by him. Some of his closest friends, however, did not have such a manifestation and became bitter enemies, declaring that Joseph Smith was a fallen prophet.

After prayer and serious reflection, Emma also came to accept it as a doctrine from heaven, but she vacillated because of its extreme difficulty. To help Emma and others who felt the weight of such a challenging principle, his supporters suggested that the time had come to write down the revelation containing the "new and everlasting covenant of marriage" (D&C 132:19). So in his upper office in the Red Brick Store on July 12, 1843, Joseph, with his brother Hyrum as a witness, dictated the revelation to William Clayton.

A month later, Hyrum read the revelation to the stake presidency and high council of the Nauvoo stake. As the news of the new doctrine spread through the membership, many revolted at it. Yet, remarkably, the vast majority did not allow it to shake their faith in the Prophet and the other doctrines they had learned through him. The revelation remains to this day in the canonized scripture of The Church of Jesus Christ of Latter-day Saints; it is found in the Doctrine & Covenants section 132. The practice of polygamy was discontinued by revelation through Church President Wilford Woodruff, who declared it would no longer be a practice of the Church until such a time as God saw fit to re-introduce it.

In February 1843, the Illinois Senate voted in opposition of Assemblyman William Smith's pleadings to preserve the Nauvoo charter, but the Assembly did not follow suit. The matter would be a point of debate and contention in the legislature throughout the coming year. The ongoing drama of the Mormons continued to appeal to readers across the country, and this obscure action by the Illinois Senate was considered newsworthy in eastern newspapers like this one:

Vol. IX. No. 14. Wednesday, April 5, 1843.

THE MORMONS.—In the locofoco [Democratic] Legislature of Illinois, on the 27th of February, the Senate repealed the law creating the Nauvoo Legion Military Corps, and also the charter of the City of Nauvoo. The locos having no longer any use for their support are about depriving them of those privileges which were granted to secure their votes. The vote in favor of repealing the city charter was 12 to 11. The members of the Senate expressed their disgust at Mormonism without reserve, and the probability is Smith will make another push westward before long, as he is not likely to get any further legislative support from the State of Illinois.

In the spring of 1843, Joseph Smith paid two visits to the Mormon settlement of Ramus, Illinois, located a few miles north and east of Carthage. Ramus boasted a population of around five hundred Mormons among a few other settlers. Here the doctrine of the eternity of marriage and family was taught to a number of the brethren. On his return, Joseph and his scribe, William Clayton, paid a visit to Judge Stephen A. Douglas at Carthage on May 18, 1843. Judge Douglas invited them to dine with him, and after dinner he requested that Joseph relate the history of the persecutions of the Saints while in Missouri, some of which he had heard in Orville Browning's testimony at Joseph's trial in Monmouth two years earlier. This Joseph did in great detail for the next three hours.[11]

He also gave an account of his visit to Washington in 1839 and his disappointing and unheeded appeals to President Martin Van Buren, Henry Clay, John C. Calhoun, Thomas Hart Benton, and others. Judge Douglas soon became well acquainted with all of these national leaders; unlike Lincoln, he won in his campaign for Congress later in 1843. Douglas was said to have listened with rapt attention and deprecated the conduct of Governor Boggs and his aids in Missouri. He said that any people who would do as the Missourians had done to the Latter-day Saints ought to be brought to judgment and punished.[12]

In the course of the conversation, President Smith abruptly changed the subject and uttered the following prophecy, which was recorded in William Clayton's journal:

> Judge, you will aspire to the presidency of the United States; and if ever you turn your hand against me or the Latter-day Saints, you will feel the weight of the hand of the Almighty upon you; and you will live to see and know that I have testified the truth to you; for the conversation of this day will stick to you through life.[13]

## MAGNANIMITY OF LINCOLN AND JOSEPH

Not a week after Joseph Smith and his Nauvoo friends left Springfield in January, John C. Bennett arrived there from Missouri. It is likely that he stopped by the Sangamo Journal office to offer more salacious disclosures on the Prophet, and he may have found Abraham Lincoln loitering there. Bennett arrived in Springfield with what he thought to big news. Francis had so completely fawned over Bennett's accusations a year earlier that he printed them ad nauseam. Bennett described his new scheme in a surprising letter to Sidney Rigdon and Orson Pratt dated January 10, 1843. Sent from Springfield, he detailed with a diabolical serenity his new plot to destroy the life of Joseph Smith:

> Dear Friends:—It is a long time since I have written you, and I should now much desire to see you; but I leave tonight for Missouri, to meet the messenger charged with the arrest of Joseph Smith, Hyrum Smith, Lyman Wight and others for murder, burglary, treason, etc., etc. . . . New proceedings have been gotten up on the old charges and no habeas corpus can then save them. We shall try Smith on the Boggs case when we get him to Missouri. The war goes bravely on, and although Smith thinks he is now safe, the enemy is near, even at the door. The Governor [Ford] will relinquish Joe up at once on the new requisition . . . He has awoke the wrong passenger.
>
> I hope that both of your kind and amiable families are well, and you will please to give them all my best respects. I hope to see you all soon. When the officer arrives I shall be near at hand.
>
> Yours respectfully,
>
> John C. Bennett[14]

Instead of rushing the news of this threat to the Prophet, Rigdon, Joseph's first counselor in the Presidency of the Church, delayed for some time before passing it to Orson Pratt. Pratt immediately disclosed it to President Smith. This led Pratt, the Prophet, and nearly all the rest of the Church leadership to question Sidney Rigdon's delay and his loyalty to Joseph Smith and the Church as a whole. Upon hearing of the letter and Rigdon's ostensible complicity with Bennett's design, John Taylor prepared an editorial on the letter's contents for the next issue of the Times and Seasons. Taylor took the piece to Joseph for his review. Joseph agreed with the accuracy of Taylor's treatment of the matter, but he advised the editor not to print it, knowing of the damage it would cause to the reputation of his longtime friend and counselor. Joseph concluded by saying, "I think you had better not [print it], we will save him if we can."[15]

President Lincoln had two similar occasions to censure others for errors, and it is interesting that he responded in a similar manner as Joseph Smith. At the conclusion of the battle of Gettysburg in July 1863, General George G. Meade sent Robert E. Lee's army retreating in disarray. Though Lincoln was grateful for the victory, he and his Secretary of War, Edwin Stanton, were deeply disappointed that Meade did not take advantage of the rare opportunity to capture Lee's retreating army, an action that Lincoln believed would have essentially ended the war. Lincoln was hesitant to condemn the General, but at Stanton's insistence, he allowed a letter of censure to be written to General Meade. In the letter, Lincoln allowed Stanton to detail their displeasure and the circumstances of the strength and position of Meade's forces in comparison to Lee's severely weakened ones. It truly was a rare opportunity to finish the great General Lee and end the war. But in the end, and to the utter dismay of Stanton, Lincoln would not allow the incensed Secretary of War to send the letter to Meade.

At the conclusion of the battle of Antietam, President Lincoln chose to pay a solemn visit to the battlefield in Northern Virginia. During the protracted years of the Civil War, the casualty counts and other challenges of his Presidency would weigh heavily on Lincoln. Often Lincoln would ask his bodyguard, Ward Hill Lamon, who had an appealing voice, to sing some of Lincoln's favorite funeral dirges, which comforted the war-weary President. On the way to Antietam, Lincoln again asked Lamon to sing. As was often the case, the song brought Lincoln to sad reflection and tears at the horrific and unrelenting casualty counts of dead and maimed young men and boys in the endless Civil War battles. En route to the Antietam battlefield, Lincoln openly wept in sadness for this and for the recent death of his own eleven–year-old son, Willie. Lamon, sensing the somber mood, thought to cheer the travelers with a well-known, lighthearted ditty.

During Lincoln's bid for reelection, the campaign team of General George McClellan twisted the story to discredit the President. They reported that Lincoln was in a laughing and lighthearted mood while passing over the hallowed battlefield and thus disrespected the tens of thousands who had fallen there. Their version was contrived and incorrect.[16] Lamon's ditty was sung hours and miles before they reached the battlefield. Lamon, like Stanton, was incensed at the misrepresentation, which took the country by storm. In the coming weeks, Lincoln bore intense criticism for the insensitivity but said nothing in his defense. Lamon insisted that a correction be issued to clarify the circumstance. Lincoln resisted, but Lamon and others pressed to the point that the President gave Lamon permission to write a clarifying document. Lincoln read the long and detailed account and concurred with its accuracy—and then ordered the stunned Lamon to throw it in the fire. With the stakes of reelection so high, one would think that Lincoln would defend his honor from the inaccurate accusations in the newspapers, but Lincoln was unyielding. He never addressed the matter and went on to defeat McClellan by a landslide.

In another surprising shift, Francis Simeon seemed to have cooled on John C. Bennett's bluster. He did not write what Bennett had hoped in his paper. In fact, Bennett's plot was not even news in Springfield. Joseph Smith had been apprised of it a week before Bennett's arrival by Governor Ford, who told Joseph that he had no intention of responding to the frivolous charges coming from Missouri. He and the people of Illinois were tiring of Bennett and Missouri's incessant and ridiculous harangue. Instead, Francis wrote the following article on the matter:

# Sangamo Journal.

Vol. XIII. Springfield, Illinois, January 12, 1843. No. 21.

We understand that another requisition will be made upon the Governor of this State for Joseph Smith, under the former indictments, which charge him with robbery, arson, treason, and murder. For this purpose the indictments referred to are to be reinstated. The requisitions will probably include many individuals. The affidavit under the last requisition was manifestly defective, but in this case, those concerned do not believe that any legal objection against the requisition can be made.

But when the new requisition for Joseph's arrest arrived, Governor Ford broke his promise to Joseph and issued yet another warrant for his arrest. Ford gave the warrant to Harmon Wilson, who was to accompany Sheriff Joseph Reynolds to apprehend Joseph. The day before Governor Ford issued the warrant, he incidentally mentioned his intentions to Judge James Adams. Adams immediately hired a messenger to rush the news to Joseph in Nauvoo, but Joseph was not in Nauvoo when he arrived.

Three days earlier, Joseph and Emma gathered their children for a joyous family outing, quite possibly the only family vacation of their lives. In the pleasant warmth of June, they took their carriage one hundred and seventy miles north to the community of Dixon, Illinois, to visit Emma's sister who had settled there. These were blissful moments for Joseph, Emma, and the children. They reveled in their time away from Joseph's responsibilities and cares in Nauvoo and focused entirely on one another. To the Smith children, for these few days, their father was all theirs. Soon after his arrival, Joseph received the urgent message from James Adams in Springfield that the state of Missouri had sent over a sheriff in yet another attempt to arrest him and take him to Missouri—on the same charges for which he had been acquitted in two previous court hearings and for which they had failed to convict him during his four-month confinement in Liberty.

William Clayton and Stephen Markham sped north to warn the Prophet, arriving before the Missouri sheriff. Upon their arrival with the news, Joseph thanked them for their sacrifice in his behalf, but he appeared to be unsurprised and free of concern over the matter. With an unexpected serenity, he told them to not be alarmed. "I have no fear, and shall not flee. I will find friends and the Missourians cannot slay me, I tell you in the name of Israel's God."[17] Joseph then instructed Markham and Clayton to not interfere.

An unknown informant apprised Reynolds and Wilson of the Smith family's location, and they nearly killed their horses in hard riding north. Once in Dixon, they presented themselves as Mormon

Elders inquiring as to the whereabouts of Joseph Smith and were readily directed to the home of Emma's sister. They arrived to find the families enjoying a pleasant meal together and asked to see "Brother Joseph."[18] As soon as Joseph stepped to the door he was presented with two cocked pistols at his chest and a string of oaths to kill him on the spot if he resisted. Joseph calmly replied:

> Kill me if you will, I am not afraid to die; and I have endured so much oppression that I am weary of life. But I am a strong man, and I could cast both of you down, if I would. If you have any legal process to serve, present it, for I am at all times subject to law and shall not offer resistance.[19]

They immediately rushed him to a wagon they had hired when Stephen Markham approached. Wilson and Reynolds warned him to stop or they would shoot, but Markham paid them no heed and continued, showing no fear until he secured the team by their bridles. He held them until Emma could bring him his coat and hat and bid him good-bye. It was a terrifying experience for Emma and the children, who watched helplessly through the windows as once again their father was taken, pistol-whipped, and threatened, though Joseph's assurance that he would be delivered comforted Emma. Joseph asked Markham to ride to Dixon for a writ of habeas corpus, because he was once again being arrested without cause. Markham found Sheriff Campbell in Dixon, who promptly rode to Joseph's aid.

This group rode into Dixon, where Joseph asked for a lawyer. When he came he was sent away at gunpoint by the kidnappers and not allowed to speak to Joseph. By this time, people were gathering in Dixon with the news that the Mormon prophet was in town and under arrest. Many observed Reynolds and Wilson's refusal to grant Joseph legal representation, and they began airing their displeasure at this unlawful action.

Early the next morning, the town was full of citizens unhappy at the actions of Reynolds and Wilson. Sheriff Reynolds yelled at the townspeople, "I want you to understand that this man is my legal prisoner, and you must disperse!" Whereupon a lame and bent old man named David Town wobbled with the support of his cane up to Reynolds and said, with the crowd listening in rapt attention:

You damned infernal puke, we'll learn you to come here and interrupt gentlemen. Sit down there, [pointing to a very low chair] and sit still. Don't you open your [mouth] till General Smith gets through talking. If you never learned manners in Missouri, we'll teach you that gentlemen are not to be imposed upon by a nigger-driver. You cannot kidnap men here. There's a committee in this grove that will sit on your case; and, sir, it is the highest tribunal in the United States, and *from its decision there is no appeal*.[20]

With Reynolds subdued at Town's rebuke, the spectators called for the Mormon prophet to preach a sermon, and while local authorities were deliberating on the case, Joseph spoke to them calmly and warmly on the subject of marriage for an hour and a half. By this time, lawyer Cyrus Walker was finally given access to the prisoner. Walker, like Lincoln, was running for office, and agreed to assist Joseph only if he could count on the Prophet's vote. Joseph gave his word and then recounted how he had been taken against his will by Wilson and Reynolds without being served any legal authorization. It was concluded by all (except Wilson and Reynolds) that Joseph would go before the nearest judge in Illinois, not directly to Missouri as his captors intended. So with Joseph in the custody of Reynolds and Wilson and they in custody of Sheriff Campbell, the curious group traveled together to the nearest judge to sort out the fiasco. The nearest judge happened to be Daniel H. Wells in Nauvoo—the last place Wilson and Reynolds wanted to take their prisoner. Wells was a resident of Commerce before the saints arrived, and he was called a "jack Mormon" like Alexander Doniphan in Missouri. At its inception, the term meant any sympathizer toward the Mormons.[21] Wells did join the Church three years after this event; he went west with them in 1846 and in later years became a counselor to President John Taylor.

As they set out, Joseph dispatched William Clayton to rush to Hyrum Smith in Nauvoo. When Hyrum heard the news, he interrupted the Sunday worship service and called the brethren to the newly constructed Masonic Hall for a meeting. He asked for volunteers to rush to the aid of their Prophet, and around three hundred stepped forward. Hyrum selected about half of them, and they sped off on horseback toward Dixon to meet the Prophet. By this time, Joseph had badly bruised sides from the continual prodding with pistol barrels.

His body displayed black and blue wounds for a circumference of 18 inches on both of his sides. He nearly fainted with the pain.[22]

While lodged at a farmhouse near Monmouth, Reynolds and Wilson were overheard planning to stir up a mob there to assist them in shuttling Joseph over the Mississippi to Missouri, avoiding the hearing in Nauvoo. Their scheme was reported to Sheriff Campbell, who promptly put an end to it. As they continued their southward journey, Reynolds and Wilson complained that they would never get out of Nauvoo alive. Upon hearing this, Joseph, in spite of their cruel mistreatment, calmly and kindly pledged to them that he would ensure that not a hair of their heads would be injured. At Joseph's direction, the Mormons did nothing to harm the two kidnappers. Soon the small traveling party was joined by portions of the posse from Nauvoo, which accompanied them the rest of the way.

By this time, Emma and her children were safely back in Nauvoo, their peaceful family outing interrupted by Joseph's enemies. About a mile north of Nauvoo, Hyrum, Emma, and a cavalcade of horsemen and carriages from Nauvoo met the entourage with a brass band to escort their Prophet back into the city. Joseph was brought his favorite horse, Old Charley, and with Emma riding at his side, Joseph led a triumphant entry before a crowd of thousands. Joseph's children ran to him, joyful that he had returned to them safely.

In anticipation of Joseph's arrival, Emma and the Relief Society prepared a banquet at the Smith home for the traveling party and Joseph's friends. In a display of remarkable magnanimity, Joseph invited Harmon Wilson and Joseph Reynolds to the banquet, sat them at the head of the table, and treated them as honored guests. In complete harmony with her husband, Emma, without a hint of resentment, courteously waited on the two ruffians who had violently torn her husband from her side and threatened his life.[23] It was a moving display of love for one's enemies as taught by Jesus in the Bible. As President, Abraham Lincoln would repeatedly demonstrate this same stirring forbearance and regard for his enemies as Joseph and Emma Smith did on this occasion.

Judge Wells later reviewed the case and promptly dismissed it as Judges Stephen A. Douglas and Nathaniel Pope had done previously.

That afternoon, Joseph addressed a crowd of thousands and gave thanks to God for his deliverance. He spoke in defense of their city charter and thanked the good and honest people of Dixon who had insisted that the law be followed in his case.[24]

In spite of Joseph's kindness and forbearance, Sheriff Reynolds bolted for Springfield and applied to Governor Ford for a posse to retake Joseph, claiming that the municipal court in Nauvoo had acted unlawfully in granting Joseph Smith his freedom. Governor Ford refused to grant Reynolds's petition. Subsequently, Governor Reynolds of Missouri demanded that Ford call out a militia to retake Joseph Smith. This Ford also refused to do, being satisfied that what had taken place in Nauvoo was proper and legal. These actions were taken after he had received complete copies of all the documents, Sheriff Reynolds's statements, and the report of an agent sent to Nauvoo to verify the truth of the matter. All demonstrated the matter had been handled judiciously, and, Ford refused to be pressured by Governor Reynolds.

In a later address to the people of Nauvoo, Joseph introduced them to his lawyer, Cyrus Walker, thanking him for his capable representation. Joseph informed the audience of his intent to vote for Walker for Congress.[25] Walker, a Whig, felt he would be well compensated for his efforts in representing Joseph Smith by receiving what he believed to be a full public endorsement from the Prophet for his people's votes. Joseph did vote as promised, but, to Walker's surprise, the majority of Nauvoo's residents voted for the Democrat Hoge—dispelling the charge that Joseph dictated how his followers should vote.[26]

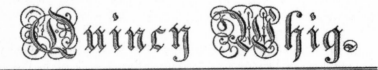

Bartlett & Sullivan. Quincy, Illinois, Wed., August 23, 1843. Vol. 6—No. 18.

The Election: In the Sixth district, it is probable that Hoge, the locofoco candidate, is elected by a few hundred votes. The Mormons have settled the question in this district.—The Rock River counties, with the exception of Lee, have given majorities for Walker, but not in sufficient numbers to offset the heavy Mormon vote.... The district is largely whig, but so little of a turn out was there, that Hardin's majority will not probably go over 800.

The election of 1843 revived the same political animosity and angst toward the Mormon bloc vote that had occurred in the past two elections. In the rest of the state, support for the Whigs and Democrats was generally divided equally, leaving the election's outcome in the hands of the Mormons. Once again, candidates like Walker sought their vote. This promised the same political repercussions as before; whichever candidate lost would blame their loss on the Mormons. Joseph Smith addressed this challenge by referring to the previous election in this way:

> With regard to elections, some say all the Latter-day Saints vote together and vote as I say. But I never tell any man how to vote, or who to vote for. But I will show you how we have been situated by bringing a comparison. Should there be a Methodist society here and two candidates running for office, one says, "If you will vote for me and put me in [as] Governor, I will exterminate the Methodists, take away their charters, etc." The other candidate says "If I am Governor, I will give all an equal privilege." Which would the Methodists vote for? Of course they would vote *en masse* for the candidate that would give them their rights.
>
> Thus it has been with us. Joseph Duncan said, if the people would elect him, he would exterminate the Mormons and take away their charters. As to Mr. Ford, he made no such threats, but manifested a spirit in his speeches to give every man his rights; hence the Church universally voted for Mr. Ford, and he was elected Governor.[27]

Despite this, the Mormons would once again feel the ire of election politics. The Democrats ceased upon the escapade of the Prophet's latest unlawful seizure to charge that the arrest was staged by the Whigs to pander the Mormon vote. Unless something dramatic was done, the saints knew that they would receive the brunt of the ire of whichever party lost the election.

# Quincy Whig.

Quincy, Illinois, Wed., July 19, 1843. Vol. 6—No.13.

The Herald of this city, follows in the wake of the State Register, in charging that the late arrest of Joseph Smith, "was a deep laid scheme, got up by the whig party for political effect." The whig party in this State must have an influence most astonishing truly, to have opperated upon such strong locos [Democrats] as stand at the head of the civil power in Missouri... The Herald gives an extract from an address, said to have been delivered at Springfield by Elder [James] Adams, a Mormon. The Sangamo Journal speaks of this address in the following terms:

MR. ADAMS' ADDRESS.—Mr. Adams, a Mormon Missionary, and a man of decided talent, recently delivered two addresses to our citizens from the door of the State House. The first was devoted to religious doctrines, and the second to Mormon persecutions. The last Register gives what it states to be a sketch of this last address, and puts language in the mouth of Mr. Adams which he never used. Mr. Adams did not mention the Sangamo Journal in his speech—he never asserted that the last arrest of Smith was the work of the whigs. The remarks published in the Register as coming from him on this subject, he never used. . . .

The Register makes Mr. Adams say that he approved of the conduct of the Governor in ordering the arrest of Smith. The Nauvoo paper takes a different view of this matter. All the movements in this affair—from the issuing of the writ, down to the false representations of the speech of Mr. Adams in the Register, show that it was got up by loco focos to effect the coming election. Our opponents can rarely suffer an election to be decided on the grounds of principles. They prefer to rely upon some trick—some scheme—for success.

Judge Adams's sermons on the steps of the State House indicate that his commitment to his religion had come a long way since his concealed membership three years earlier. He had managed to gain an appointment as a probate judge in Hancock County and was making preparations to leave Springfield to join his friends in Nauvoo. In the process of preparing for the move—and just days following his address at the State House—he contracted cholera and died on August 11, 1843, at the age of sixty. In spite of his many distinguished years in Springfield, he asked his family to bury his remains in the Pioneer Cemetery at Nauvoo, where his grave is marked to this day.

Even though Joseph returned from Washington D.C. deeply disappointed with President Martin Van Buren's unwillingness to assist the Mormons, he remained intent on pursuing compensation and justice for the extensive losses of life and property from the Missouri expulsion of 1838. With the approaching presidential election in 1843, Joseph Smith wrote a letter to each of the leading candidates for the Executive office: Henry Clay, John C. Calhoun, Lewis Cass, and Martin Van Buren.[28] He stated his views of the Constitutional rights that had so blatantly been denied the saints and asked each candidate his position, should they be elected, in pursuing justice for his oppressed followers.

Only Clay and Calhoun responded, and both cordially declined to intervene. Clay said that, if elected, he could not enter the presidency encumbered with promises or pledges to any portion of voters. Calhoun reminded Joseph Smith that his position had not changed since their conversations in Washington—redress for their losses remained a state matter, not a federal one. Joseph's impassioned rejoinder to Calhoun warned him that because of his and Congress's inaction against the violation of the saints' Constitutional rights, "God will come out of his hiding place and vex this nation with a sore vexation."[29] He then emphatically challenged Calhoun's positions by reminding him that, should a state like Missouri be guilty of insurrection or rebellion, "The President has as much power to repel it as Washington had to march against the whiskey boys of Pittsburg, or General Jackson had to send an armed force to suppress the rebellion of South Carolina"[30] twelve years earlier.

Twelve years had also passed since Joseph Smith's dramatic prophecy of an impending civil war, which was characterized as an expression of God's wrath and indignation over the suffering of His

271

saints and His avenging chastisement for the nation's sins. President Lincoln later characterized the war in very similar terms. And even though the war did not begin for another seventeen years, Joseph and his followers never wavered in their faith that God would pour out righteous judgment on the men and government who would not step forward to protect them.

The Prophet's response to Lincoln's political idol, Henry Clay, was no less fervent. Joseph exclaimed:

> When fifteen thousand free citizens were exiled from their own homes, lands and property . . . and you then upon your oath and honor occupying the exalted station of a Senator of Congress from the noble-hearted State of Kentucky, why did you not show the world your loyalty to law and order, by using all honorable means to restore the innocent to their rights and property?[31]
>
> . . . God will set a flaming sword to guard the tree of liberty while such mint-tithing Herods as Van Buren, Boggs, Benton, Calhoun and Clay are thrust out of the realms of virtue as fit subjects for the kingdom of the fallen.[32]

In spite of the Prophet's severe rebuke of Henry Clay's position, he later commented that of the pool presidential candidates, only his respect for Clay remained intact.

## JOSEPH SMITH ENTERS THE CAMPAIGN FOR PRESIDENT

Upon ascertaining that none of the presidential candidates would step forward in their defense, Church leaders began exploring other options. Meetings in Nauvoo sought ways to avoid the blame that would certainly be directed at them from the defeated political party. The more they discussed the matter, the more they warmed to the most dramatic of their options: nominating Joseph Smith as a candidate for the President of the United States. By doing so, they (and the rest of the country) could choose a candidate who was neither Whig nor Democrat. More importantly, it gave the Mormons a candidate for whom they could vote without be blamed for the defeat of the losing candidates. Joseph agreed to this solution and announced his candidacy, becoming the first Illinoisan in history to run for president. The news shocked the citizens of Illinois. It infuriated Joseph's enemies in Illinois and Missouri, but, remarkably, his candidacy was warmly received in many places across the country. He had essentially as much name recognition as did the other candidates. Even though his supporters knew from the beginning that Joseph's chances of success were remote, they developed an extensive national campaign strategy. Springfield's newspapers like the Democratic Illinois Register carried the announcement, which Lincoln was very likely to have read:

Vol. V. Springfield, Friday, February 16, 1844. No. 29.

PRESIDENTIAL.

The Nauvoo Neighbor of the 7th inst. contains the following paragraph:

"Who shall be our next President? Do you want to know? We will let it out soon. We have our eye upon the man and when the proper time comes we will publish it from "Dan to Beersheba," and then as American citizens, we will go to it with a rush."

The Neighbor has since announced Jos. Smith, the Mormon prophet, as its candidate.

Days later, the Illinois Register reported the following:

It appears by the Nauvoo papers that the Mormon prophet is actually a candidate for the Presidency. He has sent us his pamphlet, containing extracts of his principles . . . On these points he is much more explicit than Mr. Clay . . .

General Smith . . . comes right out in favor of a bank and a tariff, taking the true Whig ground, and ought to be regarded as the real Whig candidate for President, until Mr. Clay can so far recover from his shuffling and dodging as to declare his sentiments like a man.[33]

## CHAPTER ELEVEN ENDNOTES

1. Roy Basler, ed., *The Collected Works of Abraham Lincoln* (New Brunswick, NJ: Rutgers University Press, 1953), vol. 1, 297.

2. Ibid

3. Ruth Painter Randall, *Mary Lincoln: Biography of a Marriage* (Boston: Little, Brown, 1953), 66.

4. Ibid., 70.

5. Ibid.

6. Ibid., 91.

7. Ibid., 74.

8. Ibid., 73.

9. Basler, *Collected Works of Abraham Lincoln*, 320.

10. "Polygamy and the Church: A History," on The Mormons page, WGBH Educational Foundation, last modified April 1, 2014, http://www.pbs.org/mormons/peopleevents/e_polygamy.html.

11. B. H. Roberts, chap. 51, *Comprehensive History of the Church of Jesus Christ of Latter-day Saints* (n.p.: The Church and Deseret News Press, 1930), vol 2, 182 ff.

12. Ibid.

13. Taken from the daily Journal of William Clayton (the private secretary of President Smith, who was present at the interview described) as reported by B. H. Roberts, chap. 51, *Comprehensive History of the Church*, vol. 2, 182 ff.

14. Journal Histories, Church History Library, January 10, 1843.

15. Ibid.

16. Meg Thompson, posted on October 1, 2012, http://emergingcivilwar.com/2012/10/01/antietam-october-3-1862/.

17. George Q. Cannon, *Life of Joseph Smith the Prophet* (Salt Lake City, UT: Deseret Book, 1972), 444.

18. Ibid.

19. Ibid., 445.

20. Ibid., 447.

21. "Daniel H. Wells," Wikipedia, last modified January 26, 2014, http://en.wikipedia.org/wiki/Daniel_H._Wells, 1.

22. George Q. Cannon, *Life of Joseph Smith the Prophet* (Salt Lake City, UT: Deseret Book, 1972), 451.

23. Ibid., 452.

24. Ibid.

25. B. H. Roberts, The Rise and Fall of Nauvoo (repr., Provo, UT: Maasai, 2001), 228.

26. Ibid., 232–42.

27. "History of Joseph Smith," in *The Latter-day Saints' Millennial Star* (Liverpool: Asa Calkin, 1859), 668.

28. Roberts, *The Rise and Fall of Nauvoo*, 273–389.

29. Ibid., 377.

30. Ibid., 378.

31. Joseph Smith, *Views of the Powers and Policy of the Government of the United States* (repr., Heber City, UT: Archive Publishers, 2000), 38.

32. Roberts, *The Rise and Fall of Nauvoo*, 383.

33. Cannon, *Life of Joseph Smith*, 550.

# "HAVE WE NOT HAD A PROPHET AMONG US?"

## Daily National Intelligencer,

Washington: Tuesday, July 11, 1843.

THE CITY OF NAUVOO.

Few, we suspect, are aware of the rapid growth and present condition of the city of Nauvoo, the Jerusalem of the Latter Day Saints. Notwithstanding but four years have elapsed since the Mormons first made a settlement there, it is estimated that it already numbers from 16,000 to 17,000 inhabitants; and accessions are daily made to the population from the Eastern States and from Europe. The Burlington Gazette, from which we gather these facts, says:

"It is situated at one of the most beautiful points on the river, and is improving with a rapidity truly astonishing. Many of the houses are built in fine style, evincing wealth as well as taste. The Temple, which is destined to be the most magnificent structure in the West, is progressing rapidly, and will probably be completed in the course of the present and succeeding summer. Its style of architecture is entirely original—unlike any thing in the world, or in the history of the world—but is at the same time chaste and elegant. It is said to be the conception of the Prophet, Gen. Smith. It is being built by the voluntary labor of the members of the church, who devote a certain number of days in the year to the work. If the labor and materials were estimated at cash prices it is supposed that the building would cost something like a million of dollars."

In January 1844, Lincoln was finally in a position to purchase a home for Mary and five-month-old Robert. On January 16, he signed a purchase agreement for the home of Episcopal minister Charles Dresser with the understanding that they would take occupancy in April. This was the same home in which he and Mary had planned to be quietly married fourteen months earlier. Bank records show the Lincolns withdrawing funds from their family account in April to purchase furniture and yard implements for their new home. Lincoln did not travel the spring circuit that year until April. Instead, he campaigned in behalf of his candidate, Henry Clay, in nearby towns. Lincoln, Baker, Logan, and Stuart were making speeches nearly every night at various precincts in the County to large, enthusiastic audiences.

Lincoln and his fellow campaigners would have read the following announcement with surprise in the *Sangamo Journal*:

# 𝕾𝖆𝖓𝖌𝖆𝖒𝖔  𝕵𝖔𝖚𝖗𝖓𝖆𝖑.

Vol. XIII. Springfield, Ill., February 29, 1844. No. 29.

Gen. Joseph Smith, of the Nauvoo Legion, is announced in the Nauvoo paper as a candidate for President of the United States. We also hear it stated that General Hyram Smith will be a candidate for Congress for the sixth district.

By 1844, many newspapers throughout the country continued reporting the unending saga of the Mormons and their remarkable city, and none was more captivated with the tale than Washington's *Daily National Intelligencer*. They followed the real-life drama of the Mormon's taking place a thousand miles to their west with an unwavering interest.

To the surprise and approval of the Illinois Mormons, at least one of their neighboring town's newspapers formally endorsed Joseph Smith's candidacy for president. *The Politician* of Belleville, Illinois, located just across the Mississippi River from St. Louis, posted the following:

# THE POLITICIAN

Vol. I. Belleville, Illinois, April 13, 1844. No. 1.

Our paper being entirely free and independent of any sect, clique or party, we of course have the glorious privilege, of consulting our own individual judgement and preferences as to the men whom we will support for office. We shall not be whimsical, however, in our choice of candidates; nor present to the public the name of any man for office who is not fully convinced of his own fitness for the place; as the following ticket will show.

For President, Gen. JOE SMITH, OF NAUVOO. For Vice President, JAMES GORDON BENNETT, of the New York Herald.

. . . A few words in behalf of our candidates. Since it has been ascertained that Captain Tyler [incumbent John Tyler] can beat Mr. Van Buren, or Mr. Clay, or both of them together, it has occurred to us that Joe Smith is the only individual who would stand even a tolerable chance of success against the Captain, to whom, be it understood we are decidedly opposed. That Joe is qualified for the place will be evident to any one who will read with attention his recent address to the people of New Hampshire.

His availability will hardly be questioned when it is considered with what unexampled rapidity he has risen in fame and notoriety, within the last five years, while his well-known spiritual zeal precludes all doubt of his moral fitness for any political station to which he has any prospect of attaining.

James Gordon Bennett. We think there is a peculiar propriety in running this gentleman for vice President on the same ticket with Joe Smith. The only plausible objection to Smith is the fact that his hitherto exclusive devotion to spiritual concerns may lead him to give the affairs of our Government a little too much of a religious turn, resulting in a virtual union of Church and State. This result, however, will be effectually guarded against by investing Bennett with the second office in the Government.

# THE POLITICIAN

Vol. I. Belleville, Illinois, April 20, 1844. No. 2.

. . . PUBLISHED EVERY NOW AND THEN BY F. A. SNYDER &Co. . . .

For President, Gen. JOE SMITH, OF NAUVOO. For Vice President, JAMES GORDON BENNETT, of the New York Herald.

. . . All persons in favor of Joseph Smith, jr., Lieutenant commander of the Nauvoo Legion, and Chief of the Latter Day Saints, for President, are requested to meet in all the States of the Union, for the purpose of appointing delegates to the Smith Convention, to be held in Nauvoo, on the first Monday of November next.

JOSEPH SMITH
JAMES G. BENNETT
SIDNEY RIGDON
ELAM RUST,
Smith Central Committee of the United States

> JOE SMITH.—A gentleman has furnished us with a pamphlet of 12 pages, entitled, "Gen. Joseph Smith's views of the powers and policy of the Government of the United States," printed at Nauvoo. Joe appears to have become the incarnate representative of Church and State united, and . . . he obtains a considerable number of servile followers.

Now the most controversial presidential candidate of 1844, Joseph Smith's campaign supporters encouraged him to write and distribute his political platform. A pamphlet entitled *General Smith's Views of the Powers and Policy of the Government of the United States*, in which Joseph explained his views in uninhibited detail and candor, was sent to newspapers throughout the country, including those in Springfield. It is very likely that Lincoln, in one of his casual visits with editor and friend Simeon Francis at the *Sangamo Journal* office, would have not only seen the pamphlet but would have read and discussed its contents with interest.

# Sangamo Journal.

Vol. XIII. Springfield, Ill., April 4, 1844. No. 34.

### THE GLOBE AND JOE SMITH.

The Globe has a long article, attacking Joe Smith's "views of government," as lately published by him in the Nauvoo paper.—The real cause for this attack, we presume, may be found in the fact, that Smith does not choose to buckle on his armor, and support Martin Van Buren for President.

The following paragraph and quotation from Smith's "views," we copy from the Globe. If Joe never misses the truth more than in the quotation here made, he will get along quite well.

(From the Globe)
"We cannot refrain from treating our readers to the following glowing passage in which our friend Joseph so eloquently describes

the defeat of Mr. Van Buren. We have read nearly all the whig slants on this same subject; and we have met with nothing equal to the gloomy grandeur of this portentous paragraph:

"'At the age, then, of sixty years, our blooming republic began to decline, under the withering touch of Martin Van Buren. Trouble, vexation, perplexity and contention, mingled with hope, fear, and murmuring, rumbled through the Union, and agitated the whole nation, as would an earthquake at the centre of the earth, heaving the sea beyond its bounds, and shaking the everlasting hills. So, in hopes of better times, while jealousy, hypocritical pretesions, and pompous ambition were luxuriating on the ill-gotten spoils of the people, they rose in their majesty, like a tornado, and swept through the land, till Gen. [William Henry] Harrison appeared as a star among the storm-clouds, for better weather.'"

Lincoln's move to 8th Street and Jackson was not the only move he made in early 1844. He probably studied Joseph Smith's *Views* document in his new law office on the third floor of the Tinsley Building—one floor above the courtroom where Joseph Smith was acquitted. Lincoln probably liked what he read.[1] Here Lincoln amicably ended his partnership with Stephen Logan to launch out on his own as senior partner with the much younger William Herndon. These two practiced in the Tinsley building for the next nine years.

Lincoln continued his voracious reading of current events through various newspapers. William Herndon later lamented having to endure Lincoln's daily morning routine of entering the law office with a newspaper (or several) under his arm and heading straight for the couch. He would lie on the couch with one leg straddled over the back of it and commence to read the entire newspaper *aloud*. After some years, Herndon gathered the courage to ask Lincoln why he insisted in reading the paper aloud, to which his senior partner replied that by reading aloud he could retain in memory a much larger portion of the news.[2] Whether Lincoln sensed Herndon's frustration with the daily practice or not is unknown; what is known is that Lincoln continued this routine for the full eighteen years of their partnership. In the late 1850s, with the secession movement gaining traction, he even subscribed to the Charleston Mercury, the most strident voice for secession out of South Carolina, to stay abreast of developments there.[3]

## TIME AND ETERNITY

Like most Whigs, Lincoln was unhappy with Martin Van Buren's performance in the White House. Lincoln might have been intrigued to know that he had a famous ally in Joseph Smith's opposition to Van Buren's re-election. There are indications that the first line in Joseph Smith's *Views* must have immediately caught Lincoln's attention. Joseph wrote, "I ever feel a double anxiety for the happiness of all men, both in time and eternity."[4] "Happiness for all men" is clearly meant to include slaves, free blacks, and persons of all races in America. In that day, many were against slavery but not in favor of equality for blacks. Stephen A. Douglas, in his debates with Lincoln during the 1850s, often asserted the generally Democratic position that the white race was superior to all others and that Constitutional rights were reserved for whites only.

In the midst the 1860 secession movement, Alexander H. Stephens, the new Vice President of the Confederate States, declared in a speech in Savannah that the new confederate Constitution "has put at rest *forever* all the agitating questions relating to . . . the proper status of the negro in our form of civilization."[5] Then, referring to the Founding Fathers who believed that slavery was morally, socially, and politically wrong, he contended that they were the ones fundamentally wrong in their assessment of slavery:

> They rested upon the assumption of the equality of races. This was an error. . . . Our new Government is founded upon exactly the opposite idea; its foundations are laid, its cornerstone rests, upon the truth that the negro is not equal to the white man; that slavery, subordination to the superior race, is his natural and moral condition.[6]

In the first paragraph of *Views*, Lincoln observed that Joseph embraced the same unpopular position as he: that all men were created equal in the sight of God. He would probably have been astonished to know that the rest of Joseph Smith's political platform was nearly identical to the principles and beliefs that he would take to the White House sixteen years later.

The last phrase of the first paragraph, "time and eternity," is very much a Latter-day Saint phrase. It comes from the temple marriage ceremony, which Mormons believe opens the door to marriage and family relationships that extend on beyond death and into the eternities. One wonders if Lincoln's "Love is Eternal" engraving on the inside of Mary's wedding ring may have been influenced by this Mormon doctrine. It is likely that Lincoln was introduced to this phrase by Katherine Mulliner or other Springfield Mormons; the construction of the Nauvoo Temple was a hot topic throughout the state long before Joseph's *Views* was published.

Without a doubt, the phrase remained with him throughout his life; Lincoln repeated it at least twice during his Presidency. During his second State of the Union address in 1862, Lincoln said, "In times like the present, men should utter nothing for which they would not willingly be responsible through time and in eternity."[7] The other mention occurred during his run for re-election in 1864. Some constituents had warned him more than once that to win the election he would need to rescind his highly controversial Emancipation Proclamation. To one, he responded that although he may be a slow walker, he did not walk backwards.[8] The proclamation would remain in place. To another he resolutely replied that he feared he would be damned for time and eternity[9] should he ever attempt to rescind what he believed God had guided him to establish.

## POLITICAL ALLIES

Throughout the world, the name of Abraham Lincoln is associated with freeing the slaves in America. Although Abraham Lincoln and Joseph Smith were certainly not alone in their disdain for slavery, they were profoundly yet separately united in their personal pursuits for its termination. Deepening this unknown unity of purpose between Lincoln and Joseph was the fact that both were driven to end slavery by their unwavering conviction that God himself was offended and angered by the reprehensible practice, that it was evil and that it was wrong. Both repeatedly avowed that slavery should be abolished to ensure that the gates of hell not prevail against this nation. Just one year earlier, Joseph Smith affirmed his confidence in the eventual fulfillment of his prophesy on the division of this nation and subsequent civil war, which he declared eleven years earlier. His reaffirmation in April 1843 is recorded in Doctrine and Covenants Section 130, verses 12 and13:

> I prophesy, in the name of the Lord God, that the commencement of the difficulties which will cause much bloodshed previous to the coming of the Son of Man will be in South Carolina. It may probably arise through the slave question. This a voice declared to me, while I was praying earnestly on the subject, December 25th, 1832.

Just a month before his assassination, President Lincoln told an Indiana Regiment of Union soldiers who were passing through Washington that:

> I have always thought that all men should be free; but if any should be slaves it should be first those who desire it for *themselves*, and secondly those who *desire* it for *others*. Whenever [I] hear any one, arguing for slavery I feel a strong impulse to see it tried on him personally.[10]

In his platform, Joseph Smith put forth an explicit and logical strategy for ending the two-hundred-year-old blight of slavery in America:

> Petition also, ye goodly inhabitants of the slave states, your legislators to abolish slavery by the year 1850, or now, and save the abolitionist from reproach and ruin, infamy and shame. Pray Congress to pay every man a reasonable price for his slaves out of the surplus revenue arising from the sale of public lands . . . Break off the shackles from the poor black man, and hire him to labor like other human beings; for "an hour of virtuous liberty on earth, is worth a whole eternity of bondage!"[11]

It is a well-known fact that President Lincoln embraced this same strategy of compensated emancipation, but it is not known just when or how he adopted the position or if he was influenced by Joseph Smith's solution. Early into his presidency, he proposed it as an alternative to war and got very little support. Then, in his final Cabinet meeting on his last day alive, he once again appealed to his Cabinet to support a measure that would offer the Southern slave owners compensation for their freed slaves through the sale of public lands, just as Joseph Smith had proposed in 1844. His Cabinet flatly refused, and Lincoln acquiesced, knowing that the public in the North would never accept such a compassionate offering to their vanquished Southern opponents. A cogent argument can be made that, had America's leaders and public accepted Joseph and Lincoln's policy of compensated emancipation, the nation could have avoided the Civil War. This notion lends credence to both of their prophetic assertions that the war was God's chastisement for the sins of the nation.

As Lincoln read on in *Views*, he discovered that he had an ally in supporting a national bank. Joseph Smith wrote, "Let Congress show their wisdom by granting a national bank, with branches in each state and territory . . . banks shall never issue any more bills than the amount of capital stock in her vaults and the interest . . . and leave the people's money in their pockets."[12]

The Mormon prophet's next statement is also intriguing: "Abolish the practice in the army and navy of trying men by court martial for desertion; if a soldier or marine runs away, send him his wages, with this instruction, that *his country will never trust him again; he has forfeited his honor*."[13] During the war, President Lincoln infuriated his Generals and Secretary of War Edwin Stanton by frequently pardoning soldiers who were to be executed for desertion. All such orders had to be personally approved by the President. Stanton and Union generals warned Lincoln that such acts of compassion did not belong in a war and would only serve to weaken the army. Lincoln pardoned the deserters anyway.

Joseph Smith next revealed his reverence for the Declaration of Independence and his alarm at America's current state of affairs:

> My cogitations like Daniel's, have for a long time troubled me, when I viewed the condition of men throughout the world, and more especially in this boasted realm, where the Declaration of Independence "holds these truths to be self evident; that all men are created

equal: that they are endowed by their Creator, with certain unalienable rights; that among these are life, liberty, and the pursuit of happiness," but at the same time, some two or three millions of people are held as slaves for life, because the spirit of them is covered with a darker skin than ours.[14]

In his debate with Stephen A. Douglas in Peoria, Illinois, Lincoln expressed a remarkably similar view. He lamented:

This *declared* indifference, but as I must think, covert *real* zeal for the spread of slavery, I can not but hate. I hate it because of the monstrous injustice of slavery itself. I hate it because it deprives our republican example of its just influence in the world—enables the enemies of free institutions, with plausibility, to taunt us as hypocrites—causes the real friends of freedom to doubt our sincerity, and especially because it forces so many really good men amongst ourselves into an open war with the very fundamental principles of civil liberty—criticising the Declaration of Independence, and insisting that there is no right principle of action but *self-interest*.[15]

Because of this widespread erosion of the basic principles of republican freedom, both Joseph Smith and Abraham Lincoln fearfully foresaw the impending wrath of God Himself, should the nation not return to its original roots. Lincoln continued his exhortation at Peoria:

"In those days, our Declaration of Independence was held sacred by all, and thought to include all; but now, to aid in making the bondage of the negro universal and eternal, it is assailed, and sneered at, and construed, and hawked at, and torn, till, if its framers could rise from their graves, they could not at all recognize it."[16]

But the most compelling and unique thread binding these two presidential prophets together was their prophetic warning to the American people that calamity would befall them if they did not turn from their unrighteous, anarchistic ways and end their unrelenting offences toward the God who gave them the treasure of a democratic republic. On April 26, 1832, Joseph Smith recorded the following prophetic warning, now canonized in Doctrine and Covenants Section 82, verses 2 and 4:

> But verily I say unto you, beware from henceforth, and refrain
> from sin, lest sore judgments fall upon your heads. . . . And inasmuch
> as ye keep not my sayings, which I give unto you, ye become trans-
> gressors; and justice and judgment are the penalty which is affixed
> unto my law.

As President, Abraham Lincoln issued eleven proclamations to
the American people in which he boldly and emphatically called
them to repentance. In nine of them, he called for national days of
fasting and prayer. His first proclamation was issued just five months
after his election. It said, in part:

> And where as it is fit and becoming in all people, at all times,
> to acknowledge and revere the supreme government of God; to bow
> in humble submission to his chastisements; to confess and deplore
> their sins and transgressions, in the full conviction that the fear of
> the Lord is the beginning of wisdom; and to pray with all fervency
> and contrition for the pardon of their past offenses, and for a blessing
> upon their present and prospective action.[17]

Joseph Smith does nothing to conceal that, in the unlikely event
that he should be placed in the White House, he, like his fellow
prophet-president, would rely on the righteous arm of the Almighty
God for guidance:

> Wherefore, were I the president of the United States, by the
> voice of a virtuous people, I would honor the old paths of the vener-
> ated fathers of freedom: I would walk in the tracks of the illustrious
> patriots, who carried the ark of the government upon their shoulders
> with an eye single to the glory of the people; and when that people
> petitioned to abolish slavery in the slave states, I would use all honor-
> able means to have their prayers granted.[18]
>
> Now, oh! people! people! turn unto the Lord and live; and
> reform this nation. Frustrate the designs of wicked men.[19]

## YET ANOTHER APPEAL TO CONGRESS

In February 1844, Joseph's journal entry records, "I instructed the
Twelve Apostles to send out a delegation, and investigate the location
of California and Oregon, and hunt out a good location, where we can
remove to, after the temple is completed."[20] The terms *California* and

*Oregon* were the general terms then used by nearly all to refer to the entire unsettled area of the west. A number of men readily volunteered for the assignment.

The Twelve apostles also assigned Orson Pratt, John E. Page, and Orson Hyde to go to Washington D.C. with a memorial asking Congress to authorize Joseph Smith to raise a company for the purpose of establishing American colonies in the unsettled portions of the West to counteract those being established by Mexico and Russia. Hyde, Pratt, and Page were warmly received by three new Congressmen from Illinois: Joseph Hoge, whom the Mormons had supported in his bid for the House of Representatives, John J. Hardin, and Stephen A. Douglas.

Lincoln's friend John Hardin, also a Whig, won the seat for which Lincoln and Edward Baker had run. But even though Lincoln was defeated, he used the 1843 campaign to devise a strategy that would propel him to office at a later date. He managed to extract an agreement between the three Whig friends that, if elected, each would serve only one two-year term and then return to Illinois to support the other two. His strategy worked just as he had designed it. The ever-magnanimous Lincoln willingly allowed his friends to pursue the office before him. Baker, with the support of Lincoln and Hardin, replaced Hardin in 1845. In 1847, Hardin and Baker backed Lincoln, who took his place in the House of Representatives for his one and only two-year term. In the years to come, Lincoln's inimitable talent of alliance-building would be a factor in his remarkable and surprising victory over Stephen A. Douglas for President.

Douglas's political career in Washington was another matter. Having received many votes from the Mormons, he was serving his first year in Congress in 1844, but he would spend the rest of his life in Washington as a Congressman, Senator, and presidential nominee in 1860, to become one of the most powerful politicians in U. S. history.

A few days after the Apostles' first meeting with the Illinois delegation, another freshman Congressman from Illinois joined his fellow Congressmen in representing the Mormon's colonization initiative. His name was John Wentworth, the Democratic Congressman from Chicago. Two years earlier, as the editor of the *Chicago Democrat*, he had asked Joseph Smith to write him an account of the Church's origin and beliefs. Joseph obliged, writing a document that included thirteen concise statements on the beliefs of the Latter-day Saints, today canonized as the Articles of Faith. Wentworth later became an admirer of Abraham Lincoln. In 1860, even as a Democrat, Wentworth served as an influential member of Lincoln's Republican presidential campaign committee—in spite of the fact that his friend and fellow Illinoisan Stephen A. Douglas was the Democratic nominee.

Stephen A. Douglas procured a recent map of the West and a report by John C. Fremont that he apparently borrowed from Thomas Hart Benton. He gave these to Orson Hyde to pass along to Joseph Smith. Hyde wrote to Joseph, explaining, "The people are so eager for [the book] here that they have stolen it out of the library. . . . I was not to tell anyone in the city where I got it. The book is a most valuable document to any one contemplating a journey to Oregon."[21] Douglas wanted Joseph Smith to have the valuable resource and promised to meet with him in Illinois to share additional information on California that might by of interest. Douglas's willingness to once again aid the Mormons, this time in Washington, witnesses his sincere motives and friendship.

But just as before, when Joseph Smith had personally appealed to Congress in 1839 through John Todd Stuart, too few legislators were willing to stake their political careers on helping the Mormons. Missouri Senator Thomas Hart Benton was, once again, an ardent opponent to any assistance for the Mormons. No authorization was granted by Congress to assist them in a western migration, even though such a course of action would have been a welcome solution to nearly all. If the Mormons were to embark on an exodus to safety in the west, no support would be extended from the government. They would have to go it alone.

As divulged in his solitary conversation with Jonathan Browning in Quincy some five years back, Lincoln was constantly yet silently evaluating events where he heard the sounds of little things breaking, and saw big things bending dangerously near to the breaking point. His quiet observations of the years of open and unabated persecutions of the Mormons now taking place in his own state must have resounded in his mind as a dangerous breaking of the Constitutional standard of peace, order and individual rights conceived through the inspiration of the Almighty God by the Founding Fathers. Here he admitted to Browning, "Fact is, I'm so worried that I have nightmares, and not all of them when I'm asleep. I get plain scared to death when I look a few years ahead."[22]

He looked ahead with dread that greedy men might break the country in two. "That would be a welding job! It would need the fires of the inferno for the forge. And where is the anvil? Where is the hammer? Where is the blacksmith?"[21] He feared that anvil would be set before him, the hammer placed in his hand and he would be the promised blacksmith. This was reaffirmed just days before the 1860 presidential election when Lincoln told New York newspaperman Henry Villard, "Mary insists, however that I am going to be Senator and President of the United States, too."[24]

The Confederacy's defiant firing on Fort Sumter in April 1861 opened a calamity upon this nation that, as warned by Lincoln and Joseph, would be unleashed from the gates of hell. It descended upon essentially every living soul living in the states, North and South; it came in the form of a war that both Lincoln and Joseph had predicted would come as a result of a blessed people that had forgotten God. Their proclamations of God's eminent retribution were regarded by most as dross and religious extremism. But while these documented prophetic warnings of both presidential prophets have been ignored by countless historians and secularists, their historical accuracy cannot be denied.

During his stirring 1858 campaign for the US Senate against Stephen A. Douglas, Lincoln repeatedly elaborated on this scriptural theme saying that the agitation and division over slavery:

> Has not only, *not ceased*, but has *constantly augmented*. In *my* opinion, it *will* not cease, until a *crisis* shall have been reached, and passed. "A house divided against itself cannot stand." I believe that this government cannot endure, permanently half *slave* and half *free*. I do not expect the Union to be *dissolved*—I do not expect the house to *fall*—but I do expect it will cease to be divided. It will become *all* of one thing, or *all* the other.[25]

In another of his of debates with Douglas, Lincoln quoted Thomas Jefferson to describe his irrepressible foreboding of an approaching national crisis: "he trembled for his country when he remembered that God was just."[26] Lincoln then declared, "There was danger to this country—danger of the avenging justice of God."[27] Then referring to the growing support for secession, he declared that "those who did so braved the arm of Jehovah—that when a nation thus dared the Almighty, every friend of that nation had cause to dread his wrath."[28] During these debates, Stephen A. Douglas acknowledged that Lincoln was a capable and honest opponent, but he painted Lincoln's position as:

> Advocat[ing] boldly and clearly a war of sections, a war of the North against the South, of the free States against the slave States—a war of extermination—to be continued relentlessly until the one or the other shall be subdued.[29]

Of course, Douglas's attempt to discredit Lincoln for what he and many others believed to be foolish predictions later became proof of Lincoln's foresight—to the colossal misfortune of his fellow Americans who chose not to heed his warnings.

## I See the Storm Coming

During Lincoln's presidential election campaign, Springfield offered their favorite son an office on the second floor of the State House next to Newton Bateman, Superintendent of Schools for Illinois. The campaign brought in a constant flow of people and correspondence, and when Lincoln needed a rest, he often closed his office door, opened the door to Bateman's adjoining offices, and invited him over for a conversation. Eventually, Bateman became one of the select few with whom Lincoln disclosed his innermost thoughts on God. Bateman believed, like most others, that Lincoln was a man of little or no faith and was surprised when Lincoln's conversation turned to faith. Bateman observed that:

> Everything he said was of a peculiarly deep, tender, and righteous tone, and was all tinged with a touch of melancholy. He repeatedly referred to his conviction that the day of wrath was at hand, and

that he was to be an actor in the terrible struggle . . . He repeated passages in the Bible, and seemed especially impressed with the solemn grandeur of portions of Revelation, describing the wrath of Almighty God.[30]

After further reference to Lincoln's belief in God and God's involvement with the history of mankind, Bateman records that Lincoln turned the conversation to his profound dependence upon prayer. He told Bateman of his conviction that statesmen everywhere had a duty to seek God's guiding hand. Accordingly he had and would continue to rely on the Father in Heaven during his presidency.

Bateman then disclosed his surprise at Lincoln's heartfelt expressions of Deity, saying, "I had not supposed that you were accustomed to think so much on this class of subject; certainly your friends generally are ignorant of the sentiments you have expressed to me."[31] To which Lincoln gave the curious reply, "I know they are. I am obliged to appear different to them; but I think more on these subjects than upon all others, and I have done so for years, and I am willing that you should know it."[32]

Some two weeks before the election, Lincoln acquired the results of an unofficial canvass of the residents of Springfield in which they had declared their votes for president. Drawing Bateman to his side, Lincoln said, "Let us look over this book. I wish particularly to see how the ministers of Springfield are going to vote."[33] By this time, Lincoln was sure that he would be chosen for the office. In the book *Abraham Lincoln, Man of God*, John Wesley Hill describes the scene this way:

> As the leaves were turned, one by one, Mr. Lincoln frequently asked if this one or that one were not a minister, or an elder, or a member of such and such a church, and sadly expressed his surprise on receiving an affirmative answer. After they had gone through the book, Lincoln closed it and regarded in silence for some moments a pencil memorandum which lay before him. At length he turned to Mr. Bateman, his face full of sadness, and said:
>
> Here are twenty-three ministers of different denominations, and all of them are against me, but three. And there are a great many prominent members of churches, a very large majority of whom are against me. Mr. Bateman, I am not a Christian; God knows I would

be one, but I have carefully read the Bible and I do not so understand this Book (drawing from his bosom a pocket New Testament). These men well know [he continued] that I am for freedom [of slaves] in the territories, freedom everywhere as far as the Constitution and laws will permit, and my opponents are for slavery. They know this, and yet, with this Book in their hands, in the light of which human bondage cannot live a moment, they are going to vote against me. I do not understand it at all.[34]

It must be understood that Lincoln and most of America referred to the Protestant religions as the "Christian" churches. Of course, Lincoln had not united himself with any of these denominations, but there are many quotations like this one that have been misinterpreted to mean that he was not a believer in the Christian God, which is far from accurate.

When Lincoln said he was "not a Christian," he simply meant that he worshiped his God in a way that was different from the Protestant religions of his time. It clearly did not mean that he lacked faith in the Jehovah of the Old Testament or Jesus Christ of the New. On the contrary, Lincoln's religious convictions ran so deep in his soul, and he was so sure of his own interpretations of scripture, that he could not allow himself to compromise them to join a church. This aloofness from organized religion caused him countless difficulties in his personal and private life, as seen by the many ministers who were unwilling to support a candidate whom they all knew and with whom they shared their community.

Lincoln continued his contemplation on the matter of the ministers' choices as if he had forgotten that Bateman remained at his side. Eventually, he slowly rose to his feet, and Bateman saw that his cheeks were wet with tears. Lincoln continued his deep introspection, pacing back and forth across the room until, with a trembling voice addressed as much to himself as to Newton Bateman, Lincoln said:

> I know there is a God, and that He hates injustice and slavery.
> I see the storm coming, and I know that His hand is in it. If He has
> a place and work for me, and I think He has, I believe I am ready.
> I am nothing, but truth is everything. I know I am right, because I
> know that liberty is right, for Christ teaches it, and Christ is God.

I have told them that a house divide[d] against itself cannot stand, and Christ and reason say the same, and they [the ministers] will find it so. [Steven A.] Douglas don't care whether slavery is voted up or down, but God cares and humanity cares, and I care, and with God's help, I shall not fail. I may not see the end, but it will come, and I shall be vindicated, and these men [the ministers] will find that they have not read their Bible aright.[35]

After another pause, Lincoln continued, this time directly to Bateman:

Doesn't it appear strange that men can ignore the moral aspects of this contest? A revelation could not make it plainer to me that slavery or the Government must be destroyed. The future would be something awful, as I look at it, but for this rock on which I stand (alluding to the Testament which he held in his hand) especially with the knowledge of how these ministers are going to vote. It seems to me as if God had borne with this thing, slavery, until the very teachers of religion have come to defend it from their Bible and to claim for it a divine character and sanction, and now the cup of iniquity is full and the vial of wrath will be poured out.[36]

Protestant writer John Wesley Hill shared his own conviction regarding Lincoln's Divine calling to guide America through its refining fire of war:

When he spoke for the Nation he so loved, his lips were as though touched with a live coal from the alter. He seemed to be of the same fibre with the prophets of Holy Writ and it may be said, without irreverence, that he was a "priest after the order of Melchi-sedec, without beginning or end of days," combining the kingly and priestly functions essential to the service of his Nation and his time.[37]

Later Mormon prophets Heber J. Grant[38] and Reed Smoot both referred to Lincoln's prophetic role saying that he was raised up by God to save the Union and the Constitution and that his unwavering faith in God made him a prophet and a seer.

## CHAPTER TWELVE ENDNOTES

1. Lincoln Law Office Museum, Springfield, IL.

2. William H. Herndon and Jesse W. Weik, *Herndon's Life of Lincoln*, (Cleveland: Fine Editions Press, 1949), 268.

3. *The Home Front*, 175, http://books.google.com/books?id=NdoiAQA AQBAJ&pg=PA175&lpg=PA175&dq=Abraham+Lincoln+subscribe s+to+the+Charleston+Mercury&source=bl&ots=j5VuAzDqbH&sig =qUGqRZvgSwBg5iOJGfHckuF-B_U&hl=en&sa=X&ei=AO44U-rXJ6aIygGUiICoBg&ved=0CD0Q6AEwAg#v=onepage&q=Abraham%20Lincoln%20 subscribes%20to%20the%20Charleston%20Mercury&f=false.

4. Joseph Smith, *General Smith's Views of the Power and Policy of the Government of the United States* (Nauvoo, IL: John Taylor, 1844; Independence, MO: 2013), 1.

5. Charles W. Dew, *Apostles of Disunion* (Charlottesville, VA: University of Virginia Press, 2001), 14.

6. Ibid.

7. "Lincoln's Words," excerpt from Abraham Lincoln's Annual Message to Congress, December 1, 1862, last modified March 3, 2014, http://www.abrahamlincolnonline.org/.

8. Jay Monaghan, *Abraham Lincoln Deals With Foreign Affairs: A Diplomat in Carpet Slippers*, http://books.google.com/books?id=ctFf9zQesJgC&pg=PA253&dq=Abraham+Lin coln+I+never+walk+backwards&hl=en&sa=X&ei=ou44U5v1EOWsyAGUsIDYDg&ved =0CDsQ6AEwAA#v=onepage&q=Abraham%20Lincoln%20I%20never%20walk%20 backwards&f=false.

9. *The Slave in the War*, 173, http://books.google.com/books?id=eMo2AQAAMAA J&pg=PA273&dq=Abraham+Lincoln+I%27ll+be+damned+for+time+and+etern ity&hl=en&sa=X&ei=8O44U8L1PITsyQH-i4HICg&ved=0CDYQ6AEwAA# v=onepage&q=Abraham%20Lincoln%20I'll%20be%20damned%20for%20time%20 and%20eternity&f=false.

10. Roy Basler, ed., *Collected Works of Abraham Lincoln* (New Brunswick, NJ: Rutgers University Press, 1953), vol.8, 361.

11. Smith, *General Smith's Views*, 9.

12. Ibid., 9–10.

13. Ibid., 9.

14. Smith, *General Smith's Views*, 3.

15. Basler, *Collected Works of Abraham Lincoln*, vol. 2, 255.

16. Ibid.

17. Marion Mills Miller, ed., *Life and Works of Abraham Lincoln* (New York: Current Literature Publishing, 1907), vol. 6, 153.

18. Smith, *General Smith's Views*, 11.

19. Ibid., 8.

20. B. H. Roberts, *The Rise and Fall of Nauvoo* (repr., Provo, UT: Maasai, 2001), 257.

21. Ibid., 266–67.

22. Johm Browning and Curt Gentry, *John M. Browning, American Gunmaker: An Illustrated Biography of the Man and His Guns* (Garden City, NY: Doubleday, 1964), 13

23. Ibid., 14.

24. Carl Sandberg, "Abraham Lincoln: the Prairie Years and the War Years," in *Reader's Digest*, illustrated ed. (New York: Harcourt Brace Jovanovich, 1970), 131.

25. Ibid., 127.

26. Ibid.

27. Ibid 99.

28. John Wesley Hill, *Abraham Lincoln: Man of God* (New York: G.P. Putnam's Sons, 1920), 125.

29. Sandberg, "Abraham Lincoln: the Prairie Years," 127.

30. Hill, *Abraham Lincoln: Man of God*, 232

31. Ibid., 233.

32. Ibid.

33. Ibid., 229.

34. Ibid., 229–30.

35. Ibid., 230–31.

36. Ibid., 231.

37. Ibid., 251.

38. See Chapter 1, endnote 2.

*Chapter Thirteen*

# MARTYRS

## PROPHETS AMONG US?

In the weeks following South Carolina's rebellion of 1860 and the subsequent secession of the southern states, newspapers were abuzz with speculation as to where these unprecedented events might take the nation. In May 1861, the *Philadelphia Sunday Mercury* made an unexpected reference to Joseph Smith's prophesy on the southern states' rebellion that he had uttered in 1832. Referring to a Mormon pamphlet containing the prophecy, which they had in their possession, the *Philadelphia Sunday Mercury* editors printed the prophecy for its readers and then added this assessment:

> In view of our present troubles, this prediction seems to be in progress of fulfillment, whether Joe Smith was a humbug or not. The war began in South Carolina. Insurrections of slaves are already dreaded. Famine will certainly afflict some Southern communities. The interference of Great Britain, on account of the want of cotton, is not improbable, if the war is protracted . . . Have we not had a prophet among us?[1]

The Mormons were equally absorbed in the fulfillment of this prophecy, which they had been warily anticipating for twenty-nine years. By the time of Lincoln's inauguration in March 1861, they clearly observed that the rebellion did originate in South Carolina and the southern States did divide from the north, exactly as Joseph Smith and Abraham Lincoln had prophesied. And just as young Lincoln had foreseen many years earlier, he would be the presiding superintendent and God's humble instrument as the Almighty God bared his indignant arm. He unleashed His work of retribution and reclamation of the government that the American people had so severely abused.

The *Philadelphia Sunday Mercury*'s question regarding a prophet in the land elicits an even more compelling question in light of the life and exhortations of President Abraham Lincoln and Joseph Smith: Did we not have *two* prophets among us during this tumultuous time in America?

Although small pockets of people supporting Joseph Smith's 1844 bid for the presidency surfaced, the primary impact of his candidacy in Illinois was an intensification of the threats of violence from Thomas Sharp's group of Mormon-haters in Warsaw and Robert Smith's band in Carthage. Their numbers swelled, enflamed by the audacity of Joseph Smith's run for president, which to them was beyond toleration. Local elections in 1843 had resulted in more Mormons like James Adams being elected in Hancock County, adding to their frenzied clamor. While Thomas Sharp continued his call for the removal of the Mormons in the *Warsaw Signal*, the sister newspaper *Warsaw Message* suggested a more peaceful conciliation.

**WARSAW MESSAGE.**

Vol. I. Warsaw, Illinois, January 17, 1844. No. 44.

We see no use in attempting to disguise the fact, that many in our midst contemplate a total extermination of that people [the Mormons]; that the thousands of defenceless [sic] women and children, aged and infirm, who are congregated at Nauvoo, must be driven out—aye, DRIVEN—SCATTERED—like the leaves before the Autumn blast! But what good citizen, let us ask—what lover of his country and his race, but contemplates such an event with horror?

Shall not, we would ask—shall not the olive branch be at least held out to those innocent—though deluded—followers of the prophet? Shall not an attempt be made to set them right, in reference to the designs and aims of those, whom they have heretofore been taught to regard as their worst enemies?

We still persist in the opinion that a compromise may be entered into that will do much good; that will, in its operation, entirely stay the work of destruction. And we call upon all our fellow citizens to aid in bringing about such a compromise.

The *Warsaw Message* did little to soften Sharp or Smith and their growing ranks of Anti-Mormons, as evidenced by Sharp's article the following month:

**WARSAW MESSAGE.**

Vol. I. Warsaw, Illinois, February 7, 1844. No. 47.

Anti-Mormon Meeting.

The citizens of Warsaw Precinct are respectfully requested to meet at the Church in Warsaw, on SATURDAY EVENING, the 10th instant, (this week,) for the purpose of taking into consideration a proposition made by the Central Anti-Mormon Committee of the County of Hancock, and to take such other steps as the exigencies of the case require.

Thos. C. Sharp,
Wm. N. Grover,
Henry Stephens.
Precinct Committee.

Feb. 5, 1844.

### A WORD OF PARTING TO BROTHER JOE.

Now Joe, that you have been a lazy, good-for-nothing vagabond, all the days of your life, your own conscience (if you have any left) will tell you. That you have been the ruin of hundreds of your fellow beings, men, women, and children;—that you have been the means of sending many of your fellows into Eternity unprepared—that you harbored the thief and robber—directed the hand of the assassin and murder, and aided their escape from justice;—

You know that you are despised, and hated and loathed, by nineteen twentieths of all who have ever heard of your name and deeds;

And more—you cannot expect it to continue much longer in your courses of infamy and crime. Depend upon it, the day of retribution cannot be far distant, for at least some of your misdeeds. If the vengeance of the law shall overtake you, and stretch you up as quick as lightning to the gallows, and thus end your career, rest assured that individual vengeance will! Be a prophet nor the son of a prophet—yet we tell you that your career of infamy cannot continue but a little longer! Your days are numbered! The handwriting is upon the wall!

Come, now, brother Joe. Let us entreat you to begin the work of reparation. Dispoil the oxen and baptismal font of their trappings, and buy shoes and stockings for the ragged urchins of your streets; and tear down your Temple and of its materials build a hospital for the innocent victims of your ambition and licentiousness. These done, and you will have made some atonement for your past life. Until then, Joe, we shall remain as, ever, all but "your friend and most obedient servant."

In response to the unrest in these Anti-Mormon meetings, an alarmed Governor Thomas Ford issued a letter stating:

I have received the copy of the proceedings and resolutions of a meeting of the citizens of Hancock County . . .

If there is anything wrong in the Nauvoo charters, or in the mode of administering them, you will see that nothing short of legislative or [judicial] power is capable of enforcing a remedy.

I myself had the honor of calling the attention of the Legislature to this subject at the last session; but a large majority of both political parties in that body either did not see the evil which you complain of, or, if they did, they repeatedly refused to correct it. . . .

I have also been called upon to take away the arms from the

*Mormons*, to raise the militia to arrest a supposed fugitive, and in fact to repeal some of the ordinances of the city of Nauvoo.

. . . The absurd and preposterous nature of these requests gave some color to the charge that they were made for political effect only. . . .

All that I can do at present is to admonish both parties to beware of carrying matters to extremity.

. . . I wish . . . to tell the citizens of Hancock County, *Mormons* and all, that my interference will be against those who shall be the first transgressors.[2]

Three days after Governor Ford's public admonishment for peace, Joseph Smith issued a response through the Nauvoo Neighbor referring to Ford's message as a "balm of Gilead, well calculated to ease the pain which has troubled the heads and hearts of the Carthaginians, [and] Warsawvians."[3] Then he admonished his followers to remember Jesus's golden rule:

"*To do unto others as they would wish others to do unto them*," . . . Wise men ought to have understanding enough to conquer men with kindness.

"A soft answer turns away wrath," says the wise man; and it will be greatly to the credit of the Latter-day Saints to show the love of God, by now kindly treating those who may have, in an unconscious moment, done them wrong; for truly said Jesus, "*Pray for thine enemies*."[4]

It is an irony that Joseph Smith, the alleged false prophet, and Lincoln, the alleged infidel, would invoke the Christlike entreaties to love and pray for their enemies. Joseph's admonishment to his oppressed followers mirrored President Lincoln's request for the relief and forgiveness of the vanquished South by citizens in the North at the end of the Civil War and throughout his last year in office.

## DISSIDENTS

During the spring of 1844, signs of dissension among some of Joseph Smith's closest associates in Nauvoo prompted him to reveal in a meeting his belief that "we have a Judas in our midst."[5] Secret meetings were being held by apostates to plan the deaths of Joseph,

Hyrum, and other faithful Church leaders. Some invitees to these plots remained discreetly loyal to the Prophet and reported the traitors' plans back to him. Mormons living in the outlying townships began to be harassed and threatened with harm by the Anti-Mormons in Carthage and Warsaw. As was done in Missouri, haystacks were burned and livestock driven away or shot.

The Anti-Mormons' plan was to drive all of the Mormons into Nauvoo and to demand that Joseph Smith be delivered over to them—not the law. If the Joseph's followers did not comply, "a war of entire extermination should be waged to the entire destruction . . . of his adherents."[6] These conspirators included William Law, Joseph Smith's second counselor in the Presidency of the Church, and his brother Wilson Law, who just a year earlier had valiantly defended Joseph during his trial in Springfield and put up bail money for him. Their primary complaints were the doctrine of polygamy and, oddly enough, the Nauvoo charter, which they demanded be repealed. They purchased a printing press for the purpose of printing a new newspaper, which they called the *Nauvoo Expositor*, to expose their complaints. Disagreement with the polygamy doctrine is understandable, but that their opposition would escalate to the murder and expulsion of the very people they had for years defended and revered is truly a marvel.

The *Nauvoo Expositor*'s first and only issue caused an uproar in Nauvoo, prompting the city council to meet to address the upheaval. They deliberated for six hours the first day and seven more the second before Alderman Spencer summed up their concerns: "Shall [the dissidents] be suffered to go on, and bring a mob on us to murder our women and children and burn our beautiful city?"[7] They eventually emerged with a resolution to declare the new newspaper a nuisance and a threat to the safety of the city, and it was to be removed by order of the city council and Mayor Joseph Smith. The city marshal was summoned to carry out the order, and he and some selected deputies entered the *Expositor* office, removed the press, and destroyed it in the street. By this time, the leading apostates had been in secret communication with Sharp and others of the Anti-Mormon party. Although not in danger, they all fled the city as though they were,

some to Warsaw and the others to Carthage. Their coordinated strat-
agem was continuing as planned. Thomas Sharp responded with the
following call to action in the Warsaw Signal on June 12, 1844:

# THE WARSAW SIGNAL
## AND AGRICULTURAL, LITERARY AND COMMERCIAL REGISTER.

NS No. 18. Warsaw, Illinois, June 12, 1844. Whole 135.

We have only to state, that this is sufficient! War and extermination is inevitable! Citizens ARISE, ONE and ALL! Can you stand by
and suffer such INFERNAL DEVILS? to rob men of their property
and rights, without avenging them? We have no time for comment.
Every man will make his own. Let it be made with POWDER and
BALL!

Just before this revival of the hatred and violence, most members
of the Quorum of the Twelve, including Brigham Young and William Smith, had gone back east, joining the other Church leaders
who had gone to Washington weeks earlier. While there, they all
conducted a determined and well-coordinated political campaign for
Joseph Smith in Boston, New York, Philadelphia, and other cities
and towns throughout the country.

# Daily National Intelligencer

Washington: Friday, June 21, 1844.

At a meeting of the friends of "Joe Smith," held at Military Hall,
in New York, on the 11th instant, Parley Pratt, one of the Prophet's
adherents, made a speech in favor of the General, which concluded
as follows:

"Who then shall we vote for as our next President? I answer,
Gen. Joseph Smith, of Nauvoo, Illinois. He is not a Southern man
with Northern principles, nor a Northern man with Southern principles. But he is an independent man with American principles, and

he has both knowledge and disposition to govern for the benefit and protection as ALL. And, what is more, he dare do it, even in this age, and this can scarcely be said of many others.

The destruction of the Nauvoo Expositor gave the anti-Mormons a rallying cry that Governor Ford could not ignore. Rumors swirled that bodies of armed men were gathering in Missouri and Iowa and that cannons and ammunition were being accumulated for the purpose of exterminating the Mormons. In response, Ford called up militia from around the state for the sake of preventing a lawless massacre. Lincoln's friends John J. Hardin and Edward Baker were appointed commanding officers for the militia from Sangamon County and ordered to Carthage to await further orders. Just why Abraham Lincoln, with his experience as a militia captain in 1832, was not called up to lead or at least participate with his friends in the militia is unknown. Or was he called up to join the militia and, for some unknown reason, declined? These questions remain unanswered, but it is quite certain that Lincoln did not participate in this militia operation.

Two days following the destruction of the press, Judge Morrison of Carthage issued a warrant for the arrest of Mayor Joseph Smith and his entire city council on the charge of riot. The tensions were so volatile that Governor Ford left Springfield for Carthage in order to manage the situation. During these anxious days, he and Joseph Smith communicated often by messengers. Ford informed Joseph that it was necessary for him and his city council to address the charges at Carthage to assuage the violent crowds assembling there, and the Governor promised his protection to all who would come to Carthage. Under the Nauvoo Charter, the city council had the authority to address the charge in their local courts, which they did—they were acquitted by a Mormon judge. Then, for good measure, took the case to a non-Mormon judge who also acquitted the mayor and city council.

Joseph was silent and visibly troubled after reading Governor Ford's letter. After some moments of deep contemplation, he called on his personal scribe, Willard Richards, to write the following in his journal: "I told Stephen Markham that if Hyrum and I were ever taken again, we should be massacred, or I was not a prophet of God."[8]

When Richard's finished his entry, Joseph turned to Hyrum and said, "There is no mercy . . . no mercy here."[9] To which Hyrum replied, "No, just as surely as we fall into their hands we are dead men."[10]

As they considered their dire circumstances, the brothers concluded that they would, that very night, cross the Mississippi and head for the Rocky Mountains to escape the maddened mobs. Knowing that the mob wanted only them, they felt that by escaping they could eliminate the threat of an attack on the city residents. Without saying good-bye to their families, they awoke Orrin Porter Rockwell, and he conveyed them across in a rowboat.

The next day, Rockwell returned with some messengers and a letter from Emma, who had been informed that her husband had left for the west. Earlier that day, once again a posse sent to convey her husband away from her had disrupted the peace of her home. They treated her harshly and threatened her and her children when she told them that she did not know why her husband had not returned home the previous evening. In her letter, Emma, now six months pregnant and unable to bear the thought of him leaving her side, plead with her husband to return and trust in Governor Ford's promise of protection.

Emma's plea deeply touched Joseph and Hyrum. But when the messengers informed them that some of the Saints in Nauvoo felt abandoned by their leader's flight and that others had interpreted it as cowardice, Joseph mournfully replied, "If my life is of no value to my friends, it is of none to myself."[11] Hyrum also had a change of heart and suggested that they return. Joseph again warned his brother of his certainty that they would be killed, but Hyrum had begun to feel that their plan of escape was ill-conceived.

In the months prior to this pivotal moment, Joseph had made numerous allusions to premonitions that his life would be violently taken once his work as God's prophet was complete—but not until then. On the western bank of the Mississippi that day, the impression came to him that the time had finally arrived. He began to sense that after twenty-four years of unending ridicule and persecution, there remained one more sacrifice to be made in the name of God— the final offering of his own life for the work.

The brothers solemnly returned to Nauvoo. Once at his home, and after a joyful reunion with Emma and their children, Joseph penned a letter to the governor that on the morrow he and his city council would be in Carthage. He recorded that he would like to address his beloved saints for the last time, but his heart would not allow him to leave his wife and children that evening, and he cancelled the address, believing that this night would be his last with his family.

Messengers rode through the night to Carthage with Joseph's letter to the Governor and returned the next morning with fearful reports of hundreds of men gathered in Carthage calling for his blood. But Joseph appeared undaunted by the disturbing report, having concluded that he would place his trust in God's hands and face the frenzied mob.

Early the next morning, people began to gather at the front of his home, all sensing the gravity of the situation. When Joseph emerged from the home with a weeping Emma at his side and his young sons clinging to his clothing, the crowd, now numbering in the hundreds, began to implore him to change his mind and not go to Carthage. His aged mother, Lucy, then spoke for the gathering by saying, "My son, my son, can you leave me without promising to return? Some forty times I have seen you from me dragged, but never before without saying you would return. What say you now, my son?"[12]

At which point Joseph raised his hand, signaling that he would address the crowd, and solemnly said:

> My friends, my brethren, I love you. I love the city of Nauvoo too well to save my life at your expense. If I go not to them, they will come here and act out the horrid Missouri scenes in Nauvoo. I may prevent it. I fear not death; my work is done. Keep the faith and I will die for Nauvoo.[13]

With that, Joseph and his city council mounted their horses and rode toward Carthage, pausing at the nearly finished exterior walls of at the Temple. Joseph could not resist returning again to his family, whom he was certain he would never see again. Deeply preoccupied for his sons and daughters, he solemnly entreated his grieving wife to guide them to walk in the faith of their father. Then he asked Emma to name their unborn child, if a boy, David Hyrum. Their child was born fatherless in November, and Emma named him David Hyrum. After yet another tearful farewell, Joseph mournfully rode back to the party awaiting him at the Temple. Then, gazing at the unfinished edifice with deep emotion, he said to his friends, "This is the loveliest place, and the best people under the heavens; little do they know the trials that await them!"[14]

On this day, June 24, Governor Ford began making a series of inexplicable decisions that eventually led the Prophet and his traveling companions to question Ford's commitment to their protection. By ten o'clock that morning, while only four miles from Carthage, the peace-minded McDonough County militia of some sixty men led by a Captain Dunn rode toward them. Dunn informed Joseph and his party that he was under orders from Governor Ford to confiscate the state arms issued to the Nauvoo militia.

The Nauvoo Legion was the largest militia in America at the time, but they were issued only a small number of munitions. Governor Ford knew that their removal would leave the Mormons even more vulnerable to an attack by the mobs, particularly in light of their Prophet's injunction to remain passive and peaceful in the face of their oppressors. And yet Ford allowed the men from whom an unending stream of threats and black-hearted hatred was emanating to retain possession of their arms. Trusting that the residents of Nauvoo would remain safe with his surrender, and knowing that his resistance to the order would only serve to enflame the growing mob, Joseph serenely countersigned the order giving Captain Dunn permission to gather and remove the weapons.

Once pledging his submission to Captain Dunn's orders, Joseph walked over to his traveling party and explained the order and that he intended to comply with it. He then told them, "I am going like a lamb to the slaughter, but I am calm as a summer's morning. I have a conscience void of offense toward God and toward all men. I shall die innocent, and it shall yet [be] said of me, 'He was murdered in cold blood,'"[15] Captain Dunn then requested that Joseph return to Nauvoo with him to ensure that they could carry out the order without confrontation. The city council members were jubilant at Joseph's consent.

Dunn sent messengers back to Carthage to inform the governor of the party's later arrival, and they all returned to Nauvoo. As Captain Dunn had anticipated, the confiscation of arms was deeply troubling to the Nauvoo residents, but Joseph was able to orchestrate their peaceful surrender in the front of the Masonic Lodge. While there, Joseph called for a map and said, "Now I will show you the travels of this people."[16] He then traced a course across Iowa (avoiding Missouri) and on to the Rocky Mountains, pointing to a spot, saying, "Here you will come to the Great Salt Lake valley."[17] Those present, struck by the fact that Joseph had pointed out where "they" and not "we" were to go, asked Joseph where he would be at the time. He replied, "I shall never go there,"[18] continuing his ever-intensifying foreboding that his days on Earth had come to an end. Once finished at the Masonic Lodge, he then rushed one last time to his family for another tearful farewell with his young children and Emma. By early evening they were once again on the road to Carthage under the protection of Captain Dunn. They reached Carthage near midnight.

Robert Smith, a justice of the peace in Carthage, was one of the purchasers of the steamboat Nauvoo who had allowed Joseph Smith to be charged with the entire debt. He was a close associate of Thomas Sharp and now a collaborator with the Mormon apostates also assembled in the town and bent on Joseph Smith's destruction. He now commanded the Carthage Greys, which consisted of Anti-Mormon Party members who had longed for this day. He camped his militia in the public square of the town, awaiting Joseph Smith's arrival. His men were furious at Captain Dunn's protection of the prisoners, and Captain Smith did nothing to quell their disorder. The Greys' outbursts alarmed the surrounding militiamen as well as the whole town with the commotion they caused as they exclaimed:

> "Where's the d—n Prophet?" "Stand away, you McDonough boys, and let us shoot the d—n Mormons!" "G-d d—n you, old Joe, we've got you now!" "Clear the way, and let us have a view of Joe Smith, the Prophet of God. He has seen the last of Nauvoo, we'll use him up now!"[19]

Governor Ford, who was lodging nearby, heard these threats, but nothing more than Captain Dunn's militia was mustered to protect the Mormons or to bring the Carthage Greys to order. Joseph and his companions were safely delivered to the Hamilton Hotel, which they shared with Joseph's friends-turned-enemies, the Higbees, the Fosters, and the Laws. The unruly crowd remained in front of the hotel until Governor Ford, from his hotel window, finally dismissed them and promised to pass the Mormons before the assembled militias in the morning.

Early the next day, Joseph and his city council surrendered themselves to Constable Bettisworth on the charge of riot in Nauvoo. After that, Governor Ford requested that Joseph, Hyrum, and Willard Richards accompany him for a formal review before the twelve hundred militiamen that had assembled in formation on the town square. Ford first escorted them to the headquarters of Brigadier General Deming, where the Carthage Greys made another uproar, this time over the military courtesy that Governor Ford was extending to the Mormon leaders. The Greys were dismissed, and the review commenced. Governor Ford introduced Hyrum and Joseph Smith as Generals of the Nauvoo Legion. The review was orderly until they came to the Greys, who refused to receive the Smiths by their titles. Some of the officers drew their swords, vowing to introduce themselves to the Smiths in their own fashion. With difficulty, the Governor finally quieted the Greys and promised all the assembled troops that they would receive full satisfaction. The Greys were pacified until Ford concluded his address, but they then continued their frenzied hostility, and General Deming placed all of them under arrest. Governor Ford later had them released without punishment.

After the review, Joseph Smith sent a messenger to Lincoln's friend Orville Browning, asking him to represent him again in the upcoming trial. Browning was otherwise occupied, however, and could not defend Joseph as he had done in Monmouth three years earlier.

On the afternoon of June 25, Joseph, Hyrum, and the thirteen members of the Nauvoo City Council entered the courtroom to face the charge of riot. In spite of being acquitted in two previous courts, Joseph Smith determined to accept the consequences if their act of destroying the press was deemed illegal in Carthage. To their surprise, the judge presiding at their trial was not Judge Morrison, who had issued the summons, but rather Justice of the Peace Robert Smith. In Illinois, a conviction for riot carried a maximum fine of two hundred dollars, but Justice Smith promptly ordered an outrageous bail of $500 per man. He almost certainly intended to incarcerate Joseph and Hyrum. It was Justice Smith's turn to be surprised when Joseph's friends raised the excessive $7,500 and freed all the defendants on bail. Most of the city council members returned to Nauvoo, but Joseph and Hyrum remained because Governor Ford had agreed to meet with them and Joseph very much wanted to consult with the Governor.

Before the interview with Ford could begin, Constable Bettisworth intercepted Joseph and Hyrum and ordered them to the jail. Joseph and Hyrum indignantly refused, being free on bail, as Bettisworth was well aware since he was present at the hearing. Bettisworth sheepishly produced a warrant signed by Justice Smith, stating that they were now under arrest for treason.[20] He added that this new charge was addressed in the earlier hearing, which was a lie.

Under these false pretenses, Robert Smith ordered Joseph and Hyrum to be held in the jail until discharged by the court. Joseph's enemies had long sought charges of murder or treason against him, which carried the death penalty. The Smiths' lawyer, James Woods, reminded Bettisworth that under Illinois law no one could be committed to jail without a hearing before a judge and refused to allow his clients to be incarcerated. Woods went to Governor Ford with the fallacious warrant, and he and Ford went to Justice Smith.

Smith informed them that he committed them to jail because they would be safer there than in the Hamilton Hotel.[21] Ford also heard of Justice Smith's illegal actions from John Taylor, the other apostle besides Willard Richards who had not been sent east to campaign for Joseph's presidential bid. In spite of this, Governor Ford sided with Robert Smith and assured Taylor and Woods that their fears of a conspiracy to murder Joseph Smith were unfounded.

Joseph's friends feared that he and Hyrum might be shot on their way from the hotel to the jail. Captain Dunn, disturbed at the mobocratic and unlawful direction the proceedings had taken, came forward with his McDonough County militia and gallantly pledged to protect Joseph and Hyrum at the expense of his own life, if necessary. His militia surrounded the prisoners and ensured their safe arrival to the jail, which was a quarter of a mile from the hotel. Here Joseph, Hyrum, Richards, Taylor, and some other loyal Mormons spent the night in the same Carthage Jail that Lincoln had observed under construction while participating in the Fraim case in early 1839.

In the evening of June 25, jailer George Stigall, who lived at the jail with is family, moved the incarcerated Mormons from a filthy upper-level jail cell to a more comfortable debtors' apartment on the lower floor. The room was empty of furniture, so the group slept on the floor. The next morning, they shared breakfast with the Stigall family, and George suggested that they take the furnished upper bedroom, which he believed would be safer for them. On the morning of June 26, Governor Ford arrived at the jail at 9:27 for the promised interview.[22] He expressed sympathy for their circumstances but offered to do nothing to change them.

Governor Ford had heard rumors of unrest in Nauvoo. He informed the Smiths that he intended to go there, accompanied by Captain Dunn's force, to investigate. Joseph implored the governor to allow him and Hyrum to accompany him, and the governor promised to do so on the morrow.

Willard Richards recorded that Joseph was more distraught over the circumstances than he had ever seen him before. Joseph told him, "I've had a good deal of anxiety about my safety since I left Nauvoo, which I've never had before when under arrest. I cannot help these feelings, and they have depressed me."[23] Through the hot afternoon they sang hymns and read from the scriptures, whereupon Hyrum, gaining hope, asked his younger brother if he did not believe that God could deliver them. Joseph woefully replied that he did believe that God *could* deliver them, but he did not believe that He *would*.

During the day, Joseph and Hyrum spoke with their guards. When Robert Smith noticed that the guards' hatred toward the Smiths was softening, he promptly had them replaced. At midafternoon, Constable Bettisworth came to jailer Stigall and demanded that the prisoners be delivered to Justice Smith. Stigall refused. Robert Smith was only a justice of the peace, not a sitting judge, and therefore did not have the authority to demand the prisoners.

Robert Smith responded by sending some of his Greys to the jail. They threatened Stigall, who had to relent for his own safety. Lawyer Woods vehemently objected to their forced appearance but was mostly ignored. Justice Smith intended to begin a trial for treason, but because the Smith brothers had no one to speak in their behalf, Woods did prevail in gaining a continuance for the following day. In none of this did Governor Ford intervene. In fact, Ford dismissed all of the militias in Carthage except the Carthage Greys.

Prior to leaving for Nauvoo on the morning of June 27, Governor Ford issued the disturbing order to place a guard around Carthage Jail—a guard led by Frank Worrell, one of the more avowed enemies of Joseph and Hyrum, and six other bloodthirsty Carthage Greys. The Greys and many of the disbanded militiamen were jubilant that Ford was departing for Nauvoo and leaving the prisoners in their hands. Surprisingly, Ford heard their jubilation and did nothing to right the dangerous circumstances. He had been warned numerous times and by various people of the danger the Greys posed to the prisoners, yet he left the prisoners in the hands of their avowed enemies and took the most honorable remaining militia under Captain Dunn with him to Nauvoo. And if that wasn't enough, the Governor broke his promise to Joseph and Hyrum and left without them.

The reports of unrest in Nauvoo turned out to be inaccurate, inflamed, and exaggerated. Upon his arrival, Governor Ford found the people in a state of nervous calm, and he received many inquiries as to the wellbeing of Joseph and Hyrum. After passing through of the city and finding none of the chaos predicted by his informants in Carthage, he addressed the people and began heading back.

Throughout the day, the prisoners could hear menacing oaths and threats from their assigned protectors. The afternoon was muggy with rain, and their uneasiness did not subside. To cheer the forlorn group, John Taylor began to sing a new Mormon hymn, which had become a favorite among the worshipers in Nauvoo, called "A Poor Wayfaring Man of Grief":

A poor wayfaring man of grief
Hath often crossed me on my way,
Who sued so humbly for relief
That I could never answer, Nay.
I had not power to ask his name,
Whereto he went or whence he came,
Yet there was something in His eye
That won my love I knew not why.

Once when my scanty meal was spread,
He entered, not a word he spake;
Just perishing for want of bread,
I gave Him all, he blessed it, brake,
And ate; but gave me part again;
Mine was an angels portion then,
For while I fed with eager haste,
The crust was mana to my taste.

In prison I saw Him next, condemned
To meet a traitor's doom at morn;
The tide of lying tongues I stemmed,
And honored Him 'mid shame and scorn.
My friendship's utmost zeal to try,
He asked if I for Him would die;
The flesh was weak, my blood ran chill,
But the free spirit cried, "I will!"

Then in a moment to my view,
The stranger darted from disguise;
The tokens in His hands I knew,
The Savior stood before mine eyes.
He spake, and my poor name He named,
"Of Me thou hast not been ashamed;
These deeds shall thy memorial be,
Fear not, thou didst them unto Me."[24]

They all were comforted by the hymn. When Taylor finished singing, Joseph asked him to sing it again, and he did.

Shortly after five p.m., a commotion was heard coming from the south—the direction of Warsaw. The prisoners watched from their upper window and as a boisterous crowd approached the jail. In an orchestrated fashion, the guards stood as if in defense of the prisoners and even fired their weapons, but none in the mob fell as it pressed forward. The rest of the Carthage Greys watched with interest from two hundred yards away but did nothing to intervene. The guard gave way, and the jail was quickly surrounded by men with faces blackened from a mixture of water and gunpowder.

Without hesitation, a number of them ran up the stairs to the room whose door did not even have a lock, where Joseph, Hyrum, Taylor, and Richards were held. The prisoners placed their weight against the door to prevent the mob's entry. Shots were fired. One pierced the door, striking Hyrum in the face and killed him. The others continued to hold the door as best they could, but a number of gun barrels forced the door ajar. The mob fired again, and John Taylor was struck four times. He crawled near the bed. No longer able to prevent the mob's entry, Joseph stepped toward the window and was immediately struck from behind. The bullet pushed him toward the open window and the view of those outside. A volley of shots rang out, and he fell through the window to the ground below. His body was propped up against the wall of the jail, and additional balls were fired into him.

Joseph Smith was dead.[25] Days later, upon hearing the news through the newspapers, his grief-stricken Apostles made haste to return to Nauvoo.

As the mob cheered over their murders, someone cried out that the Mormons were coming from Nauvoo, and the murderers scattered like frightened children. Dr. Willard Richards, who days earlier had been told by Joseph that the day would come that bullets would fly all around him and yet not even his clothing would be harmed, stood unwounded and bewildered. After determining that Hyrum lay dead, Richards started to leave the room when he heard John Taylor call him from under the bed. Dr. Richards began administering to Taylor's wounds, all the while expecting the mob to return and finish them both. But the mob did not return. Taylor survived and recovered.

A week following the assassinations in Carthage, Lincoln would certainly have read the following in Simeon Francis's newspaper:

# Sangamo Journal.

Vol. XIII. Springfield, Ill., July 4, 1844. No. 47.

### THE MORMON DIFFICULTIES.

Notwithstanding all the rumors which are afloat, we are unable to state any thing very definite in relation to affairs at Nauvoo, or "in the region round about" that city. It is certain that the Governor has called out some of the neighboring militia—that bodies of armed men had collected without waiting a call from the Governor—that the Governor had accepted the services of militia at St. Louis under certain contingencies—that he had demanded of Smith the State arms at Nauvoo—that it had been reported that they were given up—that Smith and his Council had given themselves up to be tried by our laws for alleged offences. Thus far our news seems to be certain. Rumor says further, that on Thursday of last week Joe Smith, Hyram Smith, and Dr. Richards were shot by a mob at Carthage. We are incredulous in regard to the truth of this rumor. We cannot think that under the circumstances of the case—the excitement against these men among the anti-mormons—Gov. Ford would have received them as prisoners, to be tried under our laws—had pledged himself for their protection—and then placed them in a situation where they would be murdered. The rumor is too preposterous for belief.

We await with much anxiety to hear the truth on this subject; and this feeling is general in this community.

Shortly after editor Simeon Francis wrote this article, the rumors were confirmed. Lincoln and his Springfield friends would soon know that the Mormon prophet and his ever-loyal brother Hyrum were indeed murdered while in the custody of law enforcement and civil officials in Carthage. While Lincoln's reaction to this news is not recorded, it can be safely inferred that his feelings regarding lawlessness and mobocracy, as expressed earlier in his Lyceum speech, governed his response.

The wives and children of Joseph and Hyrum would hear the news the day following the murders. Adding to the anguish of the brothers' mother, Lucy Smith, was the death of her son Samuel only days later. Samuel kept a inn on the road between Nauvoo and Carthage, and he was pursued so intently by mobbers that he died from what the family believed were complications from the determined and extended pursuit.

The murders of Joseph and Hyrum Smith did little to quell the unrest that surrounded the saints. Just as Joseph had prophesied, the pressure to leave Illinois continued, and the saints there began to experience persecutions similar to those experienced in Missouri. Governor Ford appeared to be unable to control the mounting hostilities toward the Mormons in his state, and the Mormons seemed to sense that in spite of their renowned and beautiful city and Temple, they would find no peace or protection from governing officials anywhere in the United States.

Their thoughts and conversations began to focus westward, as Joseph had counseled them earlier. Ford appointed a team of negotiators led by Stephen A. Douglas to meet with Brigham Young and other Mormon leaders to find an acceptable solution. Both sides eventually came to the conclusion that the saints would conduct a planned and measured exodus to the Rocky Mountains. But the persecutors persisted unabated, forcing a cruel and premature departure over the frozen Mississippi in 1846.

Even then, the state of Illinois did nothing to support or protect or aid them in this massive migration. The Mormons went with only their God to guide and support them. They finished their magnificent temple shortly before their exodus and then walked away from it, their homes, and their farms as they had before. Speculators knew that by waiting they could avoid paying market value for the Latter-day Saints' properties. They simply took them over at little or no cost once vacated.

## PRESIDENT OF THE UNITED STATES

In May of 1860, the newly formed Republican Party, which Abraham Lincoln had labored hard to organize in Illinois, held their national convention in Chicago. Lincoln, in spite of his defeat to Stephen A. Douglas in the 1858 Senate race, had become renowned for his political acumen and the stirring moral messaging that he demonstrated in his debates with Douglas. These had propelled him into being what most people considered a lesser candidate for the Republican presidential nomination. The Republican heavyweights were in Chicago as well: William Seward, Salmon Chase, and Edward Bates, and all of them had the credentials to capture the nomination. These brought with them years of public service in Washington as well as the governorships of their respective states. In 1860, Lincoln had not held any political office for eleven years—since the end of his two-year term in Congress in 1849.

The results of the balloting were astonishing. The procedure dictated that the delegates cast their votes in rounds until a candidate reached two hundred and thirty votes. The candidates with the fewest votes in the first round were eliminated, and their delegates were to then cast their votes for any of the remaining candidates. To the utter bewilderment of Bates and Chase, Lincoln came in second to Seward in the first round, eliminating them from the race. To be beaten by Lincoln was completely unexpected, and Bates and Chase began resenting Lincoln from that day forward, in spite of the fact that President Lincoln later invited them both to serve in his cabinet.

With Bates and Chase eliminated, it was now Seward's turn for consternation. The second round of voting resulted in 184 votes for Seward and 181 votes for Lincoln. By the third round Lincoln had eclipsed Seward, and by the end of the balloting, Lincoln, needing only 230 votes, held 354, a resounding and startling majority to nearly everyone—with the exception of Mary and Abraham Lincoln, who seemed to have long anticipated this day.[26]

Upon hearing the news of Lincoln's nomination, many Republicans throughout the country felt that there had been some mistake in the voting process. Surely Lincoln could not have defeated Bates or Chase—and triumphing over the renowned William Seward was unthinkable. But, in fact, he had. For the first time since George Washington, a presidential nominee had been selected based on the merits of integrity, social morality, and an unwavering devotion to God, not political prowess—and that man was Abraham Lincoln.

## The Book of Mormon in the White House

In November 1861, six months into the war, Lincoln took a walk to the Library of Congress and checked out four books about the Mormons. Three of these were generally critical of the sect, and these he returned a few days later. But one book, the Book of Mormon, he retained. In fact, the register at the Library of Congress indicates that the President did not return the book until July 1862. He kept the Book of Mormon in the White House for eight months.

Just two months after its return, Lincoln penned a note to himself, which apparently no one saw until after his assassination in 1865. Lincoln had a practice of turning ideas over and over in his mind and writing his musings and conclusions on the backs of envelopes and pieces of paper and then placing them in his tall stovepipe hat or in nooks and drawers in his desk. One such written meditation was not discovered or made public until after his death. It is of singular significance in glimpsing Lincoln's faith and conviction that God was the silent architect of the horrible war ravaging the country. John Hay, Lincoln's private secretary, discovered this personal notation among a number of other such notes and kept it. In 1872, Hay gave it a title: "Meditation on the Divine Will." He included it in a biography of Lincoln published in 1890, describing it as a private meditation that was not meant to be seen by men.

### Meditation on the Divine Will
September 2(?) 1862, sixteen months into the war

The will of God prevails. In great contests each party claims to act in accordance with the will of God. Both <u>may</u> be, and one must be wrong. God cannot be for, and against the same thing at the same time. In the present civil war it is quite possible that God's purpose is something different from the purpose of either party—and yet the human instrumentalities, working just as they do, are of the best adaptation to effect His purpose. I am almost ready to say this is probably true—that God wills this contest, and wills that it shall not end yet. By His mere quiet power, on the minds of the now contestants, He could have either <u>saved</u> or <u>destroyed</u> the Union without a human contest. Yet the contest began. And having begun He could give the final victory to either side any day. Yet the contest proceeds.[27]

## PREMONITIONS OF MARTYRDOM

Once elected, Lincoln embarked on the most challenging presidency in American history. On the February 1861 morning of his emotional departure from Springfield, he told William Herndon, his law partner of twenty years, of a troubling foreboding that he would never return alive to his beloved Springfield. Since his election three months earlier, he began to receive threats against his life, which he simply placed in a file labeled "Assassination."

On the final leg of his journey to Washington, the evidence of a plot to kill the new President during his scheduled stop in Baltimore was so strong that Lincoln reluctantly followed the urgings of his security staff to bypass Baltimore entirely. Lincoln arrived in Washington quietly and unnoticed in the early morning hours, in disguise, bypassing the planned fanfare to avoid the plot.

As the war approached its close in 1865, the Assassination file had become stuffed with threatening letters received throughout his presidency. Lincoln did not know the day, but he carried a deepening impression that his earthly end was imminent. Like Joseph Smith, Abraham Lincoln had premonitions of his looming assassination. Just after Lincoln's reelection in November 1864, he told trusted friend Owen Lovejoy that he was dubious about another term as President. Lincoln said, "This war is eating my life out . . . I have a strong impression that I shall not live to see the end."[28]

One evening just days before his assassination, Lincoln was talking with Mary, Ward Hill Lamon, and a few others when he turned dreadfully solemn and began talking about dreams. "I had one the other night which has haunted me ever since,"[29] Lincoln told them. He continued to say that upon awakening from the dream, he opened his Bible, and on every page he turned, his eyes fell on passages about dreams, visions, and visitations of heavenly messengers. "'You frighten me!' Mary exclaimed. 'What is the matter?'"[30] Lincoln responded apologetically that maybe he had done wrong in mentioning it "but somehow the thing has got possession of me."[31] Mary pressed him to reveal the dream. After hesitating, Lincoln described in a sad and subdued voice that:

> About ten days a go I retired very late. I had been up waiting for important dispatches from the front. I could not have been long in bed when I fell into a slumber, for I was weary. I soon began to dream. There seemed to be a death-like stillness about me. Then I heard subdued sobs, as if a number of people were weeping. I thought I left my bed and wandered downstairs. There the silence was broken by the same pitiful sobbing, but the mourners were invisible. I went from room to room; no living person was in sight, but the same mournful sounds of distress met me as I passed along. It was light in all the rooms; every object was familiar to me; but where were all the people who were grieving as if their hearts would break? I was puzzled and alarmed. What could be the meaning of all of this? Determined to find the cause of a state of things so mysterious and so shocking, I kept on until I arrived at the East Room, which I entered. There I met with a sickening surprise. Before me was a catafalque, on which rested a corpse wrapped in funeral vestments. Around it were stationed soldiers who were acting as guards; and there was a throng of people, some gazing mournfully upon the corpse, whose face was covered, others weeping pitifully. "Who is dead in the White House?" I demanded of one of the soldiers. "The President," was his answer; "he was killed by an assassin!" Then came a loud burst of grief from the crowd.[32]

"'That is horrid!' Mary said. 'I wish you had not told it.' 'Well,' Lincoln said, 'it is only a dream, Mary. Let us say no more about it.'"[33]

Lamon, Lincoln's security marshal, could not help being troubled by the disclosure. Turning to him, Lincoln tried to relieve the uneasiness in the room by saying:

> For a long time you have been trying to keep somebody—the Lord knows who—from killing me. Don't you see how it will turn out?

In this dream it was not me, but some other fellow, that was killed. It seems that this ghostly assassin tried his hand on someone else.[34]

Then, growing solemn again, Lincoln said, "Well, let it go. I think the Lord in His own good time and way will work this out all right."[35]

That Lincoln would have such a dream is not uncommon, but his response to it was. He seemed to have felt a need to share it with Mary and his closest friends, as if to prepare them for such an event. He appeared to believe it was imminent. Ward Hill Lamon, who was with the President daily, said this regarding Lincoln's belief in dreams: "The moving power of dreams and visions of an extraordinary character he ascribed, as did the Patriarchs of old, to the Almighty Intelligence that governs the universe."[36]

## THE SACRIFICE

That Lincoln believed that he would be assassinated in office is evidenced further by a conversation with a friend from Illinois, Father Charles Chiniquy. Lincoln and Chiniquy shared a common challenge and bond as neither was affiliated with an organized religion, which fact caused them both to suffer criticism and derision. Chiniquy, a French Canadian from Montreal, was one of the most renowned Catholic priests in North America. He had a large following and was a requested speaker throughout Canada and the United States. In the mid 1800s, he led a group of thousands of Roman Catholic Canadians to settle in Illinois. One night, after a powerful sermon to several thousand listeners in Montreal on the role of the Virgin Mary as an intermediary between mankind and Jesus Christ, he claimed to hear a voice with the power of thunder in his mind telling him that what he had just preached was false doctrine.[37] After a long night of reading the New Testament and hours of prayer, he came to the conclusion that the voice he had heard was correct. The next morning he went to his bishop, telling him that he believed the voice he heard to be the voice of God and that he could no longer embrace this tenet of the Catholic faith.

Thus, with his excommunication, he was left without affiliation to any organized religion, much like Lincoln. Yet they both admired each other's faith and determination to follow Jesus and the prophets as written in the Bible. Chiniquy became one of the few with whom he openly confide on his deepest thoughts on God and religion.

Lincoln and Chiniquy first met when a Jesuit priest accused Chiniquy of attempting to sexually assault his sister shortly after Chiniquy's excommunication. The charge was generally believed to be retaliation by the Roman Catholic bishop in Chicago for Chiniquy's highly publicized falling away. The trial took place in Urbana, Illinois, one of Lincoln's circuit stops, and Lincoln and two other lawyers were assigned to defend Chiniquy. The prosecutor presented the charges, and Lincoln did his best to refute them, but at the day's end, Lincoln told Chiniquy, "There is not the least doubt in my mind that every word he has said is a sworn lie; but my fear is that the jury thinks differently."[38] Lincoln went on to tell Chiniquy that he believed that the alleged victim (who, it was said, could not attend the trial because of sickness) had plotted with her brother to press the false charges. "And I know," Lincoln continued, "nothing so difficult as to refute such female testimonies, particularly when they are absent from the court. The only way to be sure of a favorable verdict tomorrow is, that God Almighty would take our part and show your innocence! Go to Him and pray, for He alone can save you."[39] Chiniquy recorded, "Mr. Lincoln was exceedingly solemn when he addressed those words to me, and they went very deep into my soul."[40]

At three a.m. that morning, a knock came on Chiniquy's door. The former priest had remained awake, praying for God's deliverance as Lincoln had admonished. At the door was Lincoln, who elatedly announced, "Cheer up, Mr. Chiniquy, I have the perjured priests in my hands. Their diabolical plot is all known, and if they do not fly away before the dawn of day, they will surely be lynched. Bless the Lord, you are saved."[41] And fly they did.

Two women who knew of the plot read of the trial in the Chicago newspapers. They had promised not to reveal the secret but were later persuaded to change their minds. One, Miss Philomene Moffat, boarded a night train to Urbana with the intent to testify against the false charges. The plaintiffs, aware of this possibility, stayed awake through the night to check the passenger roster and found her name at the top of the list. Upon her arrival, she met with Lincoln and revealed the plot. The accusing priests left town on the next train. The truth was revealed, the case was dismissed, and a lasting friendship between Lincoln and Chiniquy began. Chiniquy paid the other two lawyers their fees of one thousand dollars, but to Chiniquy's astonishment, Lincoln would only accept fifty.

Charles Chiniquy visited President Lincoln in the White House in August 1861, June 1862, and June 1864 to warn Mr. Lincoln of plots, which Father Chiniquy believed to be masterminded by Jesuits, against the life of the President. Chiniquy believed that the pro-slavery, pro-secession, and pro-Confederacy Roman Catholic Church would seek Lincoln's life. On the last of these visits to the White House, June 9, 1864, in the course of a warm and extended conversation, Chiniquy recorded a remarkable disclosure that Lincoln made regarding his role in the redemption of the nation:

> "You are not the first to warn me against the dangers of assassination. My ambassadors in Italy, France, and England, as well as Professor [Samuel] Morse, have, many times, warned me against the plots of murderers whom they have detected in those different countries. But I see no other safeguard against these murderers, but to be always ready to die, as Christ advises it. As we must all die sooner or later, it makes very little difference to me whether I die from a dagger plunged through the heart or from an inflammation of the lungs. Let me tell you that I have, lately, read a message in the Old Testament which had made a profound, and, I hope, a salutary impression on me. Here is that passage."
>
> The President took his Bible, opened it at the third chapter of Deuteronomy, and read from the 22nd to the 27th verse [wherein Jehovah is conversing with Moses]:
>
> 22. Ye shall not fear them: for the Lord your God he shall fight for you.
>
> 23. And I besought the Lord at that time, saying,
>
> 24. O Lord God, thou hast begun to shew thy servant thy greatness, and thy mighty hand: for what God is there in heaven or in earth, that can do according to thy works, and according to thy might?
>
> 25. I pray thee, let me go over, and see the good land that is beyond Jordan, that goodly mountain, and Lebanon.

26. But the Lord was wroth with me for your sakes, and would not hear me: and the Lord said unto me, Let it suffice thee; speak no more unto me of this matter.

27. Get thee up into the top of Pisgah, and lift up thine eyes westward, and northward, and southward, and eastward, and behold it with thine eyes; for thou shalt not go over this Jordan.

After the President had read these words with great solemnity, he added:

"My dear Father Chiniquy, let me tell you that I have read these strange and beautiful words several times, these last five or six weeks. The more I read them, the more it seems to me that God has written them for me as well as for Moses.

"Has He not taken me from my poor log cabin, by the hand, as He did Moses, in the reeds of the Nile, to put me at the head of the greatest and most blessed of modern nations just as He put that prophet at the head of the most blessed nation of ancient times? Has not God granted me a privilege, which was not granted to any living man, when I broke the fetters of 4,000,000 of men, and made them free? Has not our God given me the most glorious victories over my enemies? Are not the armies of the Confederacy so reduced to a handful of men, when compared to what they were two years ago, that the day is fast approaching when they will have to surrender?

"Now, I see the end of this terrible conflict, with the same joy of Moses, when at the end of his trying forty years in the wilderness; and I pray my God to grant me to see the days of peace and untold prosperity, which will follow this cruel war, as Moses asked God to see the other side of Jordan, and enter the Promised Land. But, do you know, that I hear in my soul, as the voice of God, giving me the rebuke which was given to Moses?

"Yes! every time that my soul goes to God to ask the favor of seeing the other side of Jordan, and eating the fruits of that peace, after which I am longing with such an unspeakable desire, do you know that there is a still but solemn voice which tells me that I will see those things only from a long distance, and that I will be among the dead when the nation, which God granted me to lead through those awful trials, will cross the Jordan, and dwell in that Land of Promise, where peace, industry, happiness, and liberty will make everyone happy; and why so? Because He has already given me favors which He never gave, I dare say, to any man in these latter days.

"Why did God Almighty refuse to Moses the favor of crossing the Jordan, and entering the Promised Land? It was on account of the nation's sin! That law of divine retribution and justice, by which one must suffer for another, is surely a terrible mystery. But it is a fact which no man who has any intelligence and knowledge can deny. Moses, who knew that law, though he probably did not understand it better than we do, calmly says to his people: 'God was wroth with me for your sakes.'

"But, though we do not understand that mysterious and terrible law, we find it written in letters of tears and blood wherever we go. We do not read a single page of history without finding undeniable traces of its existence.

"Is not our Christian religion the highest expression of the wisdom, mercy, and love of God! But what is Christianity if not the very incarnation of that eternal law of Divine justice in our humanity?

"When I look on Moses, alone, silently dying on the Mount Pisgah, I see that law, in one of its most sublime human manifestations, and I am filled with admiration and awe.

"But when I consider that law of justice, and expiation in the death of the Just, the divine Son of Mary, on the Mount of Calvary, I remain mute in my adoration. The spectacle of the Crucified One which is before my eyes is more than sublime, it is divine! Moses died for his People's sake, but Christ died for the whole world's sake! Both died to fulfill the same eternal law of the Divine justice, though in a different measure.

"Now, would it not be the greatest of honors and privileges bestowed upon me, if God in His infinite love, mercy, and wisdom would put me between His faithful servant, Moses, and His eternal Son, Jesus, that I might die as they did, for my nation's sake!

"My God alone knows what I have already suffered for my dear country's sake. But my fear is that the justice of God is not yet paid. When I look upon the rivers of tears and blood drawn by the lashes of the merciless masters from the veins of the very heart of those millions of defenseless slaves, these two hundred years; when I remember the agonies, the cries, the unspeakable tortures of those unfortunate people to which I have, to some extent, connived with so many others a part of my life, I fear that we are still far from the complete expiation. For the judgments of God are true and righteous.

"It seems to me that the Lord wants today, as He wanted in

the days of Moses, another victim—a victim which He has himself chosen, anointed and prepared for the sacrifice, by raising it above the rest of His people. I cannot conceal from you that my impression is that I am the victim. So many plots have already been made against my life, that it is a real miracle that they have all failed. But can we expect that God will make a perpetual miracle to save my life? I believe not.

"But just as the Lord heard no murmur from the lips of Moses, when He told him that he had to die before crossing the Jordan, for the sins of his people, so I hope and pray that He will hear no murmur from me when I fall for my nation's sake.

"The only two favors I ask of the Lord are, first, that I may die for the sacred cause in which I am engaged, and when I am the standard bearer of the rights and privileges of my country.

"The second favor I ask from God is that my dear son, Robert, when I am gone, will be one of those who lift up that flag of Liberty which will cover my tomb, and carry it with honor and fidelity to the end of his life, as his father did, surrounded by the millions who will be called with him to fight and die for the defense and honor of our country."

Father Chiniquy continued, saying:

> Never had I heard such sublime words. . . . Never had I seen a human face so solemn and so prophet-like as the face of the President when uttering these things. Every sentence had come to me as a hymn from heaven, reverberated by the echoes of the mountains of Pisgah and Calvary. I was beside myself. Bathed in tears, I tried to say something, but I could not utter a word. I knew the hour to leave had come. I asked from the President permission to fall on my knees and pray with him that his life might be spared; and he knelt with me. But I prayed more with my tears and sobs than with my words. Then I pressed his hand on my lips and bathed it with tears, and with a heart filled with an unspeakable desolation, I bade him adieu.[42]

## THE ALMIGHTY HAS HIS OWN PURPOSES

These solemn sentiments shared by the President of the United States with Father Chiniquy enlighten our understanding of why Lincoln, in the course of his presidency, called for nine different national days of fasting, prayer, repentance, and thanksgiving to the "Almighty and merciful Ruler of the universe."[43] In these eloquent messages, Lincoln never failed to acknowledge his unwavering faith in God and his deepest gratitude to the Almighty for His righteous justice and mercy. On March 30, 1863, Lincoln proclaimed to the American people:

> And insomuch as we know that by his divine law nations, like individuals, are subjected to punishments and chastisements in this world, may we not justly fear that the awful calamity of civil war which now desolates the land may be but a punishment inflicted upon us for our presumptuous sins, to the needful end of our national reformation as a whole people? We have been the recipients of the choicest bounties of Heaven. . . . but we have forgotten God.[44]

Later that year, in October, President Lincoln sent the third of three proclamations to America wherein he reminded the people that in spite of the severity of the war, God had continued to prosper them in industry, natural resources, and agriculture:

> No human counsel hath devised, nor hath any mortal hand worked out these great things. They are the gracious gifts of the most high God, who, while dealing with us in anger for our sins, hath nevertheless remembered mercy.[45]

The similarity of this and Joseph Smith's message in his 1832 revelation on war is striking:

> Verily, thus saith the Lord concerning the wars that will shortly come to pass, beginning at the rebellion of South Carolina, which will eventually terminate in the death and misery of many souls. . . . For behold, the Southern States shall be divided against the Northern States . . . after many days, slaves shall rise up against their masters, who shall be marshaled and disciplined for war. (D&C 87:1–4)
> . . . And thus, with the sword and by bloodshed the inhabitants of the earth shall mourn; and . . . be made to feel the wrath, and indignation, and chastening hand of an Almighty God . . . That the cry of the saints, and the blood of the saints, shall cease to come up into the ears of the Lord of Sabaoth, from the earth, to be avenged of their enemies. (D&C 87:6–7)

The unique and common thread that bound these two presidential prophets together was their conviction that the Civil War had a divine purpose that transcended freeing the slaves, preserving the Union, or saving the Constitution. It was the celestial purpose of divine justice. As both Abraham Lincoln and Joseph Smith articulated, the sins of the American people, including two hundred fifty years of enslaving millions, simply could not go unpunished. Lincoln believed that the horrors of the Civil War still fell short of a full recompense. He reiterated this sentiment just five weeks before his final sacrifice in his Second Inaugural Address:

> Neither party expected for the war, the magnitude, or the duration, which it has already attained . . . Each looked for an easier triumph, and a result less fundamental and astounding . . . Both read the same Bible, and pray to the same God; and each invokes His aid against the other. It may seem strange that any men should dare to ask a just God's assistance in wringing their bread from the sweat of other men's faces; but let us judge not that we be not judged. The prayers of both could not be answered; that of neither has been answered fully.[46]
>
> . . . The Almighty has His own purposes.[47]
>
> Yet, if God wills that it continue, until all the wealth piled by the bond-man's two hundred and fifty years of unrequited toil shall be sunk, and until every drop of blood drawn with the lash, shall be paid by another drawn with the sword, as was said three thousand years ago, so still it must be said "the judgments of the Lord, are true and righteous altogether."[48]

Abraham Lincoln came to understand that he, like Moses and Jesus, would be called upon to pay a redemptive price for bringing to pass what he considered God's work. In like manner, Joseph Smith came to believe the same thing about himself. As said on the way to Carthage, "I am going like a lamb to the slaughter; but I am calm as a summer's morning . . . I SHALL DIE INNOCENT, AND IT SHALL YET BE SAID OF ME—HE WAS MURDERED IN COLD BLOOD" (D&C 135:4).

The price each man paid included suffering lifelong persecution for their uncommon understanding of God's will and nature, agonizing at the trials of their followers, and, in the end, publicly giving their lives for the work which they completed in the name of God. Moses' final sacrifice was remaining outside the promised land while all the hosts of Israelites passed over the Jordan. Jesus's death on the cross was likewise public. In lesser degrees, so were Joseph Smith's and Abraham Lincoln's. Joseph's bullet-riddled body fell from the second story jailhouse window in view of hundreds, and Abraham Lincoln took Booth's bullet to the head before the stunned audience at Ford's Theater. Their final sacrifices, effected before the public as they both were, are the ultimate display of the presidential prophets' devotion to their God.

## CHAPTER THIRTEEN ENDNOTES

1. Kenneth Alford Editor, *Civil War Saints* (Salt Lake City, UT: Religious Studies Center, Brigham Young University, in cooperation with Deseret Book Company 2012), 41.

2. B. H. Roberts, *The Rise and Fall of Nauvoo* (repr., Provo, UT: Maasai, 2001), 270–72.

3. Ibid., 272.

4. Ibid., 274–75.

5. Ibid., 281.

6. Ibid., 286.

7. Ted Gibbons, *Sealing the Testimony: An Eyewitness Account of the Martyrdom* (Provo, UT: Maasai, 2001), 14.

8. Ibid., 24.

9. Ibid.

10. Ibid.

11. Ibid., 27.

12. Ibid., 32.

13. Ibid.

14. Roberts, *The Rise and Fall of Nauvoo,* 298.

15. Gibbons, *Sealing the Testimony,* 33.

16. Ibid., 35.

17. Ibid.

18. Ibid.

19. Roberts, *The Rise and Fall of Nauvoo,* 300.

20. Ted Gibbons, *Sealing the Testimony* (Provo, UT: Maasai Publishing, 1988), 43.

21. Ibid.

22. Ibid., 48.

23. Gibbons, *Sealing the Testimony,* 50.

24. Text: James Montgomery, 1771–1854; Music: George Coles, 1792–1858, alt.; See B. H. Roberts, *History of the Church of Jesus Christ of Latter-day Saints* (Salt Lake City, UT: Deseret Book), vol. 6, 614–15.

25. Joseph's death may mark the first time a candidate for President of the United States was murdered in pursuit of the office.

26. William Lee Miller, *Lincoln's Virtues: An Ethical Biography* (2002; repr., New York: Vintage Books, 2003), 401–4.

27. Ron L. Anderson, *Abraham Lincoln: God's Humble Instrument* (Salt Lake City, UT: Millenial Mind Publishing, 2009), 200–201.

28. Stephen B. Oates, *With Malice Toward None: A Life of Abraham Lincoln* (New York: Harper Perennial, 1994), 380.

29. Ibid., 425.

30. Ibid.

31. Ibid.

32. Ibid., 425–26.

33. Ibid., 426.

34. Ibid.

35. Ibid.

36. Ward Hill Lamon, *Recollections of Abraham Lincoln, 1847–1865* (repr., Lincoln, NE: University of Nebraska Press, 1994), 121.

37. Charles Chiniquy, *Fifty Years in the "Church" of Rome: The Life Story of Pastor Chiniquy, who was for Twenty-five Years a Priest in the Roman Catholic Church*, abridged ed., (London, England: Protestant Literature Depository, 1886; Chino, CA: Chick Publications, 1985), 179.

38. Ibid., 275.

39. Ibid.

40. Ibid.

41. Ibid., 276.

42. William E. Barton, *The Soul of Abraham Lincoln* (New York: George H. Doran Company, 1920; repr.,University of Illinois Press, 2005), 188–92.

43. Marion Mills Miller, ed., *Life and Works of Abraham Lincoln* (New York: Current Literature Publishing, 1907), vol. 6, 164.

44. Ibid., 156 .

45. Ibid., 160.

46. Ronald C. White, Jr., *The Eloquent President: A Portrait of Lincoln through his Words* (New York: Random House, 2005), 290–91.

47. Ibid., 293.

48. Ibid., 298–99.

# ABOUT THE AUTHOR

R on L. Andersen is a noted career management consultant for thousands of clients throughout the United States and Latin America.

He has been a pioneering innovator in the conception and developed of two major initiatives that have been embraced by his global organization to help thousands more find greater success in their careers through more that 150 career development center around the globe.

Mr. Andersen has been a dynamic, compelling public speaker throughout the country on the remarkable life of Abraham Lincoln. In these presentations he draws his audiences into life and world of Lincoln's incomparable leadership, unmatched magnanimity, and placid spirituality. He maintains a following of thousands of loyal Lincoln admirers through his Lincoln Leadership Society, which he founded in 2009 and through the sale of his first book *Abraham Lincoln—God's Humble Instrument*.

This gifted writer and storyteller will release his second book on Lincoln in June 2014.

Ron currently sits on the board of largest young men's organization in the world, promoting integrity and faith in the lives of over 600,000 youth in nearly every country in the world.

0   26575 14160   3